VOICING DISSENT

VOICING DISSENT

New Perspectives in Irish Criticism

Edited by
Sandrine Brisset
and Noreen Doody

IRISH ACADEMIC PRESS
DUBLIN • PORTLAND, OR

First published in 2012 by Irish Academic Press

2 Brookside,
Dundrum Road,
Dublin 14, Ireland

920 NE 58th Avenue, Suite 300
Portland, Oregon,
97213-3786 USA

www.iap.ie

British Library Cataloguing in Publication Data
An entry can be found on request

ISBN 978 0 7165 3138 8 (cloth)

Library of Congress Cataloging in-Publication Data
An entry can be found on request

Printed and bound by CPI Group (UK) Ltd, Croydon CR0 4YY

Contents

Part 5. Pop Culture and Heroic Misfits

Contributors

Sandrine Brisset was awarded her PhD jointly from St Patrick's College, Drumcondra, and from the Sorbonne Nouvelle (Paris 3). She is Teaching Fellow in the English Department of St Patrick's College, Drumcondra.

Amy Galvin is an editor at an educational publishing company in Boston, Massachusetts. She received her MA in English literature from Boston College in December 2010.

Shannon Hipp completed her doctorate at Emory University in August 2011, specializing in modernist literature and contemporary Irish poetry. Her dissertation, 'Eliot among the Women', reconsidered T.S. Eliot's relationship to the female figures of his poetry and drama according to a paradigm of self-loathing, empathy and devotion. She has also worked extensively in the Medbh McGuckian archives at Emory, publishing an analysis of McGuckian's notebooks in *Irish University Review* (Spring/Summer 2009). She currently teaches in Atlanta, Georgia.

Caitríona Ní Chléirchín is an Irish-language lecturer in University College Dublin and is completing a doctorate on the poetry of Nuala Ní Dhomhnaill and Biddy Jenkinson at present. She spent a year in Lyon, France, studying for a master's degree in French literature and was very influenced by *l'écriture féminine*. She was a Government of Ireland Scholar 2006–08. *Crithloinnir*, her début collection of poetry, won first prize in the Oireachtas competition for new writers in 2010. She has published poetry in *Comhar, Feasta, Blaiseadh Pinn, Cyphers, The SHOp, An t-Ultach* and *An Guth*. She also writes reviews, academic and journalistic articles in *The Irish Times, Comhar*, and *Taighde agus Teagasc* and others.

Simon Workman was educated at Trinity College Dublin where he completed a doctoral thesis on the poetry and radio drama of Louis MacNeice. He has published on twentieth-century Irish poetry, and has a particular interest in Irish writers working at the BBC. He is currently a lecturer in English at St Patrick's College Carlow.

Sheila McCormick recently received her PhD from the National University of Ireland, Galway. Her main area of interest is verbatim and documentary theatre. At present, she is developing a practice as research project that will examine the use of documentary theatre in the applied theatre setting.

Ian R. Walsh is a graduate of University College Dublin, where he completed his doctoral research, and is now teaching there in the School of English, Drama and Film. He is currently working on a monograph which examines experimental Irish drama in the period 1939–53. He has also worked as a theatre reviewer for *Irish Theatre Magazine* and RTE Radio 1's *Arena* and as a freelance director of Theatre and Opera; his most recent production was of Mozart's *The Magic Flute* in the D.L.R. Glasthule Opera Festival 2011.

Brian Gourley completed a PhD on carnivalesque and grotesque transgression in the writings of John Bale, at the Queen's University of Belfast. His essay on the representation of apocalypse in Bale's plays appeared in *Renaissance Medievalisms* published by the Centre for Reformation and Renaissance Studies (CRRS) at the University of Toronto. His PhD thesis has also been provisionally accepted for publication by the CRRS.

Irina (Ira) Ruppo Malone is a graduate of the Hebrew University of Jerusalem, Trinity College Dublin, and the National University of Ireland,Galway, where she teaches courses on Irish and European drama, James Joyce, and contemporary Irish fiction. She is the author of *Ibsen and the Irish Revival* (Palgrave Macmillan, 2010). Irina's current project, *Ibsen and Chekhov on the Irish Stage*, a collection of essays and interviews dedicated to the memory of the co-author, Ros Dixon, is due to be published by Carysfort Press in February 2012.

Jessica Dougherty-McMichael has recently completed her doctorate in literature at The University of Notre Dame. She focuses on contemporary Irish and Native American literatures. She is currently a lecturer at the University of Montana.

Katherine O'Keefe received her BA from Point Loma Nazarene University, and her MA and PhD in Anglo-Irish Literature and Drama from University College Dublin. Her thesis was titled *Synthesizing Wilde: Intertextuality, Nationality, and Dialectic in the Fairy Tales of Oscar Wilde*. Other research interests include contemporary Irish drama, children's literature, speculative fiction, and the relation of contemporary non-mimetic fiction to the literary fairy tale.

Kelly Matthews completed her PhD at the University of Ulster in 2009, and is currently Assistant Professor of English at Framingham State University in Framingham, Massachusetts. Her book project, *Opening Windows: The Bell Magazine and the Representation of Irish Identity*, discusses the cultural and material history of *The Bell* and its attempt to transform conceptions of Irishness in the mid-twentieth century. Her essays have appeared in *Éire-Ireland* and in *Proceedings of the Harvard Celtic Colloquium*.

Stefanie Lehner is currently Postdoctoral Fellow at the John Hume Institute for Global Irish Studies at University College Dublin. She is the author of *Subaltern Ethics in Contemporary Scottish and Irish Literature: Tracing Counter-Histories* (Palgrave Macmillan, 2011).

Sharon Tighe-Mooney completed her doctoral research in 2010 at the School of English, Media and Theatre Studies, National University of Ireland, Maynooth. She obtained a BA and an MA in English, Sociology and Theology from the National University of Ireland. She is co-editor, with Deirdre Quinn, of *Essays in Irish Literary Criticism: Themes of Gender, Sexuality, and Corporeality* (Lampeter: Edwin Mellen, 2008).

Graham Price is a tutor and occasional lecturer in University College Dublin and St Patrick's College, Drumcondra. He received his PhD from University College Dublin in 2008. The topic was the influence of Oscar Wilde on twentieth-century Irish authors. Graham has taught courses on Irish literature, critical theory and twentieth-century drama. He has published articles on Oscar Wilde, John McGahern and Brian Friel.

Anthea E. Cordner researches in Irish studies (specifically Northern Irish prose), trauma theory, gender studies, regional and cultural theories, and theories relating to memory and identity. She has presented her research at various conferences and has articles published in Queen's University Press *Crosscurrents* (2005) and Greenwood's *A–Z of Irish Women Writers* (2006), Bath Spa UP *New Voices in Irish Studies* and Routledge's *Irish Studies Review*. She is completing her PhD at the University of Newcastle on contemporary Northern Irish prose as it intersects with gender and trauma theories.

Lori Bennett has a Masters of Philosophy in Anglo-Irish Literature from Trinity College Dublin and has authored dissertations on Irish women short story writers as well as the use of Irish mythology in W.B. Yeats's poetry. Lori is currently finishing her final year at Fordham University School of Law in New York. Today, her literary efforts focus on writing fiction.

Libe García Zarranz, 2010 Trudeau and Killam Scholar, is a PhD candidate in the Department of English and Film Studies at the University of Alberta, Canada. She has published on the representation of gender in the work of Merlinda Bobis, Raymond Carver and William Trevor. She has also published on the evolution of the female heroines in Walt Disney's movies from the 1990s. In the spring of 2009, she co-edited the second issue of *The Raymond Carver Review* on 'Carver and Feminism'. Areas of interest include transnational and globalization studies, contemporary women's writing and queer theory.

Michael Flanagan is currently lecturing in the areas of Film and Popular Culture in All Hallows College (DCU), and is a former Deputy Principal of the Central Model School. He has an interest in children's literature and has been published in such collections as *Treasure Islands: Studies in Children's Literature*, edited by Celia Keenan and Mary Shine Thompson (Dublin: Four Courts Press, 2006); *Divided Worlds: Studies in Children's Literature*, edited by Mary Shine Thompson (Dublin: Four Courts Press, 2007) and *Ireland, Design and Visual Culture: Negotiating Modernity 1922–1992*, edited by Linda King and Elaine Sisson (Cork University Press, 2011).

Jenny O'Connor received her doctorate from University College Dublin in April 2009. Her thesis examined the way that film studies and Deleuzian philosophy interact. During the course of her PhD studies, she presented at conferences in Ireland and abroad, contributed to postgraduate publications, published a paper in the peer-reviewed online journal *Rhizomes*, and contributed to three published collections of essays. She is currently employed as a lecturer in the School of Humanities at Waterford Institute of Technology.

Sorcha de Brún is from Dublin. She holds a BA in Irish and Politics from UCD, an MA in Politics from UCD, an MA in Irish from St Patrick's College and DCU, an LTCL in Piano Teaching from Trinity College London and a DipABRSM in Organ Performance from the Associated Board of the Royal Schools of Music London. A recipient of the John and Pat Hume Scholarship, she is currently completing her doctorate on contemporary Gaeltacht prose writers in the Department of Modern Irish in the National University of Ireland Maynooth. She has published essays on aspects of the Irish language translation of *Dracula* in *Bliainiris*, and essays on the teaching of Irish are forthcoming. She has won several awards for prose, including the Máirtín Ó Cadhain short story competition and Duais Foras na Gaeilge. Poetry she has written for children has been published in the anthology *Seo, Siúd agus Uile* (An Gúm, 2009), and a short story for children was chosen for the collection *Sin Scéal Eile* (An Gúm, 2011). She was the President of the Irish Jury for the European Prize for Literature (Ireland) in 2009.

Leo Keohane completed his PhD at NUI Galway and teaches at the Centre for Irish Studies there. His special areas of interest include the application of critical theory to counter hegemonic thinking and early-twentieth-century Irish socialist history, in particular, the writings of James Connolly. He is currently writing a biography of Captain Jack White DSO.

Noreen Doody is Head of the Department of English in St. Patrick's College, Drumcondra, a college of Dublin City University. Her research interests are in Irish Studies and Nineteenth Century Literature and focus on the works of Oscar Wilde and W. B. Yeats. She has published widely on Yeats and Wilde.

Acknowledgements

The editors are grateful for the support and help given to us during the writing and editing of this book. In particular, we would like to express our appreciation to Dr Derek Hand, Dr Julie Anne Stevens and Dr Mary Shine Thompson who gave generously of their time and advice in the initial preparation of this book. We would also like to offer our thanks and appreciation to Justine Doody for her expert assistance in the final stages of this book.

Voicing Dissent: New Perspectives in Irish Criticism arose from a conference in the New Voices in Irish Criticism series that was held in St Patrick's College, Drumcondra. We would like to express our sincere gratitude to Professor Declan Kiberd and Dr P.J. Mathews for their generous participation in the conference. We are grateful to all of those who contributed to and helped in the organization of the conference, especially David Meehan, Anne Marie Byrne and Limear Hegarty.

We are indebted to the College Research Committee, St Patrick's College, Drumcondra, for its generous support of this publication.

Introduction

Voicing Dissent: New Perspectives in Irish Criticism is an edited volume of critical essays on the idea of dissent in contemporary Irish Studies. In this book, energetic young scholars add their voices to the debate, breaking new literary ground and bringing to light fresh interpretations and original critical insights in Irish literature and culture. The essays foreground radical points of view, alternative readings, contentious texts and some unusual and innovative approaches to canonical works. Dissent is the focal point through which critical perceptions on key arguments and subsidiary themes in the field of Irish Studies are debated, and this critical use of dissent is sustained throughout all of the essays in the collection, giving cohesion and clarity to the book. The aim of these essays is to catch an argument or debate at the moment of refusal, capturing something of its dynamism – to go beneath the surface of prevailing opinion and to look for alternative meaning and answers.

While the book is primarily concerned with dissent in changing cultural and social contexts within literature, it also addresses several different fields of academic research, including history, cinema and gender studies. Some essays examine how twentieth and twenty-first-century poets configure poetry as an act of dissent. Others explore questions of myth and versions of truth in drama of various historical periods. Elsewhere, by looking at postcolonial trauma in works of fiction, Irish identity is interrogated. Representations of femininity, sexuality and patriarchy are challenged by rebellious women – whether as characters, writers or critics. Dissenting voices are examined as they appear in popular cultures, illustrating how dissident attitudes in works of art can conjure ordinary individuals into public celebrities.

Voicing Dissent: New Perspectives in Irish Criticism is a lively collection of essays that will both challenge and inform current critical thinking. The book represents exciting developments in Irish literary and cultural criticism: it offers new ways of perceiving not only central topics of critical debate but also anomalies, those things traditionally consigned to its margins. *Voicing Dissent* opens a door upon a space in which to examine shifts in power, acts and figures of rebellion, resistance itself, and all of those who break the law of what is commonly accepted and acceptable, and who dare to question respectability in arts, literature or in the broader context of society at large.

This collection focuses on Irish literature and includes within its ambit some essays not directly related to Ireland, but which provide an interesting contextual dimension to the phenomenon of dissent. The contents have been grouped thematically and according to genre, although in keeping with the theme of the book some latitude in this order has been allowed.

The first section of the book, 'Verse and Subversion', examines how five twentieth and twenty-first-century poets – Brendan Kennelly, Thomas Kinsella, Nuala Ní Dhomhnaill, Cathal Ó Searcaigh and Louis MacNiece – transform poetry into an act of dissent. While Brendan Kennelly has recourse to an original treatment of myth and mythology, Thomas Kinsella, who famously provided modern readers with a translation of the *Táin*, dismantles the clocks and rejects the dictum of passing time. Sandrine Brisset opens the section with an exploration of myth as a dynamic component of Kennelly's work, and Amy Galvin analyses Kinsella's treatment of time in the earliest stages of his career. The poet Nuala Ní Dhomhnaill's personal papers are explored by Shannon Hipp, who examines the act of dissent involved in the unusual genesis of poems with multiple authors in her chapter, 'Cribs and Collaborations in the Poetry of Nuala Ní Dhomhnaill'. In the chapter 'Marginal Figures and Subversion in the Poetry of Cathal Ó Searcaigh', Caitríona Ní Chléirchín shows how marginality is rooted in the verse of contro-versial poet Cathal Ó Searcaigh. Simon Workman peers into Louis MacNiece's ambiguous political position in a piece of work entitled, ' "Of them but not of them": Louis MacNiece and the "Thirties poets" '. Workman interrogates MacNiece's association with W.H. Auden and the group of English poets from the 1930s and highlights how the poet's childhood spent in Ireland affected his sense of independence.

'Dissent on Stage' deals with a wide breadth of drama, ranging from medieval morality plays to tribunal theatre. Sheila McCormick guides her reader through a reflection on the political and social power of verbatim theatre; her chapter, 'Tribunal Theatre and the Voice of Dissent as seen in *Bloody Sunday: Scenes from the Saville Inquiry*', analyses tribunal theatre between cathartic witness-bearing and mythification of historical events. Ian Walsh demonstrates, in 'Exploding the Kitchen Comedy: Maurice Meldon's *Purple Path to the Poppy Field*', how Meldon disrupts the idea commonly agreed upon in the 1950s, that the Irish Kitchen comedy should follow the rules of realism. Taking us to another era and another setting, in 'A Brief Consideration of Dissent in Two Reformation Moralities', Brian Gourley considers how *Love Feigned and Unfeigned* and *Three Laws* offer an expression of religious dissent. Alternative interpretations of Ibsen by twentieth-century Irish playwrights are examined by Irina Ruppo in 'Irish Nationalist [Mis]readings of Ibsen: Padraig Pearse, Lennox Robinson, and Thomas MacDonagh'.[1]

The section 'Postcolonialism and Irish Identity' focuses on dissent in a postcolonial context. In her chapter, 'Murder in the Margin: Descent and Dissent in Patrick McCabe's *Winterwood* and Sherman Alexie's *Indian Killer*', Jessica Dougherty-McMichael shows how in these two novels both writers attack the postcolonial literary structure from which they have emerged. The literary fairy tale is interrogated in its colonial context by Katherine O'Keefe's chapter 'Serious Fancy: Oscar Wilde, Charles Dickens and the Literary Fairy Tale in Colonial Discourse'. Stefanie Lehner's essay, 'Postcolonial Trauma – Postmodern Recovery? Gender, Nation and Trauma in Contemporary Irish and Scottish Fiction', elucidates issues of identity resulting from postcolonial trauma across Ireland and Scotland. Matters of identity are also Kelly Matthews' concern in 'A Dissenting Vision of Irish Identity: *The Bell* Magazine', in which she investigates how the newspaper became an instrument of dissent, providing an alternative model of Irishness that conflicted with the political tenets of the time.

'Rebellious Femininity' explores challenging representations of femininity. Graham Price studies the Wildean component of dandyism in John McGahern's *Amongst Women* and sheds light on female characters' subtle ways of bending the rules of patriarchy while apparently respecting them. Anthea E. Cordner plunges to the core of more violent expressions of dissent as she investigates 'Anything Neurotic, Exotic, Experimental or New' in women's writing on the Troubles. Lori Bennett writes about Irish representations of femininity, sexuality and patriarchy in the short stories of Mary Lavin, Clare Boylan and Emma Donoghue. Emma Donoghue is also at the centre of Libe García Zarranz's attention as she examines how the writer uses intertextuality and parody as political strategies, and the 'heterosexist ideology of canonical fairy tales and novels'. In ' "What Kate Did": Subversive

Dissent in Kate O'Brien's *The Ante Room*', Sharon Tighe-Mooney brings this section to a close by challenging the perception of Kate O'Brien as a conservative popular writer of romantic fiction.

The final section in the volume, 'Pop Culture and Heroic Misfits', is concerned with how dissenting voices emerge in popular cultures and how challenging behaviours represented in works of art can turn marginal individuals into characters who attract admiration and earn heroic status. Michael Flanagan begins with a study of the 'moral panic' that accompanies the growing success of the 'Penny Dreadful' genre in Victorian society. In 'Disobeying Gilles Deleuze: Is Quentin Tarantino the Voice of Dissent?', Jenny O'Connor compares Deleuze's considerations on cinema with Quentin Tarantino's *Pulp Fiction* and *Reservoir Dogs*.[2] Sorcha de Brún reflects on traditional conceptions of heroism and observes how these relate to the status of heroes in the work of Pádraig Ó Cíobháin. The collection comes to a close with a portrait by Leo Keohane of a flamboyant figure and radical thinker of early twentieth-century Ireland: 'Captain Jack White, DSO – Anarchist and Proleptic Post-structuralist'.

Sandrine Brisset
Noreen Doody

NOTES

1. This essay first appeared in *Ibsen and the Irish Revival* by Irina Ruppo Malone, published by Palgrave Macmillan, 2010.
2. A version of this essay by Jenny O'Connor, 'Quentin Tarantino Gilles Deleuze's Cinematic "Falsifier"', was published in C. Siegel and E.E. Berry (eds), *Rhizomes: Cultural Studies in Emerging Knowledge*, 16 (Summer 2008), http://www.rhizomes.net/.

PART 1
VERSE AND SUBVERSION

1

'Stabbed up the line': Myth and Dissent in the Poetry of Brendan Kennelly

Sandrine Brisset

The reception of Brendan Kennelly's works is notable for the extreme reactions of some of their readers and listeners. In 1984, the poet was punched in the face for allowing Oliver Cromwell a voice and for presenting an alternative portrait of this near-mythical figure. Years later, in the early 1990s, *The Book of Judas* gave rise to fierce and abusive reviews. Something in Kennelly's poetry seems to deeply arouse certain readers to disproportionate reactions. One possible explanation for this sort of reaction, which this paper wishes to investigate, is that Kennelly's original treatment of living myth – a form of myth to which we are directly connected, as opposed to mythology – can be experienced as profoundly unsettling because it forces us to question our own reality. Living myth, then, acts as an impetus to dissent and provides a way of interrogating the reader's or the listener's system of values.

In its negative form, living myth can be understood as a lie, but myth is also that which feeds the human need for explanation when a rational and logical chain of events cannot be provided. In ancient Greece, philosophers such as Socrates and Plato had recourse to myth in order to provide possible explanations of diverse phenomena. Living myth satisfies the need for cosmogonic understanding and thus brings peace to the intellect. As shown by Jean-Pierre Vernant, living myth is always political and finds its relevance for the individual in its relation to the group.[1] Brendan Kennelly's childhood was spent in a rural community where living myth constituted a fundamental condition of life. No space was allowed to question the communal system of values. As he became progressively distanced from this community, Kennelly came to realize the poetic richness of living myth and its potential for opening up a new mode of thinking.

Brendan Kennelly's Background

Living myth always comprehends a certain amount of something fabulous. Myth is also *fabula* (story, tale, etc.) which in an Irish context often takes the form of storytelling. In Ballylongford, Brendan Kennelly's native village, living myth defines the landscape through stories. Every ruin, road, path, hill, wall, pond, church and nearly every bush is related to the world of myth. In Ballylongford, living myth is rooted in the supernatural but also in history and violence: 'The Shannon has provided an avenue for invaders. It has brought trouble in, and around Ahanagran lie burned abbeys and the blasted castle of Carrigafoyle. The land itself testifies to violence and conquest: to the troubled times that stretch back for half a millennium and more.'[2] In this region of Ireland living myths are orally transmitted. Like most oral narratives, they become distorted: the teller makes them his or her own, according to his or her own personality but also according to the demands of the present, for myth only remains alive as it continues to be told and to maintain its relevance to the present listeners. The link to what really happened does not matter so much; what matters is the truth of the teller – that is, their genuine feelings about the myths told – and the belief and sense of awe and wonder generated among their listeners: 'Kerry wants not just the story but the very facts themselves to meet the times. Kerry wants a past that meets the demands of the present; it wants present events and past events to connect and even to merge. Kerry is inventive: it will alter the cut of the past to fit present fashions.'[3] It often happens that when living myths have been transmitted to the storyteller in a powerful way through repetition and through good narration, the teller is capable of convincing himself/herself that they lived and witnessed things they never attended, including events that took place long before they were born. This conviction leads to sincerity in the delivery. A living myth that belongs to collective memory thus becomes personal memory. Richard White, a historian who studied the village of Ballylongford, encountered the phenomenon among some of its people, including a woman named Teresa:

> 'I used to hear the stories', Teresa says, 'I used to tell the stories as a child.' The stories were so compelling that she [Teresa] actually became part of the stories. She was hiding out on the dike when the Black and Tans came. She was in the fields 'on the moonlight night'. But Teresa says now, 'I wasn't even born.'[4]

Living myths also structure time and space in Ballylongford and

provide explanations for the present state of the village. Richard
White says: 'Little was what it seemed in this landscape. Nothing
was reliably only the here and now.'[5] The fox announced impending
death; fairies lived in mounds in fields; there was a holy well at the
Hollys'; Guyney's Hole inspired fear – a horse had been drowned
there. 'Between Ballylongford and Ballybunion there was an
enchanted village that appeared from beneath the waters once
every seven years.'[6] Treasure hunters had been deterred by underground bulls that came out from the earth as they dug. Galvin's Gate
was haunted and should be avoided at night. These local myths
were strongly rooted in the place: as White attests, 'In Dublin these
stories are out of place. When they were alive in memory, they were
part of the land itself. They were about the land and its features.
They were the landscape people moved through.'[7] In Ireland's capital
city, Brendan Kennelly was a dislocated Kerryman, yet these Kerry
myths continued to mark his verse, even if discreetly so. In 'Dream
of a Black Fox'[8] and 'The Black Fox, Again'[9] the black fox is a source
of fear, not only because the poet's sleep is being disturbed by nightmare, but also because in Kerry the fox announces impending death:

> The black fox, big as a pony,
> Circled and circled,
> Whimsical executioner,
> Torment dripping like saliva from its jaws.[10]

In 'Family Affairs', myths and collective and personal history are
tightly interwoven through reference to a ballad, 'Margaret' (also
known as 'Lady Margaret'), a date, 'the sixth of April', and the allusion
to rebel martyrs as the poet remembers:

> Tidying up the parish graves on April
> The sixth. With Martyrs, dates are precise.
> With landlords, monuments are understandable.[11]

The word 'understandable' sets up two opposing types of logic. On
the one hand, the logic of history is evoked: landlords have their
monuments because of their wealth and power. A figure in the
poem, Norman Sande, bears the name of a much-hated family of
landlords who gave their name to the village, Newtownsandes,
where the events in this poem occur. This place name was for a long
time a matter of debate and was eventually changed to Moyvane.
On the other hand, monuments to rebels are of a different type in
Kerry. They belong to the logic of myths and are often mysterious

and vague, if not somewhat irrational. This was pointed out by Manus O'Riordan as he commented on the commemorative plaque to Michael Lehane, in his unpublished paper, 'In Search of Michael Lehane': 'In true Kerry Republican tradition, the inscription is as intriguing as it is informative, shedding light on but one aspect of his heroic life and none whatsoever on the context or even date of his death.'[12] Martyrs enter the realm of collective memory where historical truth becomes entangled with collective feelings for heroes and heroism, just like the ivy is upon the grave, so that the speaking voice in the poem is in a position comparable to that of an historian trying to distinguish truth from myth:

> Norman Sande had one, all ivy and moss.
> I know I got involved with the ivy,
> Ripping it off yet not finding a source,
> Piling it high amid gravel and stones.

The poem is not only restricted to the collective aspect of myth. The poet's personal history is also attached to the piece. On 6 April, Brendan Kennelly as a child was indeed sent by the local priest with other children to clean the graveyard. The day was believed to mark the destruction of Carrigafoyle Castle by the Cromwellians.[13] The poem poignantly expresses the power of living myth through the way in which it weaves collective and personal beliefs and experiences. This combination makes the last lines even more effective:

> I saw the hare near a headstone, busy
> As I was. Investigating the place
> I spied him munching offsprings to their bones.

The figure of the hare appears as a cross between the Easter hare and the mythical hare of Ballylongford. In the village it was believed that if you hurt yourself in a graveyard your wound would never heal. It is told that once, two hunters let their hounds loose in the Aghavallen churchyard, and the hounds caught a hare. One of the men had a stick and beat the captured animal dead. The hare cried a human cry as it was struck. Following the episode the hand that had held the stick began to rot. No doctor could heal the man. There was something unearthly about the wound and the man died not long after.[14] Hares are also known in Kerry for feeding on human flesh in graveyards. Indeed, one feels that the hare described in the poem 'Family Affairs' is something more than a common animal. The consumption of one's own progeny is not unconnected to the idea that parents own their children and can freely dispose of them, a conception of the family that facilitates incest and that was challenged and denounced in many of Kennelly's poems.

Reviving Mythology into Living Myth

Brendan Kennelly found in his personal background the elements that familiarized him with living myth. As the notion implies close connections between the personal and the collective sphere, any subversive treatment of living myth can be perceived as a threat and is potentially dissident. However, the beauty and power of old myths often becomes extinct in our modern society, as myth is strongly dependent on place and transmission in time. An ancient myth often becomes frozen mythology, folklore or is simply forgotten. Much of the fragility of living myth has to do with its oral mode of transmission. Brendan Kennelly's approach to mythology, both Greek[15] and Irish, is original and challenging in so far as it attempts to reinforce mythology – that is, near-extinct myth – and its connection to life, both at a personal and collective level. In other words, Kennelly's approach contests linear time and the seemingly inescapable transformation of living myth into a forgotten mythology. Kennelly's ambitious purpose, both in his teaching and in his poetry, is to turn petrified mythology back into living myth. Myth belongs both to the collective and to the personal, but mythology is often experienced as estranged from us, being part of a different time and space, detached from our day and age. Kennelly worked on restoring mythology and its connection to us. As a professor, he would therefore ask his students to rewrite or stage great mythological stories. The personal and emotional link that existed between these stories and their audience when they were still at the stage of living myth was worked upon through titles of essays such as 'Imagine you are Juno'.[16] Similarly, in his poetry, mythological traces fuse within poems in a manner which allows the reader to identify with the situation that is presented to them. Mythology is in attendance in a non-invasive way.

Kennelly chose to keep ancient mythology at a secondary level, enriching the poem but not obscuring it, since mythology, unlike living myth, has nowadays lost its close connection with the majority of people and few of them would currently have any acquaintance with mythological stories. Thus the links to mythology are subtle, as in 'By the Ears':

> Janey Mary grabbed him by the ears and said
> 'Sweep the caution out of your heart, stand up and sing,
> what use to man or God if you're clever and tame-blooded?'[17]

Janey Mary's action directly recalls that of Deirdre of the Sorrows. She becomes a heroine in the wake of great heroines from Irish mythology and pushes her lover to prove himself a hero rather than a contemplative artist.

In 'No Solution', Deirdre and Emer become two middle-class women, the 'new rich' type whose sorrows flow in the Sunday newspapers:

> Corner table, Deirdre of the Fashionable Sorrows,
> Black-hatted, literate paradigm of
> Middle-class prosperity:
>
> > 'And how are you?'
> > 'Actually, to be brutally true,
> > I've just been having a ferocious tête-à-tête
> > With Emer on the subject of estranged husbands.'[18]

This Deirdre is not the usual 'literate paradigm' in so far as this woman is extremely mundane and, as such, most readers would recognize her as somebody they know. Humour makes an entrance in this mythological reference as the ruthlessness of the epic story is maintained through expressions casually used in everyday conversation – 'to be brutally true' and 'a ferocious tête-à-tête' – so that the attempted shift from mythology to parodical myth is boosted with comical power. The linguistic snobbish habit, typical of some elements of the Dublin middle class, of dropping French words into conversation is signalled by the phrase 'tête-à-tête'. While in the context of epic myth 'a ferocious tête-à-tête' would amount at least to headbutting and most possibly to a good deal of blood, here, despite the exaggeration in the talk, it most certainly refers to a one-to-one confidential type of conversation.

In his *Preface to Plato*, Eric Havelock underlines how, in order to be personal, a living myth has to be political. It has to echo the society of the individual listeners:

> The men who act [in the myth] must be the kind of men whose actions would involve the public law and the family law of the group. They must therefore be 'political' men in the most general sense of that term, men whose acts, passions, and thoughts will affect the behaviour and the fate of the society in which they

live so that the things they do will send out vibrations into the farthest confines of this society, and the whole apparatus becomes alive and performs motions which are paradigmatic.[19]

This explains Kennelly's need to readjust mythological references to modern society and create situations in which his readers and listeners will recognize themselves. In re-establishing links between mythology and society, Kennelly also tries to revive the necessary personal link in which the individual relates to living myth.

Dismantling Living Myths towards Tragedy

As the collective and the individual are closely joined in living myth, living myth somehow preserves the peaceful cohesion of a group. This also means that any opposition to a living myth becomes an act of dissent. Brendan Kennelly's treatment of living myth is not restricted to trying to revive mythology, it also involves questioning and debunking living myths, which cannot but lead to a tragic situation for the reader who feels personally connected to these myths. As demonstrated by Jean-Pierre Vernant, tragedy cannot proceed when myth is maintained. This is the reason why in Greek tragedies the myths that people commonly believed in have been transformed so that 'the hero ceases to be regarded as a model and becomes instead an object of debate'.[20] While living myth provides answers, tragedy forces us to interrogate the human condition and exposes enigmatic questions that do not have any solution. Therefore, through examining the living myths of *Cromwell* and *Judas*, and also the living myth of the Irish poet in *Poetry My Arse*, Kennelly obliges his readers to question their own myths, leading to the excessive reactions already observed. The poet, for instance, depicts Judas in such a way that readers are bound to recognize something of themselves in Judas, who has been established as the ultimate monster, the absolute other with whom no association is possible. The recognition damages the personal link the reader has to the mythical Judas and leads to a crisis comparable to that experienced in tragedy.

In his assault against living myth the poet is doing violence to the reader, who retaliates with verbal, occasionally physical, and often politely written violence, especially in literary reviews. The circularity of the process appears in 'Child of the Sword'.[21] In this poem, a reference to Irish mythology is made explicit and is related to a present event, a murder. One notes that the typical goriness of epic mythology endures in the present of the poem, which is also the present of newspapers' headlines. The victim can be viewed as any Irishman, but also as the poet himself who, like other poets and artists in Ireland, is protected by his holy patron, Saint Bridget. This is confirmed by the word 'line', that can refer to the train in which the characters are travelling but can also refer to poetry:

> Somebody stabbed somebody up the line,
> I ran to the victim, his neck was bloody.
>
> There beside him lay Saint Bridget's Peace Cross.
> It said 'One day, a beggar called to her
> Asking for alms. Bridget looked in the man's eyes
> And seeing whatever she saw there
>
> Gave him her father's sword.' Today, right here,
> A child of that sword stabbed a man in the neck,
> He's quiet in his blood now, tonight he'll be raving.

REFERENCES

Havelock, E., *Preface to Plato* (Oxford: Blackwell, 1963).
Kennelly, B., *Cromwell* (Newcastle-upon-Tyne: Bloodaxe, 1987).
Kennelly, B., *Poetry My Arse* (Newcastle-upon-Tyne: Bloodaxe, 1995).
Kennelly, B., *The Book of Judas* (Newcastle-upon-Tyne: Bloodaxe, 1991).
Kennelly, B., *Familiar Strangers* (Tarset: Bloodaxe, 2004).
Kennelly, B., *When Then Is Now: Three Greek Tragedies* (Tarset: Bloodaxe, 2006).
My Education, RTÉ Radio, 1993.
O'Riordan, M., 'In Search of Michael Lehane', unpublished paper, n.d.
Vernant, J.-P., *Myth and Thought among the Greeks*, trans. J. Lloyd (New York: Zone Books, Cambridge, MA: MIT Press, 2006).
White, R., *Remembering Ahanagran: A History of Stories* (New York: Hill & Wang, 1998).

NOTES

1. J.-P. Vernant, *Myth and Thought among the Greeks*, trans. Janet Lloyd (New York: Zone Books; Cambridge, MA: MIT Press, 2006), p.196.
2. R. White, *Remembering Ahanagran: A History of Stories* (New York: Hill & Wang, 1998), p.18.
3. Ibid., p.19.
4. Ibid., p.56.
5. Ibid.
6. Ibid.
7. Ibid., p.560.
8. B. Kennelly, *Familiar Strangers* (Tarset: Bloodaxe, 2004), p.364.
9. Ibid.
10. Ibid.
11. B. Kennelly, *Cromwell* (Newcastle-upon-Tyne: Bloodaxe, 1987), p.26.
12. M. O'Riordan, 'In Search of Michael Lehane', unpublished paper, n.d.
13. *My Education*, RTÉ Radio, 1993.
14. White, *Remembering Ahanagran*, p.58.

15. See the collection of his three plays, *Antigone, Medea* and *The Trojan Women*, which bears a telling title: *When Then Is Now*. B. Kennelly, *When Then Is Now: Three Greek Tragedies* (Tarset: Bloodaxe, 2006).

16. Personal correspondence with Prof. Joris Duytschaever.

17. B. Kennelly, *Poetry My Arse* (Newcastle-upon-Tyne: Bloodaxe, 1995), p.337.

18. B. Kennelly, *The Book of Judas* (Newcastle-upon-Tyne: Bloodaxe, 1991), p.213.

19. E. Havelock, *Preface to Plato* (Oxford: Blackwell, 1963), p.167.

20. Vernant, *Myth and Thought*, p.196.

21. Kennelly, *Book of Judas*, p.163.

2

The Passing of Time in Thomas Kinsella's Early Poetry

Amy Galvin

The phrase 'passionate transitory' first emerged as the last words of Patrick Kavanagh's poem 'The Hospital' (1954), a poem that begins by paying regards to a sterile, nondescript institutional space, and then articulates the beauty of naming ordinary things:

> This is what love does to things: the Rialto Bridge,
> The main gate that was bent by a heavy lorry,
> The seat at the back of a shed that was a suntrap,
> Naming these things is the love-act and its pledge;
> For we must record love's mystery without claptrap,
> Snatch out of time the passionate transitory.[1]

'Passionate transitory' denotes an emotion that lasts for only a brief moment. In his poetry Kavanagh responds to that possibility of transience with the impulse to 'snatch out of time' – essentially to freeze time and to claim the moment as wholly his. Thus time is rendered subject to or in the control of the poet, not as a condition of being that exists apart from him.

The exploration of the 'passionate transitory', and thus of the relationship between the poet and time, also appears in the work of Louis MacNeice – most evidently in 'Meeting Point' (1941) with the recurring line 'time was away and somewhere else'.[2] Like Kavanagh, MacNeice manipulates time to assume control over it:

> Time was away and she was here
> And life no longer what it was,
> The bell was silent in the air
> And all the room one glow because
> Time was away and she was here.[3]

The two poets' 'passionate transitory' focuses completely on the present, always opposing the passage of time. In Kavanagh and

MacNeice's vision of time, there is no past, no future, little action and no process. Although the reader gains access to the poet's private experience, this focus on the passionate transitory undermines the possibility for invention and creation.

Unlike his two Irish contemporaries, Thomas Kinsella writes not to capture the 'passionate transitory' that MacNeice's recurring line seeks, but to envision time as a function of life's processes, as real as the structures, the people and the moments of clarity of which he writes. He sees the *movement* of time (not the freezing of it) as essential in determining the significance of what it means to be human. But how does he portray this movement? This essay explores how Kinsella uses time in his early poetry (1956–73) to reflect the past, present and future as possibilities within which to create, invent and preserve the significance of human existence.

In 'King John's Castle' Kinsella turns his subject to a medieval ruin and tracks the process of time by describing a castle and the tourists who now visit it without knowing what the structure once represented. The poem's description of the castle emphasizes the process of erosion:

> Now the man-rot of passages and broken window-casements,
> Vertical drops chuting through three storeys of masonry,
> Draughty spiral stairways decaying in the depths,
> Are a labyrinth in the medieval dark.[4]

The first word in the stanza – 'Now' – steers readers into the present, as they experience the castle within contemporary time. The 'man-rot of passages', the 'spiral stairways decaying in the depths' and the 'medieval dark' all indicate the seemingly endless epochs in which the castle has existed. Unlike a biological creation, the stone of which this building is constructed resists elements of decomposition – decaying only through long and persistent outside pressure. By including references to the ancient craft of stonemasons, Kinsella establishes the castle's age, its long presence in time. Seamus Deane, however, points out what Kinsella *excludes* from this description: 'Castles and museums are not haunted, in Kinsella's poetry, by nostalgic voices.'[5] Kinsella has another purpose for them, which we unravel through further reading of the poem.

Focusing not just on the age and history of the structure, Kinsella also describes its use:

> King John directs at the river a grey stare, who once
> Viewed the land in a spirit of moderation and massacre.[6]

The terms 'moderation' and 'massacre' are at odds with each other, and, furthermore, in choosing to put the word 'massacre' at the end of the line (the word also marks the end of the stanza) Kinsella allows that final word to assume much greater weight than 'moderation'. Through such choices, he illuminates a violent, medieval society, where conditions that do not logically belong together (like 'moderation' and 'massacre') function within the same space. Yet what most endures in this ancient land – the reality of historical massacre – is lost to the unknowing contemporary tourists who wander aimlessly around this relic:

> Contemplatives, tiny as mice moving over the green
> Mounds below, might take pleasure in the well
> Of quiet there, the dark foundations near at hand.
> Up here where the winds weep bleakly, as though in remembrance
> Against our own tombstones, the brave and great might gather.
> For the rest, this is not their fortress.[7]

Were Kinsella speaking in the 'passionate transitory' he might have narrated the poem through the point of view of a visitor making a case, merely, for moments of pleasure and silence inflected by a romantic nostalgia. Through such a visitor's point of view, the poem would convey only what can be experienced from the now quiescent 'green mounds below'. But with a focus, rather, on the passing of time, Kinsella reveals that the tourist's limited experience is insufficient – that to see the castle as simply a romantically recalled ancient structure generates erroneous interpretation. The poem, then, restores the significance of a castle whose meaning has been eroded through the passing of time – a thematic focus common to the poet's early work. Thomas Jackson suggests that Kinsella's poetry 'is at best a holding force resisting the inevitable processes of entropy'.[8] Describing the ruin as it now exists, indicating what it once represented, and revealing how its original role in a particular society has been erased or forgotten, 'King John's Castle' acknowledges the passing of time – but also seeks to *preserve* for its subject that deep historical significance unavailable to the contemporary viewer.

Not only does the passing of time preserve the significance of what is lost, but it also acknowledges and recaptures conditions that are simply overlooked. Kinsella also uses the passing of time, with the aid of a mirror, as a process for self-recognition.[9] In the poem 'Mirror in February', the simple act of a morning shave leads to an acknowledgement of time passing and thus to a greater understanding of self:

> I towel my shaven jaw and stop, and stare,
> Riveted by a dark exhausted eye,
> A dry downturning mouth.[10]

The poem takes as its action a grooming routine, performed automatically at the start of the day. But this day it is different, as the speaker *stops*, apprehending his role within the relentless progression of time. Then he *stares* into the mirror at his reflection, 'dark' and 'downturning'.

The simple process of the morning routine becomes significant through the poet's momentary pauses, indicating that something has been discovered today. But what has been discovered, and why is this discovery significant?

> It seems again that it is time to learn,
> In this untiring, crumbling place of growth
> To which, for the time being, I return.
> Now plainly in the mirror of my soul
> I read that I have looked my last on youth
> And little more;[11]

The phrase 'It seems *again*' (emphasis added) signals the moment of understanding of a process with which the speaker is familiar but not always engaged – hence, 'for the time being' and 'it is time to learn'. The mirror image represents the poet's simultaneous existence on two planes: one of assumption and inattention, where he has resided before the 'time to learn'; and another plane of reality that acknowledges the passing of time beyond human control. Significantly, this acknowledgement brings the 34-year-old speaker, writing at almost the same age reached by Christ, to a wisdom appropriate to his own age and place in life: 'I have looked my last on youth.' If time is the great enemy, consciously living within time, nevertheless, becomes the only means for human existence, 'Not young and not renewable, but man.'[12]

In 'Mirror in February', the speaker's sudden pause and realization – the 'stop' – suggests no epiphany, no stopping of time within a moment of 'passionate transitory'. Instead the speaker acknowledges that time *fails* to stand still. Although his moment of clarity seems to give pause, he does not, illogically, attempt to 'freeze' the moment of realization that illuminates how time does not halt for him. In Kinsella's poetry, observes Dillon Johnston, 'Discoveries replace epiphanies, and discovering is more like uncovering, too close at hand to be comfortable.'[13] We witness such a process of discovery when the speaker folds his towel 'in slow distaste'; his realization is neither joyous nor terrible – but it strikes a chord of truth that is not easy to digest. By acknowledging time's role in limiting his humanity, the poet, paradoxically, acknowledges the fullness of that humanity (and the evolution towards who he will become) which is another example of how the poet creates significance in human existence.

'The Route of The Táin' was written after Kinsella's 1969 acclaimed translation of the early epic, *Táin Bó Cúailnge*, an achievement that made an ancient national saga tradition accessible and stimulating to contemporary audiences.[14] In undertaking this monumental work of translation, the poet sought both to preserve an epic whose meaning had become obscure through the passing of time and to bring a lost literary tradition into contact with more recent literature. Kinsella states that 'it is not necessary to abandon one aspect of Ireland's literature in order to deal with the other … We have a dead language with a powerful literature and a colonial language with a powerful literature. The combination is an extremely rich one. I don't see why it's necessary to separate the elements.'[15] Such a commitment to joining Ireland's past literary achievement with its more contemporary writing suggests that if a literary endeavour focuses on significance, then nothing needs to be lost. The mark of Kinsella's poetry, as we have seen in 'King John's Castle' and 'Mirror in February', as well as his views on Ireland's literature, is that it is wholly inclusive. Even though the passing of time can distort and create uncertainty, poems like 'The Route of The Táin' demonstrate how this uncertainty opens up a space for discovery and creation.

The poem begins with the speaker and a few of his friends attempting to retrace the path of the Táin, 'content to "enrich the present/honouring the past" '.[16] By including specific references to the contemporary search (a 'map' in line 1; a waiting 'car' in line 5) and to the past Táin culture (hundreds of 'charioteers' in line 9, whose route the speaker and his friends seek to discover) the poem immediately offers its dilemma: has the passing of time rendered it impossible to retrace the steps made in history? At first this seems the case:

> We ourselves, irritated,
> were beginning to turn down toward the river

back to the car, the way we should have come.

We should have trusted our book.[17]

The reader enters the scene at this stopping point, at a moment of frustration with what now appears to be 'a waste of hours'.[18] The narrator and his friends cannot continue on as they fear they have taken the wrong path. Had they been more faithful to the interpretation of the ancient text, would they still be lost?

Such frustration disappears as a red fox streaks by, for in watching the animal's swift passing the travellers apprehend a landmark from the Táin they had not seen before:

> For a heartbeat, in alien certainty,
> we exchanged looks. We should have known it by now
> – the process, the whole tedious enabling ritual.
> Flux brought to fullness, saturated;
> the clouding over; dissatisfaction,
> spreading slowly like an ache;
> something reduced shivering suddenly
> into meaning along new boundaries;[19]

Kinsella represents the journey along the route of the Táin as signifying how one must approach the process of life. 'For a heartbeat' reveals that the moments of profound understanding (this 'alien certainty') are quick yet intense. The clarity must come from a source of struggle, a source of uncertainty – 'flux brought to fullness' – and such moments of clarity move in real time to the next stage of the process – the discovery of 'meaning along new boundaries':

> Before us
> the route of the *Táin*, over men's dust,
> toward these hills that seemed to grow
> darker as we drove nearer.[20]

That the hills grow darker as the travellers move closer suggests that the supposed clarity they possessed earlier in the journey will no longer help them at this new state of illumination. The speaker now acknowledges that he enters a new path of discovery and uncertainty, 'over men's dust', a process that he cannot engage in alone – for many men have taken this journey and many will continue to do so.

In a series of poems engaging with very disparate subject matter – the evocation of a castle, an ordinary grooming ritual, or the retracing of a path based on an ancient text – Kinsella reveals time as pausing, moving backwards in history and forward into new clearings of possibility. Reading his poetry, we must be alert to the meaning behind the stone face looking over the land. We must also acknowledge mortality as we witness the speaker's reflection in the mirror, and observe what the fleeing fox reveals. The awareness of time's role in our lives, even if impalpable and seemingly abstract, allows us to interrogate the significance of each moment. Time for Kinsella is always dynamic; throughout his poetry he notes the importance of each second to bring clarity. Reading his poetry, the reader begins to comprehend all experience within a continuum of time, rather than through Kavanagh's epiphanic moments of 'passionate transitory' that would stop time. And in the open, unknown space of time that Kinsella offers us, the process of human self discovery is most fully experienced.

REFERENCES

Badin, D.A., *Thomas Kinsella* (New York: Twayne, 1996).
Deane, S., 'Thomas Kinsella: "Nursed out of Wreckage" ', in S. Deane, *Celtic Revivals: Essays in Modern Irish Literature 1880–1980* (London: Faber & Faber, 1985), pp.135–45.
Jackson, T.H., *The Whole Matter: The Poetic Evolution of Thomas Kinsella* (New York: Syracuse University Press, 1995).
Johnston, D., 'A Response to Hugh Kenner: Kinsella's Magnanimity and Mean Reading', *Genre: A Quarterly Devoted to Generic Criticism*, 13, 4 (Winter 1980), pp.531–7.
Kavanagh, P., 'The Hospital', in P. Crotty (ed.), *Modern Irish Poetry: An Anthology* (Belfast: Blackstaff, 2004), p.49.
Kinsella, T., *Collected Poems* (Manchester: Carcanet, 2001).
MacNeice, L., 'Meeting Point', in P. Crotty (ed.), *Modern Irish Poetry: An Anthology* (Belfast: Blackstaff, 2004), pp.823.
Quinlan, K., 'A Review of *Collected Poems, 1956–1994*', *World Literature Today*, 72, 3 (Summer 1998), p.662.

NOTES

1. P. Kavanagh, 'The Hospital', in P. Crotty (ed.), *Modern Irish Poetry: An Anthology* (Belfast: Blackstaff, 2004), p.49.
2. Crotty (ed.), *Modern Irish Poetry*, p.83.
3. Ibid.
4. T. Kinsella, *Collected Poems* (Manchester: Carcanet, 2001), p.18.
5. S. Deane, 'Thomas Kinsella: "Nursed Out of Wreckage" ', in S. Deane, *Celtic Revivals: Essays in Modern Irish Literature 1880–1980* (London: Faber & Faber, 1985), pp.135–45.
6. Kinsella, *Collected Poems*, p.18.
7. Ibid.
8. T.H. Jackson, *The Whole Matter: The Poetic Evolution of Thomas Kinsella* (New York: Syracuse University Press, 1995), p.8.
9. Phrase adapted from D.A. Badin, 'The Phases of Kinsella's Poetic Career: Aims and Continuities', in D.A. Badin, *Thomas Kinsella* (New York: Twayne, 1996), pp.11–26.
10. Kinsella, *Collected Poems*, p.53.
11. Ibid.
12. Ibid.

13. D. Johnston, 'A Response to Hugh Kenner: Kinsella's Magnanimity and Mean Reading', *Genre: A Quarterly Devoted to Generic Criticism*, 13, 4 (Winter 1980), pp.531–7.
14. K. Quinlan, 'A Review of *Collected Poems, 1956–1994*', *World Literature Today*, 72, 3 (Summer 1998), p.662.
15. D.A Badin, 'Excerpts from 14–15 August 1993 Interview', in Badin, *Thomas Kinsella*, p.193.
16. Kinsella, *Collected Poems*, p.120.
17. Ibid.
18. Ibid.
19. Ibid., p.121.
20. Ibid.

3

Cribs and Collaborations in the Poetry of Nuala Ní Dhomhnaill

Shannon Hipp

Contemporary Irish poet Nuala Ní Dhomhnaill's decision to write solely in Irish has its roots in both aesthetics and linguistics. In essays about her work, Ní Dhomhnaill has always maintained that 'For some reason that I can never understand, the language that my soul speaks, and the place it comes from, is Irish. At sixteen I had made my choice. And that was that. It still is. I have no other.'[1] The careful diction of Ní Dhomhnaill's sentiment suggests that the Irish language chose her, itself a kind of muse determining the words she would write. Translation, however, has allowed Ní Dhomhnaill's poetry a wider readership and political arena. In a review of Ní Dhomhnaill's 1992 collection *The Astrakhan Cloak*, Bríona Nic Dhiarmada stated that the 'unprecedented visibility in the wider world for a writer in modern Irish has been due in no small part to Nuala Ní Dhomhnaill's willingness to be translated' by her colleagues who have forged their own poetic careers writing in English.[2] But what relationship do these translations bear to her own original works, particularly in books like *Pharaoh's Daughter*, in which each poem's two iterations are printed on facing pages beneath the poet's or the translator's name? Furthermore, beyond aesthetics, what precisely is the function of translation within Ní Dhomhnaill's poetic project? How does it change the way we read her, and her translators, and conceive of language itself? In his book *After Babel*, linguist George Steiner sheds light on these questions by suggesting that 'When we read or hear any language-statement from the past ... we translate. The schematic model of translation is one in which a message from a source-language passes into a receptor-language via a transformational process.'[3] The 'transformational process' of discovering meaning in a Ní Dhomhnaill poem via a translator's English version, then, is both complex and creative. In the very act of reading, Steiner explains, 'We re-enact, in the bounds of our own ... consciousness, the creation by the artist.'[4] By allowing her poems to be re-created in both translation and reading, Ní Dhomhnaill not only brings Irish into new literary arenas, but also takes an intellectual and creative risk in order to foster a collaborative dialectic, joining her own voice to that of her translator in a unison of dissent. To Julia Kristeva, such an act realizes the possibility of revolt that is not violent but rather 'a dialectical process ... a state of permanent questioning, transformation.'[5] This is the very interchange Ní Dhomhnaill has always initiated with her translators. In the archives of Emory University, personal letters and manuscripts belonging to three of Ní Dhomhnaill's most well-known translators – Medbh McGuckian, Ciaran Carson and Paul Muldoon – illuminate this revolutionary, bilingual dialogue unique within contemporary poetry.

Like the girl in 'Teist Mhuintir Dhún Chaoin ar an Oileán/The Testimony of the People of Dunquin',[6] from her series 'Immram/The Voyage',[7] Ní Dhomhnaill's personal, historical and political attachment to the Irish language forces her to 'stay put',[8] alone on the Hy-Breasil (enchanted island) of her choice in order to effect the potency of language as a force for revolt. The title of a 2002 collection of interviews with Julia Kristeva, *Revolt, She Said*, enacts Kristeva's thesis that the concept of revolt must be reinterpreted as an act of articulation. Kristeva's drive 'to strip the word "revolt" of its purely political sense',[9] allowing for its 'Sanskrit root that means to discover, open, but also to turn, to return to the surface',[10] parallels the linguistic agenda of Ní Dhomhnaill's poetry. In her article 'Lashings of the Mother Tongue: Nuala Ní Dhomhnaill's Anarchic Laughter', Mary O'Connor asserts the poet's awareness of such larger political implications, claiming that her 'postrational line of talk in interviews, insofar as it includes an anti-intellectual stance, is partly a pose; she is well-versed in the works of Freud and Jung ... and stays *au courant* with the contemporary critical theorists, especially the French feminists'.[11] If Ní Dhomhnaill is to be read as revolutionary for her recovery of Irish, she fulfils the role equally by participating in revolt as 'a dialectical process'[12] of exchange between herself and her English translators.

Probing into the archive of McGuckian, Carson and Muldoon reveals that the poet relies on her colleagues as interpreters, translators and personal friends in order to collectively achieve poetic dialogue. The collection of correspondence sent to Muldoon numbers twenty-five handwritten letters, notes and postcards, consistently written in English and suggesting his exceptional role as a mentor to Ní Dhomhnaill. Within such correspondence are references to what Ní Dhomhnaill calls cribs, line-by-line English translations completed by the poet herself. For example, in a 1989 letter to Muldoon, Ní Dhomhnaill wrote: 'I enclose a crib as I find it helps people even with good Irish if they see roughly what it means. That can give you more leeway to add the "je ne sais quoi" that makes for an excellent translation.'[13] Indeed, for each of the translation manuscripts found in the McGuckian, Carson and Muldoon archives, there is a Ní Dhomhnaill crib among the drafts and the correspondence. In a personal interview, Muldoon explained that Ní Dhomhnaill 'originally made up the cribs because those translating her didn't have any Irish at all. She sent them out to guide the translators, and she still sends them, even to me, just as a matter of course.'[14] After a bit more thought as to why she might still be doing so, even for those practiced in Irish, Muldoon surmised that 'the cribs are maybe for herself, really, just a matter of course in her own writing'.[15] If translation is at the root of her own authorial process, then Ní Dhomhnaill certainly complicates the role of her colleagues who follow suit.

Understanding the presence of the cribs in the Ní Dhomhnaill translations presents an opportunity to parse language at the level of its operation within the project. With the Irish original and the English crib in hand, are McGuckian, Carson, Muldoon and others truly translating? If Ní Dhomhnaill herself generates her poems' cribs, why does she engage the pens of others? Personal notes from the archive reveal her own aesthetic limitations with English as one possible reason. A letter to Carson dated 6 August 1989, requesting his translation of 'An Ceann', reveals the complaint: 'I find it almost impossible myself to get that exact "raconteur" tone in English (that's where you come in!).'[16] A similar sentiment surfaces in a handwritten postscript included on the crib of 'The Unfaithful Wife', sent to Muldoon: 'Sounds pretty brutal in English, doesn't it? In Irish it is much more "<u>natural</u>", the words don't hit you in the face just as much. How do you get the equivalent in English?'[17] Thus, just as Ní Dhomhnaill is in dialogue with her colleagues, so poem and crib exist in dialogue with one another in order to engender the English translation.

The archive of Medbh McGuckian reveals the organic process of translation most clearly, though it also remains least connected to the person of Nuala Ní Dhomhnaill. No personal correspondence between the two women poets is found within McGuckian's papers at Emory, though her file is the only one to include a crib written in Ní Dhomhnaill's own hand. An examination of the translation process for 'Geasa/The Bond'[18] must thus begin with the crib itself, a white sheet of paper on which Ní Dhomhnaill attached a printed version of the Irish poem with paper clips, then scrawled the following in the margins:

Any time I touch the inner sanctum
that I build a bridge over the river
every thing the bridge [???][19] build by day
is knocked down again before morning.

Up the river at night comes a boat
a woman is standing in it.
There are fierce lights (lit candles) in her eyes
and in her hands/she holds two oars.

She takes out a deck of cards
'Will you play forfeits' she asks me
We play and she always wins
and puts as a demand on me

Not to ~~spend the~~ eat two meals in one house
nor spend two nights under the one roof
not to sleep twice in any one bed
until I find her. When I ask where she dwells

'If it were west I'd say east' she says 'if east west'
She leaves [???][20] off in a flash of lightning
and I am left alone on the bank
the two candles are still beside me.
She has left me the oars.[21]

From this crib, McGuckian's papers reveal her process to be both organic and intellectual. On sheets of loose-leaf paper, McGuckian next wrote through the poem in neat cursive penmanship, trying out synonyms for operative words and literally listing them side by side. Of the title, for example, McGuckian wrote 'Geasa—a solemn injunction, spell, taboo'; the poem's first line became: 'If I put one hand on the repunge/sanctuary/asylum/protection/aegis/blessed ... '[22] A reading of McGuckian's initial stab at translation, then, reveals her interpretation of its most crucial elements and shows her to be involved in verbal selection. McGuckian is most involved in selection in lines seven and twelve. Ní Dhomhnaill – as illustrated by the crib – even revised her own translation of line seven – 'There are fierce lights (lit candles) in her eyes' – the same line that, in McGuckian's hand, becomes: 'There are candles glowing/burning/blushing/ripe/blazing/ kindled/shining/inflamed/flashing/glowing.'[23] Likewise, line twelve, the admittedly awkward 'and she puts as a demand on me' becomes 'and she puts a question/problem/difficulty/riddle/examination/a sentence/judgment/penance/doom/greatobligate/murder/load/deeds ... '[24]

The McGuckian archive contains two more copies of 'Geasa/The Bond' among her papers – another version handwritten on loose-leaf and one typed manuscript. By the time McGuckian wrote the poem out a second time, she had decided on 'The Bond' as the appropriate translation of the title and made some more determined decisions. The first and the twelfth lines, however, still evoke hesitation. On the handwritten draft, the first line reads 'If I put/place one hand on the ~~sanctuary~~ forbidden place', indicating a revision of one of the synonyms McGuckian discovered during her play with the language. Similarly, line twelve, which generated thirteen synonyms for 'demand' on the first draft, retains its complexity. The draft reads 'And she puts three ~~penalties~~ ~~promises~~ banns on me.'[25] Both 'forbidden' and 'banns' arise for the first time on this second version, and their respective sinful and nuptial connotations must have satisfied McGuckian. Both words remain in the final translation, though McGuckian adjusted the first line one last time. The final manuscript opens with: 'If I use my forbidden hand', thereby attaching immorality quite literally to the speaker's body.[26] These examples represent only a portion of McGuckian's work on the poem. The original crib read alongside the complete published version presents the full picture. It is this translation process that results in 'The Bond' belonging to McGuckian's oeuvre, even if it owes its origins to Ní Dhomhnaill.

Ciaran Carson's collected papers reveal a similar translation process with regard to Ní Dhomhnaill's poem 'An Ceann/The Head', including a typed crib, two handwritten drafts and a final typed manuscript. A letter of introduction accompanies the poem. In it, Ní Dhomhnaill describes 'An Ceann' as both 'deliberately mundane ... [and a] protest against the minimalist lyric that has begun to dominate in poetry in Irish – playing to the lowest common denominators – a mere smattering in Irish.'[27] Against this trend, Ní Dhomhnaill offers 'An Ceann', a weighty poetic folk tale of seven stanzas ranging in length from four to sixteen lines each. Carson's 'The Head'[28] retains the heft of the original, as it is comprised of six long stanzas, one of which stretches to nineteen lines. Read against even the early drafts of Carson's translation, Ní Dhomhnaill's crib falls flat. In order to be effective, the poem's speaker must be able to spin one yarn that can itself generate a second. The crib reads like the work of a rushed journalist; the translation like that of a practised teller of place-lore:[29]

Crib, Ní Dhomhnaill
My aunt's husband, Thomas Murphy is a man
who can recognize a head above all others.
There is not a single tomb opened in St. Caitlin's graveyard
in the parish of Ventry that he's not aware of, and can tell you
every skull that is in it, just by counting the teeth (Alas poor Yorick)
And when he comes upon a shinbone broken with the signs of knitting
still noticeable, he knows who he has there, the name and the surname of its
owner, and even the story of how the accident happened.

First Translation Draft, Carson
My aunties man, Tom Murphy, is a man who ...
Or rather, you might ~~say~~ call him a phrenologist
For there's not a skull he wouldn't ~~know~~ recognize anytime
They'd open up a ~~grave~~ sepulcher, I think they call it
Over there in Ventry parish. He turns them by their teeth
And when he comes ~~across~~ chanced upon a badly knitted bone
He reads the jagged line like script/an open book to him. He'll have the name,
the surname, and a story about how it happened
as long as your 2 arms.[30]

Already in this first draft, Carson's stanza evokes the tone of legend, transforming the formal 'aunt's husband' to the colloquial 'aunties man' and integrating original similes so familiar as to be almost clichéd: in the seventh line – 'reads the jagged line like script' and in the ninth, the story is described as 'as long as your 2 arms'. These colloquialisms make the translation successful, for 'The Head' retains the spoken qualities of self-correction and hesitation throughout. In stanza two of the final manuscript of 'The Head', the speaker says, 'The stick broke in two bits/While Tommy ... Tommy never turned a hair', allowing the pause of the ellipsis to draw suspense. Likewise, phrases such as 'come to think of it' in the fourth stanza – 'About ten years, come to think of it, before The Massacre/In Dingle' – and strategic ambiguities such as the fifth stanza's 'He walks into the Child's place – he was some relation of the mother' resonate with the mutability of tall tales that comprise oral culture in English.

Talk itself assumes further primacy in the final stanza of Carson's translation. Ní Dhomhnaill's original crib for 'An Ceann' ends with the poem's speaker and children flashing SOS beams at their vision of the Big Child across the bay, 'trying to get him to understand our message,/and to come over to our side, trying to see if we could only/make contact with him somehow, at last'.[31] While Carson maintained the beauty of the SOS signal (reproducing the 'on/off, on/Off , on/off' exactly as in the crib), his last lines express a desire for intimacy through spoken language: the speaker and children flash their lights 'Hoping he would get the message, trying to see if he would talk to us,/Or, finally, if we could talk to him.'[32] For all of these developments Ní Dhomhnaill endorsed Carson's 'The Head' in the 1989 letter to Muldoon. After mentioning the ' '"je ne sais quoi" that makes for a good translation', she wrote: 'I'm thinking in particular of one Ciaran Carson did recently called "An Ceann" where just that very thing happened.'[33]

The dialectical nature of Ní Dhomhnaill's interaction with her translators is best exemplified by her relationship with Paul Muldoon, perhaps because their exchange transcends poetic language in order to approach nuances of content and sound. Muldoon describes his relationship with Ní Dhomhnaill simply – 'we're very good friends' – but acknowledges the complex exchange of their poetic sensibilities, even to the extent that he claims, 'after I started translating her work, I think it changed the way she wrote along the way. So it's a dialogue, a dialogue, yes, along the way.'[34]

In addition to the many notes, postcards and letters from Ní Dhomhnaill found in Muldoon's papers are the crib and the working manuscript for 'An Bhean Mhídhílis/The Unfaithful Wife', which offer productive means for understanding the dialogue of their translation endeavour. Although each stanza of Muldoon's translation includes words and phrases that exactly match Ní Dhomhnaill's cribs, he claims that 'To tell the truth, I pay not all that much attention to them because sometimes they're not really quite accurate. You know, a line would not have the particular resonance necessary. Nuala has her own take, but that may not be my take. What you must know is that the poem becomes a new thing in English.'[35] In the case of this particular poem, in which the title character speaks frankly of casual sex in a stranger's car, Ní Dhomhnaill had specific hopes for the English iteration. These hopes, articulated in a letter, belie her own frustration with the conventional expectations for the Irish woman poet. She explains that the poem 'has caused my considerable distress already with men sidling up to me after readings and making nasty remarks on the principle that a woman who would write something like that would do anything'. Thus, the letter expresses her desire for the poem not to be provocative but rather 'simultaneously less romantic, more sordid, more honest, and at the same time exhultant [sic] and celebratory'.[36] Consideration of the first stanza of the crib and of Muldoon's translation suggests exactly how his poetic language achieved this dichotomy:

Crib, Ní Dhomhnaill
He picked me up
at the counter
and after a spot of banter
he offered me
a drink
which I didn't refuse
and then we sat down talking
We went from drink to drink
and from joke to joke
and he had me stretched out, in stitches
but no matter how drunk I got,
I never told him I was married.

First Translation Draft, Muldoon
He started coming on to me
at the spirit-grocer's ~~incredibly~~ warped and wonky counter
and after a spot of banter
offered to buy me a glass of porter;
I wasn't one to demur
and in no time at all we were talking
the hind legs off a donkey.
A quick succession of snorts and snifters
and his relentless repartee
had me splitting my sides with laughter.
However much the drink had loosened my tongue
I never let on I was married.[37]

In the richness of its imagery as well as its toying with English itself (such as in the second line's 'wonky'), the translation domesticates and thus tempers the poem's crucial pick-up scene. The bar where the pick-up occurs becomes the 'spirit-grocer', that last word a place where even the most conventional wife would appropriately linger, and the translation's feminine rhyme works like the porter to ensnare even the most conservative reader. Wonky/talking/donkey, banter/porter/demur and even snifter/laughter possess even more force when they are heard aloud, according to the spoken 'repartee' of the sly male character himself. In fact, only a listener might catch the man's early intent to mount her, in the resonance of the third line's last word, 'counter'.[38]

In addition to its associative power, Muldoon's rhyme represents an aesthetic means by which he recasts the original in his translation: 'Sometimes I represent not the original form but rather an indicator of formal constraint in the original. For example, I'll use rhyme independently of the original, with assonantal and consonantal rhyme.'[39] Thus freed from the necessity for exact mimesis, Muldoon opens up his translation to the possibility of achieving the 'effect on the ear'[40] of Ní Dhomhnaill's Irish originals. Further explaining his attention to rhyme in translation, Muldoon says: 'There is no full rhyme in Irish. It tends to be assonantal, so sometimes I keep that in mind. But always I think of my work as the poem becoming a new thing.'[41] In the case of 'The Unfaithful Wife', Muldoon's rhyme makes palatable, even enjoyable, the poem's potentially shocking content – just as Ní Dhomhnaill intended.

Unlike the processes suggested by McGuckian's and Carson's handwritten drafts, Muldoon's translations are cleanly typed; only rarely does he physically strike through a word and replace it. The last stanza of 'The Unfaithful Wife', however, must have posed a particular challenge, for Muldoon's scrawling black pen suggests second thoughts and the possibility of reversing Ní Dhomhnaill's ending. Its strike-throughs and brackets, all written in Muldoon's hand and reproduced here, recall McGuckian's invocation of synonyms in her drafts of 'Geasa/The Bond':

> As I ~~beat~~ led myself up my own ~~front~~ garden-path
> I burst into song and whistled a little tune
> and vowed never to breathe a word
> to a soul about what I'd done.
> And if, by chance, I run into him again
> at a disco or in some shebeen
> [the honourable thing, [surely] would be to keep break faith]
> and [never] let on I was married.[42]

In the draft, two possible endings coexist, best demonstrated in the side-by-side placement of keeping and breaking faith in the stanza's seventh line and the possible exclusion of 'never' in the last line. Below the typed draft, Muldoon further worked out possible translations by scrawling the following phrases: 'for surely; , I suppose,; , I guess, only course; decent thing; [and below the rest] betray our trust.'[43] The complexity of the wife's moral conundrum has exceeded the capacity of the poet's language, a condition that he eventually ascribed to the woman herself. In the translation's final form, she stammers to the conclusion that 'the only honourable course – the only decent thing – /would be to keep faith and not betray his trust/by letting on I was married.' Thus, just as Muldoon did in working to achieve his translation, the unfaithful wife simultaneously aligns the opposing concepts of deceit and decency, betrayal and faith.[44]

The extent to which Muldoon has become Ní Dhomhnaill's primary translator attests to a mutual understanding between the poets. Nic Dhiarmada suggests that 'the imagination of these two poets inhabits the same territories' and explains Muldoon's role as 'not simply to translate but to find an equivalence which would strike the same type of memory chord in a reader in English'.[45] His translations are then associative in nature. Muldoon himself remains modest about his role, explaining that after Ní Dhomhnaill accepted his first translation, 'As for the Quince', 'I allowed myself a certain amount of play, and well, she continues to ask me to translate her poems, so presumably there's a reason.'[46] In a 2003 article in *Critical Survey* on Ní Dhomhnaill, Eavan Boland and Eiléan Ní Chuilleanáin, Helen Kidd invokes the folkloric figure of Sheela-na-gig, who 'incorporates male and female, demonstrating the necessity of the two', and suggests her as a metaphor for 'the bisexuality of language, moving between the singularity of meaning and the plenipotential of possibilities'.[47] As individual poets, Ní Dhomhnaill and Muldoon handle language in just this way; together in dialogue, perhaps they constitute the male/female overlap of the metaphoric Sheela-na-gig.

For all the writing that Ní Dhomhnaill does, not only in her verse but also in her personal and cultural essays and her private correspondence, the politics of her art are best summed up in six words she uttered in a 1996 interview with the *Irish Literary Supplement*: 'While I live, Irish doesn't die.' Stripped of aesthetics and linguistics, the maxim endorses sheer survival. As evidenced by the correspondence, cribs and manuscripts left behind in the archive, Ní

Dhomhnaill writes her poems in Irish and initiates a dialogue wherein they are translated into English, thereby sacrificing creative control in the hopes of creating an Irish poem in conversation with an English poem. The two independently authored works thus, in the words of Steiner, 'make tangible the implication of a third, active presence ... that "pure speech" which precedes and underlines both languages'.[48] This kind of poetry exceeds empire, transcends understanding and supersedes cultural difference. Ní Dhomhnaill's soul may speak Irish, but her project encompasses letters, cribs, drafts and poems engaged in dialectic, generative revolt beyond the trappings of language.

REFERENCES

Carson, C., Translation Draft for 'An Ceann/The Head', Ciaran Carson papers, ca. 1970–2002, Manuscript, Archives and Rare Book Library, Emory University.

Kidd, H., 'Cailleachs, Keens and Queens: Refiguring Gender and Nationality in the Poetry of Eiléan Ní Chuilleanáin, Nuala Ní Dhomhnaill and Eavan Boland', *Critical Survey*, 15, 1 (2003), pp.34–47.

Kristeva, J., *Revolt, She Said* (Cambridge, MA: MIT Press, 2002).

McGuckian, M., Translation Draft for 'Geasa/The Bond', Medbh McGuckian papers, 1967–99, Manuscript, Archives and Rare Book Library, Emory University.

Muldoon, P., Crib and Translation Draft for 'An Bhean Mhídhílis/The Unfaithful Wife', Paul Muldoon papers, 1968–96, Manuscript, Archives and Rare Book Library, Emory University.

Muldoon, P., Personal interview, 12 December 2006.

Ní Dhomhnaill, N., Crib for 'An Bhean Mhídhílis/The Unfaithful Wife', Paul Muldoon papers, 1968–96, Manuscript, Archives and Rare Book Library, Emory University.

Ní Dhomhnaill, N., Crib for 'Geasa', Medbh McGuckian papers, 1967–99, Manuscript, Archives and Rare Book Library, Emory University.

Ní Dhomhnaill, N., Letter to Paul Muldoon, lá le Caitlíona 1989, Paul Muldoon papers, 1968–96, Manuscript, Archives and Rare Book Library, Emory University.

Ní Dhomhnaill, N., Letter to Ciaran Carson, 6 August 1989, Ciaran Carson papers, ca. 1970–2002, Manuscript, Archives and Rare Book Library, Emory University.

Ní Dhomhnaill, N., *The Astrakhan Cloak* (Loughcrew: Gallery Press, 1992).

Ní Dhomhnaill, N., *Pharaoh's Daughter* (Winston-Salem, NC: Wake Forest University Press, 1990).

Ní Dhomhnaill, N., *Selected Essays* (Dublin: New Island, 2005).

Nic Dhiarmada, B., Rev. of Nuala Ní Dhomhnaill and Paul Muldoon, *The Astrakhan Cloak*, manuscript copy, Paul Muldoon papers, 1968–96, Manuscript, Archives and Rare Book Library, Emory University.

O'Connor, M., 'Lashings of the Mother Tongue: Nuala Ní Dhomhnaill's Anarchic Laughter', in T. O'Connor, *The Comic Tradition in Irish Women Writers* (Gainesville, FL: University Press of Florida, 1996), pp.149–70.

Steiner, G., *After Babel: Aspects of Language and Translation* (London: Oxford University Press, 1975).

Teicher, C.M., 'Lyrical Latitudes', *Poets & Writers* (November/December 2006).

NOTES

1. N. Ní Dhomhnaill, *Selected Essays* (Dublin: New Island, 2005), p.13.

2. B. Nic Dhiarmada, Rev. of Nuala Ní Dhomhnaill and Paul Muldoon, *The Astrakhan Cloak*, manuscript copy, Paul Muldoon papers, 1968–96, Manuscript, Archives and Rare Book Library, Emory University, Atlanta, GA [hereafter MARBL], p.1.
3. G. Steiner, *After Babel: Aspects of Language and Translation* (London: Oxford University Press, 1975), p.28.
4. Ibid., p.26.
5. J. Kristeva, *Revolt, She Said* (Cambridge, MA: MIT Press, 2002), p.120.
6. N. Ní Dhomhnaill, *The Astrakhan Cloak* (Loughcrew: Gallery Press, 1992), p.88.
7. Ibid., p.72.
8. Ibid., p.89.
9. Kristeva, *Revolt*, p.99.
10. Ibid.
11. M. O'Connor, 'Lashings of the Mother Tongue: Nuala Ní Dhomhnaill's Anarchic Laughter', in T. O'Connor (ed.), *The Comic Tradition in Irish Women Writers* (Gainesville, FL: University Press of Florida, 1996), p.152.
12. Kristeva, *Revolt*, p.120.
13. N. Ní Dhomhnaill, Letter to Paul Muldoon, lá le Caitlíona 1989, Paul Muldoon papers, 1968–96, MARBL.
14. P. Muldoon, Personal interview, 12 December 2006.
15. Ibid.
16. N. Ní Dhomhnaill, Letter to Ciaran Carson, 6 August 1989, Ciaran Carson papers, ca. 1970–2002, MARBL.
17. N. Ní Dhomhnaill, Crib for 'An Bhean Mhídhílis/The Unfaithful Wife', Paul Muldoon papers, 1968–96, MARBL.
18. N. Ní Dhomhnaill, *Pharaoh's Daughter* (Winston-Salem, NC: Wake Forest University Press, 1990), p.12.
19. A word follows 'bridge' in Ní Dhomhnaill's crib, though I could not make it out.
20. The same is true here. The word appears to be 'hives', but may in fact be 'hooks', which surfaces in McGuckian's translation.
21. N. Ní Dhomhnaill, Crib for 'Geasa', Medbh McGuckian papers, 1967–99, MARBL.
22. Ibid.
23. M. McGuckian, Translation Draft for 'Geasa/The Bond', Medbh McGuckian papers, 1967–99, MARBL.
24. Ibid.
25. Ibid.
26. Ibid.
27. Ní Dhomhnaill, Letter to Ciaran Carson, 6 August 1989.
28. Ní Dhomhnaill, *Pharaoh's Daughter*, p.15.
29. Ní Dhomhnaill, *Selected Essays*, p.30.
30. C. Carson, Translation Draft for 'An Ceann/The Head', Ciaran Carson papers, ca. 1970–2002, MARBL.
31. Ibid.
32. N. Ní Dhomhnaill, *Pharaoh's Daughter*, p.19.
33. Ní Dhomhnaill, Letter to Paul Muldoon, lá le Caitlíona 1989.
34. Muldoon, Personal interview.
35. Ibid.
36. Ní Dhomhnaill, Letter to Paul Muldoon, lá le Caitlíona 1989.
37. P. Muldoon, Crib and Translation Draft for 'An Bhean Mhídhílis/The Unfaithful Wife', Paul Muldoon papers, 1968–96, MARBL.
38. Though imaginative and somewhat speculative in nature, this type of reading is indicative of Muldoon's own work as both a reader and writer of poetry. In Craig Morgan Teicher's profile of Muldoon, 'Lyrical Latitudes', in *Poets & Writers*, he explained that Muldoon believes both reading and writing to be 'highly associative' activities: *Poets & Writers* (November/December 2006), p.40.
39. Muldoon, Personal interview.
40. O'Connor, 'Breaking the Rules', p.79.
41. Muldoon, Personal interview.
42. Muldoon, Translation Draft for 'An Bhean Mhídhílis/The Unfaithful Wife'.

43. Ibid.
44. Ní Dhomhnaill, *Pharaoh's Daughter*, p.109.
45. Nic Dhiarmada, Rev. of Nuala Ní Dhomhnaill and Paul Muldoon, *The Astrakhan Cloak*, manuscript copy, pp.3–4.
46. Muldoon, Personal interview.
47. H. Kidd, 'Cailleach, Keens and Queens: Refiguring Gender and Nationality in the Poetry of Eiléan Ní Chuilleanáin, Nuala Ní Dhomhnaill and Eavan Boland', *Critical Survey*, 15 (2003), p.35.
48. Steiner, *After Babel*, p.64.

4

Marginal Figures and Subversion in the Poetry of Cathal Ó Searcaigh

Caitríona Ní Chléirchín

Cathal Ó Searcaigh is a poet and dramatist who writes in Irish and was born in Meenalea, Gortahork, in 1956, in the heart of the Donegal Gaeltacht. He studied French, Russian and Irish at the National Institute of Higher Education in Limerick, at the same time as his fellow poets Michael Davitt, Nuala Ní Dhomhnaill, Liam Ó Muirthile and Gabriel Rosenstock who were part of the *Innti* group, studying Irish in University College Cork. Having lived abroad in London for a year, he returned to study in Maynooth University and then to work in RTÉ. He published poems in *Comhar*, *Feasta*, *Scríobh* and *Innti* magazines. He has published thirteen collections of poetry, both in Irish and bilingually: *Miontraigéide Cathrach* (1975), *Tuirlingt* (1978), *Súile Shuibhne* (1983), *Suibhne* (1987), *An Bealach 'na Bhaile* (1991), *Homecoming/An Bealach 'na Bhaile* (1993), *Na Buachaillí Bána* (1996), *Out in the Open* (1997), *Ag Tnúth leis an tSolas* (2000), *Caiseal na gCorr* (2002), *Seal I Neipeal* (2003), *Na hAingle ó Xanadú* (2005) and *GúrúigClúidíní* (2006).

The bilingual collection *Homecoming/An Bealach 'na Bhaile* won the Sean Ó Ríordáin and Bord na Gaeilge prizes in 1993. The collection includes English translations from thirteen poets, including Seamus Heaney, John F. Deane, Frank Sewell and Gréagóir Ó Dúill. Ó Searcaigh was able to reach a wider readership because of this bilingual collection. He was writer in residence at the University of Ulster, Coleraine, between 1992 and 1995, and at NUI Galway in 1996. The NUI awarded him an honorary doctorate in 2000 and his *Ag Tnúth leis an tSolas* collection was awarded *The Irish Times* Literature Prize for Irish Language Books in 2001. As regards criticism of his work, Lillis Ó Laoire, Frank Sewell and Caoimhín Mac Giolla Léith were among the first to write critical essays on his poetry. Ó Laoire once claimed that 'critical analysis of his work has been mainly confined to short reviews and articles in literary journals'.[1] Since then, however, a collection of critical essays in English, *On the Side of Light*, was published in 2002, as well as a major critical study in Irish by Pádraig de Paor, *Na Buachaillí Dána: Cathal Ó Searcaigh, Gabriel Rosenstock agus ról comhaimseartha an fhile sa Ghaeilge*, in 2005.

Marginal Voices: 'Maigdiléana' and 'An Díbeartach'

Cathal Ó Searcaigh writes in Irish, more specifically in the Donegal dialect, which is perceived by many as the most marginalized and least understood of the three main Irish dialects. The poet writes consciously as a native speaker from within his own marginalized heritage.[2] His is a chosen marginality, which gives him the freedom to explore and map liminal territories from an actively constructive position. Lillis Ó Laoire has already highlighted the dissenting voice in Cathal Ó Searcaigh's poetry, as a voice that openly celebrates homosexual love.[3] Ó Searcaigh often deals with the tensions that occur between the individual and the immediate community or large and powerful institutions.

Brian Lacey traces the history of homosexuality in Ireland in his study *'Terrible Queer Creatures': A History of Homosexuality in Ireland*. He illustrates how in the past homosexual people have been outlawed as criminals and excommunicated from the Catholic Church. In his poetry, Cathal Ó Searcaigh confidently subverts dominant discourses within the Irish-language literary tradition, eroding the heterosexual consensus in order to give voice to the homosexual speaking subject.

In his poetry, Ó Searcaigh reappropriates discourses of authority, subverting received notions of those who live on the edge of society as being in a position of deficit. His poetry develops as a safe place for the threatened and the fearful to speak: 'Maigdiléana'[4] is a poem describing the life of a prostitute; 'An Díbeartach/Outcast'[5] is about the poet as outcast. Ó Searcaigh celebrates nomadic identities from his own community in poems such as 'Bean an tSléibhe/Mountain Woman'[6] and the inspirational poem 'Do Jack Kerouac/For Jack Kerouac'.[7] I will use Stephen Menell's theory of social identities and Julia Kristeva's theories on the stranger, as well as Rosi Braidotti's theories on the nomad, to analyse the subversive element of Ó Searcaigh's poems dealing with marginality.

The poem 'Maigdiléana', first published in *Suibhne* in 1987 and translated into English by Gabriel Fitzmaurice in 1993, deals with the life of a prostitute living in present-day London. Ó Searcaigh conveys the desolate loneliness of her life through images of darkness and emptiness. Maigdiléana goes to work at twilight, 'I dtrátha an ama a dtachtann sealán aibhléise aoibh shoilseach na spéire/about the time the noose of electric light chokes the luminous beauty of the sky'.[8] The poet continues with the deathlike imagery to describe this lady of the night 'agus í ar a *beat* ag *cruiseáil* go huaigneach sa mharbhsholas chnámhach/on her beat cruising lonely in the skeletal half-light'.[9]

The name Maigdiléana given to this lady of the night evokes the figure of Mary Magdalene from the New Testament, a faithful follower of Jesus. Although she was cast out by others as a sinner and a prostitute, Jesus treated her as a person of worth. Ó Searcaigh also values the Maigdiléana of his poem, portraying her human frailty with compassion. Ó Searcaigh evokes the sadness of this figure 'ag spléachadh go fáili ar scáilí na gcros teilifíse ag cuartú a Calvaire go heaglach/glimpsing on walls the crosses of TV aerials as she seeks her Calvary in fear'.[10] In Christianity, Calvary and the cross are symbols of failure, crucifixion and death, but also of redemption. They symbolize suffering but also hope, as it was on the cross that Christ died in order to save humanity, according to Christian belief. With the images of Calvary and the television-aerial crosses, the poet identifies Maigdiléana with Mary Magdalene.

The Maigdiléana of the poem leads a lonely and fearful existence. Ó Searcaigh is profoundly aware of her isolation as she returns at break of day on the Underground to Paddington:

> Nuair nach labhraíonn éinne leat, a ghrá,
> Thíos ansiúd, dubh bán nó riabhach
> Bhéarfaidh na fógraí béal ban duit agus béadán
> i dtumba folamh an *underground*
>
> no b'fhéidir scéala ón Ghalailéach.
>
> When nobody speaks to you, love,
> down there, black, white or in-between,
> the ads will softsoap you with gossip
> in the empty tomb of the Underground
>
> or maybe bear tidings of the Galilean.[11]

No one will speak to her and she herself is silent. Her isolation is complete: the only ordinary human communication she has is in the form of the advertising messages in the Underground.

Ó Searcaigh continues with images from Christ's Passion and death in the final verse of the poem. Maigdiléana has followed Christ into the tomb and the message there is that he is risen: that he has overcome death, sin and pain. The 'tidings of the Galilean' refer to the sentences from the Gospel that sometimes appear in the Underground to remind people that Jesus died for them and that he rose from the dead after that, according to the Christian faith. These tidings would seem to be a possible source of hope to this woman working at night on the streets.

The depth of empathy and understanding for the marginalized and condemned figure of the prostitute here demonstrates the humanist sensibility of Ó Searcaigh's writing. The pathos of this poem is in the sound of plaintive lamenting cries as each line falls further and further into the lower regions of voice and silence:

> I dtrátha an ama a dtachtann sealán aibhléise
> Aoibh shoilseach na spéire
> Tím uaim í de ghnáth, ...
> Agus í ar a beat ag cruiseáil go huaigneach.

> About the time the noose of electric light chokes
> The luminous beauty of the sky,
> I see her usually, ...
> On her beat cruising lonely.[12]

Like 'Maigdiléana', the poem 'An Díbeartach/Outcast' appeared for the first time in *Suibhne* in 1987, and was published again with an English translation by Frank Sewell in *Out In the Open* in 1997. This poem deals with the poet's relationship to his public. He sees himself as a marginal figure both misunderstood and ridiculed.

An tír seo bheith ag fonóid faoi gach rabhán dá ndéan tú de cheol

(i) Ní thuigeann siad an buachaill seanchríonna
a bhíonn ag cumadh ar feadh na hoíche
thuas i gcnoic Bharr an Ghleanna.
Tá a bhfuil ar siúl aige amaideach
A deir siad thíos i dtigh an leanna –
Macasamhail an mhadaidh bháin
a bhíonn ag cnaí chnámh na gealaí
I bpolláin uisce ar an bhealach.

And the country scoffing at your half-baked songs ...

(i) They don't get it. The boy,
older than his years, versing
all night, away up in the glen
what he's up to is daft,
they say down the pub.
Like the white dog
baying for the bone he sees
in a puddle on the road – the moon.[13]

In 'Outcast',[14] the community sees what he does as 'daft' and futile. The poem begins with an extract from 'Úirchill an Chreagáin', an Ulster *aisling* poem from the eighteenth century by Art Mac Cumhaigh. A 'spéirbhean', or vision woman, from the otherworld attempts to entice the poet away and points out that the country is mocking his verse. Lillis Ó Laoire reminds us in his essay 'Dearg Dobhogtha Cháin/The Indelible Mark of Cain: Sexual Dissidence in the Poetry of Cathal Ó Searcaigh' that poets in Gaelic society often saw themselves and were seen by their communities as outside the bounds of accepted patterns.[15] This marginality gave them freedom, but it came at a price:

> Ach fós beidh a chuid amhrán
> ina n-oileáin dóchais agus dídine
> i bhfarraigí a ndorchadais.

> And yet his songs will be
> islands of hope and protection
> in their mind-dark seas.[16]

Interpreting this poem from the perspective of marginality, it would seem that when the public must face their own dark minds in private moments as individuals, it is poetry that will provide hope. In the next verse, Ó Searcaigh speaks about the sacrifices the poet must make in order to write. Writing is a solitary activity that sets him apart from the crowd. Most of the people around him are working on the land, but his fields are poems.[17] ('Anseo tá achan chuibhreann mar a bheadh rann ann i mórdhán an mhíntíreachais/Here every enclosed field is like a verse in the great poem of land reclamation.'[18]) Ó Searcaigh sees writing as work where the land becomes word as in Seamus Heaney's poem 'Digging'. The pen that replaces the spade becomes the poet's tool and the boundaries between physical and cultural labour disappear. Heaney holds a special place in Ó

Searcaigh's imagination as a source of inspiration and courage, having himself given voice to the marginalized speech of a northern dialect of Hiberno-English.

Excluded from the Catholic Church and the community because of his sexuality, the first person of this poem feels that for him there will be no 'loving under licence', no marriage, but only secret, forbidden love:

(ii) Ní duitse faraor
dea-fhód a dhéanamh den domasach
ná an Domhnach a chomóradh mar chách
ná grá na gcomharsan lá na cinniúna
ná muirniú mná faoi scáth an phósta
ná dea-chuideachta an tí ósta.

Duitse faraor
Dearg do-bhogtha Cháin
A bheith smeartha ar chlar d'éadain.

(ii) Not for you, it seems,
making the best of the badland,
suiting Sunday like everyone,
a Samaritan when you're in need,
loving under licence,
the good cheer of the pub.

For you, it seems,
The indelible mark of Cain
Engraved in your forehead.[19]

The last verse of the poem refers to the Old Testament. The poet compares himself with Cain, 'marked' like Cain with a physical sign on his forehead that lets others know he is different from them. Cain and Abel were the sons of Adam and Eve, born after the Fall of Man.[20] Cain committed the first murder by killing his brother after God had rejected his sacrifice but accepted Abel's. Cain was a tiller of the land while his younger brother Abel was a shepherd. Cain offered fruit and grain as a sacrifice to God and Abel offered fat and fatlings. God favoured Abel's offering and subsequently Cain murdered Abel. God put a curse on Cain to wander the earth. Cain was afraid of being murdered, and so God placed a mark on Cain so that he would not be killed.

Although the story could be interpreted in many ways, Ó Searcaigh in 'An Díbeartach' chooses to concentrate on the continual struggle within the human person between the need to belong, to settle, to put down roots, and the longing to wander and be free. In 'An Díbeartach', Ó Searcaigh identifies with Cain as the outcast, driven to wandering, yet haunted by the need to belong.

Identity and Marginality: 'Bean an tSléibhe'

'Bean an tSléibhe'[21] deals with the difficulty of being and of identity. In her essay 'Identity and Marginality', Rebecca Kay tells us that 'Identities are a way of making sense of who we are and as such may be the result of a very individual process of reflection and choice and empowering beliefs, tastes and values.'[22] She also points out that 'identities are socially constructed and determined by wider social, cultural, political and economic contexts'.[23] We are individuals but we are also in relation to those around us. Kay quotes Stephen Menell's theories on the multifaceted and layered nature of identities. Each person's self is formed by a reflexive process, in which our perception of how others see us plays a paramount part: 'individual self-images and group we-images are not separate things'.[24] Socially constructed identities may be imposed upon certain groups or individuals by others, often as a result of inequalities of power and authority. In this case identities may be divisive and repressive or even rebellious and subversive.

The poet celebrates marginal figures from his own community in a series of poems in *An Bealach'na Bhaile*, which commemorates men and women from the area who influenced him as a child.[25] One of these poems, 'Bean an tSléibhe', is written to the woman living alone on the mountain. He shows a great appreciation for the individuality and resilience of this woman in the face of her fate. She encourages the young poet and the other boys to question authority:

> 'Bhfuil jizz ar bith ionaibh, a bhuachaillí?' a deireadh sí
> nuair a bhíodh leisc orainn easaontú lena tuairimí.
> 'Oró tá sibh chomh bómanta le huain óga an earraigh,
> ach sin an rud atá na sagairt is na TDs a iarraidh,
> is nuair a thiocfas sibhse i méadaíocht, a bhuachaillí,
> ní bheidh moill ar bith orthu sibhse a thiomáint mar chaoirigh.'

> 'Have you any jizz at all in you boys,' she'd say,
> when we were embarrassed to disagree with her.
> 'Arrah, you are as stupid as young spring lambs,
> But that's what the priests and the TDs want

And when you grow up, boys,
They'll have no trouble driving you like sheep'.[26]

Everywhere in Ó Searcaigh's poetry is the celebration of life and
freedom of expression, the transgression of boundaries and the
refusal to conform. His poetry is full of the subversive humour of the
powerless.[27] At the same time, Ó Searcaigh is profoundly aware of
the loneliness of the human condition and the universality of suffering. The price to be paid for being different is to be seen as strange
or other. Society can easily forget its marginal figures, like the drunk
who dies alone in the poverty of his cabin.[28]

'L'Étranger'

Ó Searcaigh is also deeply engaged (as a kind of 'outsider within') in
Irish-language poetry, with those who are excluded and marginalized. In *Strangers to Ourselves*, Julia Kristeva speaks about the loss
and challenge experienced by the foreigner: 'A secret wound, often
unknown to himself, drives the foreigner to wandering.'[29] The word
foreigner is translated here from the French word 'l'étranger', which
can also mean stranger or outsider. Free of ties with his own people,
the foreigner feels 'completely free', yet terribly alone. We get a
sense of the great solitude that comes with this freedom in Ó
Searcaigh's poem, 'Piccadilly: Teacht na hOíche'.

Tá mé ag fanacht ar dhuine inteacht
ar feadh na hoíche.
Anseo i gceartlár Phiccadilly,thart
fá bhéal bagrach an fhostaisiún

Níl de chara ag Cumhaidh ach Cuimhne
ach mar ghrianghraf a fhliuchfaí
tá sin fein ag gabháil as aithne
i dtruacántas.

I am waiting for somebody
In the dusk.
Here in the centre of Piccadilly, around
The menacing mouth of the Underground

...

I am alone and alone has no friend
But memory, but memory is a snap-shot

That wept upon, goes out of focus,
blurs.[30]

Kristeva speaks about the strangeness within ourselves that we can recognize in the Other: 'The foreigner is within us. And when we flee from or struggle against the foreigner, we are fighting our unconscious – that "improper" facet of our impossible "own and proper".'[31] Ó Searcaigh is a poet who is continually engaged in conversation with the other, the one who is eternally absent, and his poems bravely break silences. According to Rosi Braidotti, the nomad is a transgressive identity, whose transitory nature is precisely the reason why he/she can make connections at all. Nomadic politics is a matter of bonding, of coalitions, of interconnections.[32] Whether he is evoking the figure of Suibhne, 'Mad Sweeney', the central character in the medieval Gaelic saga *Buile Shuibhne*, who is transformed into a bird-man at the battle of Magh Rath and becomes a restless and solitary fugitive, exiled to the treetops and mountain slopes, or the figure of Maigdiléana the prostitute, or the 'buachaillí bána' or white boys or other marginal figures from his own community, his approach is always one of humanity and understanding.[33]

Cathal Ó Searcaigh's poetry celebrates those who dare to transgress society's laws. His is a poetry of nomadic subjects. Rosi Braidotti tells us that the Nomadic subject 'is a figuration for the kind of subject who has relinquished all idea, desire or nostalgia for fixity. This figuration expresses the desire for an identity made of transitions, successive shifts and coordinated changes, without and against an essential unity.'[34] For Rosi Braidotti, the Nomadic subject is a utopian figuration that is not about displacement but about a discursive freedom from dominant narratives. Ó Searcaigh's poetry, however, shows us the reality and suffering of the Nomadic subject, in isolation and poverty.

Crossing Frontiers

Ó Searcaigh, described by Máirín Nic Eoin as an Irish nomad/*fánaí gaelach*, gives voice to the silenced: those who live on the margins of society. 'Cuireadh', the first poem of his collection *Gúrú i gClúidíní* (2006), is an invitation to all those who are 'lost' or wandering to come into his poetry. He welcomes those whom the world has forgotten and cast aside: madmen, prostitutes, drunks, the lonely and the hungry. The poet's words remind the reader of Christ's welcome for these figures:

Sibhse ar fad atá ar seachrán
ar an duibheagán, atá ar fán
i mbéal athá na beatha, atá caillte i ngleann
na ngealt,

...

Taraigí, a bhacaigh, a bhithiúnaigh, a bhitseacha
taraigí, a scraitsí agus a striapacha,
taraigí, a lucht an drabhláis, a lucht an uaignis,
sibhse atá eaglach, ocrach, aonarach[35]

As Máire Ní Annracháin illustrates in her article 'An creideamh eaglasta agus nuafhilíocht na Gaeilge',[36] there are often biblical echoes in Ó Searcaigh's work. Poetry itself is seen as a form of salvation and the poet compares himself with Christ. Ní Annracháin highlights the complexity of the relationship between Irish poetry and religion, and the figurative use of religious language to celebrate sexual love in Ó Searcaigh's poem 'Searmanas/Ceremony'.[37]

Ó Searcaigh emphasizes the need to face serious social issues in his poetry. It is important to say that he does not look on the victims of social injustice/inequality as pitiable creatures but as people in their own right, with their own identity. According to Ó Searcaigh, those not tied down by middle-class social conventions have a unique energy of their own. He describes the work of other writers that inspired him in *Na hAingle ó Xanadú*: beat poets such as Ginsberg, Corso, Snyder, Kerouac and O'Hara, who refused to conform to the status quo.

Ó Searcaigh's poem 'To Jack Kerouac'[38] begins with an extract from Kerouac's *On the Road*, which celebrates nomadic existence:

> The only people for me are the mad ones, the ones who are mad to live, mad to talk, mad to be saved, desirous of everything at the same time, the ones who never yawn or say a commonplace thing but burn, burn like fabulous yellow roman candles

> *Beat* buile inár mbeatha. Spreagtha ... Thrasnaigh muid teorainneacha agus thrasnaigh muid taibhrithe. Cheiliúraigh muid gach casadh ar bhealach ár mbeatha./ ... a mad beat to our lives. Crazed ... We crossed frontiers and we scaled dreams. Celebrations at every turn of life's highway ... [39]

Cathal Ó Searcaigh is a poet who celebrates those marginal figures who are willing to take risks in subverting the norms, in pushing the boundaries of the status quo. In his poetry he also illustrates how these marginal figures must also be willing to pay the price for their unique search for authenticity and freedom, even if that search may lead them into madness, loneliness and despair.

REFERENCES

Braidotti, R., *Nomadic Subjects: Embodiment and Sexual Difference in Contemporary Feminist Theory* (New York: Columbia University Press, 1994)

Kay, R., 'Identity and Marginality', *eSharp*, 6, 1, http://www.gla.ac.uk/media/media_41175_en.pdf, accessed 31 July 2011.

Kristeva, J., *Strangers to Ourselves*, trans. L.S. Roudiez (New York: Harvester Wheatsheaf, 1991).

Mennell, S., 'The Formation of We-Images: A Process Theory', in C. Calhoun (ed.), *Social Theory and the Politics of Identity* (London: Blackwell, 1994), pp.175–87.

Ní Annracháin, M., 'An creideamh eaglasta agus nuafhilíocht na Gaeilge', in C. Ó Searcaigh and M. Ó Cearúil (eds), *Aimsir Óg*, 200, 2, 2 (Dublin: Coiscéim, 2000), pp.104–17.

Ó Laoire, L., 'A Yellow Spot on the Snow', in C. Ó Searcaigh, *An Bealach 'na Bhaile* (Indreabhán, Conamara: Cló Iar-Chonnachta, 1991).

Ó Laoire, L., 'Dearg Dobhogtha Cháin/The Indelible Mark of Cain: Sexual Dissidence in the Poetry of Cathal Ó Searcaigh', in E. Walshe (ed.), *Sex, Nation and Dissent in Irish Writing* (Cork: Cork University Press, 1997), pp.221–34.

Ó Searcaigh, C., *An Bealach 'na Bhaile* (Indreabhán, Conamara: Cló Iar-Chonnachta, 1991).

Ó Searcaigh, C., *Out in the Open*, trans. F. Sewell (Indreabhán, Conamara: Cló Iar-Chonnachta, 2000).

Ó Searcaigh, C., *Gúrú i gClúidíní* (Indreabhán, Conamara : Cló Iar-Chonnachta, 2006).

NOTES

1. L. Ó Laoire, 'Dearg Dobhogtha Cháin/The Indelible Mark of Cain: Sexual Dissidence in the Poetry of Cathal Ó Searcaigh', in Éibhear Walshe (ed.), *Sex, Nation and Dissent in Irish Writing* (Cork: Cork University Press, 1997), p.221.
2. 'The partition which came with self-determination served to cut Donegal off to a large extent from its natural hinterland. It is joined to the rest of the country only by a narrow band of land in the extreme south of the county. Therefore Donegal is in many senses an island, isolated and distinct with its own unique mindcast', L. Ó Laoire, 'A Yellow Spot on the Snow', in C. Ó Searcaigh, *An Bealach 'na Bhaile* (Indreabhán, Conamara: Cló Iar-Chonnachta, 1991), p.13.
3. Ó Laoire, 'Dearg Dobhogtha Cháin/The Indelible Mark of Cain'.
4. Ó Searcaigh, *An Bealach 'na Bhaile*, p.66.
5. Ó Searcaigh, *Ag Tnúth leis an tSolas*, p.146.
6. Ó Searcaigh, *An Bealach 'na Bhaile*, p.116.
7. Ibid., p.188.
8. Ibid., p.66.
9. Ibid.
10. Ibid.
11. Ibid., p.67.
12. Ibid.
13. C. Ó Searcaigh, *Out in the Open*, trans. Frank Sewell (Indreabhán: Cló Iar-Chonnachta, 2000), pp.48–9.
14. Ó Searcaigh, *Ag Tnúth leis an tSolas*, p.146.
15. Ó Laoire, 'Dearg Dobhogtha Cháin/The Indelible Mark of Cain', p.221.
16. Ó Searcaigh, *Out in the Open*, pp.48–9.
17. 'Bend like your fathers' fathers to land-worship and work like you were born to this

heirloom. The harvest will be yours: every field a poem', from the poem 'Submit', Ó Searcaigh, *Out in the Open*, p.57.

18. Ó Searcaigh, 'Anseo ag Stáisiún Chaiseal na gCorr', *An Bealach 'na Bhaile*, p.95.
19. Ó Searcaigh, *Out in the Open*, pp.48–9.
20. Genesis 4:1–17.
21. Ó Searcaigh, *An Bealach 'na Bhaile*, p.116
22. R. Kay, 'Identity and Marginality', *eSharp*, 6, 1, http://www.gla.ac.uk/media/media_41175_en.pdf, accessed 31 July.2011, p.1.
23. Ibid.
24. S. Mennell, 'The Formation of We-Images: A Process Theory', in C. Calhoun (ed.) *Social Theory and the Politics of Identity* (London: Blackwell, 1994), p.179.
25. Ó Searcaigh, *An Bealach'na Bhaile*, pp.112–39.
26. Ibid., p.117.
27. See 'We are all brothers … like Cain and Abel' in the poem 'Briathra agus Bráithre/Words of a Brother', Ó Searcaigh, *An Bealach 'na Bhaile*, p.131.
28. See 'Fiacha an tSolais' in Ó Searcaigh, *An Bealach 'na Bhaile*, p.120.
29. J. Kristeva, *Strangers to Ourselves*, trans. Leon S. Roudiez (New York: Harvester Wheatsheaf, 1991), p.5.
30. Ó Searcaigh, *An Bealach'na Bhaile*, p.73.
31. Ibid., p.191.
32. R. Braidotti, *Nomadic Subjects: Embodiment and Sexual Difference in Contemporary Feminist Theory* (New York: Columbia University Press, 1994), p.35.
33. Heaney has also written about Sweeney in 'Sweeney Astray' and 'Sweeney's Flight', based on a revised text of 'Sweeney Astray'. He talks about the 'migrant solitude' of this figure in 'The King of the Ditchbacks'.
34. Braidotti, *Nomadic Subject*, p.22.
35. C. Ó Searcaigh, *Gúrú i gClúidíní* (Indreabhán, Conamara: Cló Iar-Chonnachta, 2006), p.11.
36. M. Ní Annracháin, 'An creideamh eaglasta agus nuafhilíocht na Gaeilge', in C. Ó Searcaigh and, M. Ó Cearúil (eds), *Aimsir Óg*, 200, 2, 2 (Dublin: Coiscéim, 2000), pp.104–117.
37. Ó Searcaigh, *An Bealach 'na Bhaile*, p. 156
38. In his notes to this poem, Ó Searcaigh, describing Kerouac as 'the strange solitary crazy Catholic mystic', the inspirational hero of the 'beat generation', tells us that Kerouac made him a 'rucksack romantic'. *On the Road* became his guide for an inner journey.
39. Ó Searcaigh, *An Bealach 'na Bhaile*, pp.188–9.

5

'Of them but not of them': Louis MacNeice and the 'Thirties Poets'

Simon Workman

In recent years[1], critics have sought to revise and complicate limiting constructions of Louis MacNeice's national identity which have, on the one hand, reduced the poet to the 'professional lachrymose Irishman',[2] while on the other, posited him as insufficiently Irish (because of his formative years spent in an English education system and his professional life working for the BBC). MacNeice was left to languish between two national polarities being 'too English for the Irish and too Irish for the English'.[3] And as Terence Brown notes, MacNeice could not escape his split identity even if he wanted to: 'the English tended to think of him as Irish, critics referred to his nationality when they reviewed his books'.[4] Bracketed as an outsider in both the English and Irish literary traditions, MacNeice is granted 'at best resident alien status' in the literary canons of both nations.[5] One solution which critics have found is to frame MacNeice as an 'Anglo-Irish' poet, yet even this revision carries its own dangers as it risks aligning MacNeice with the class which Yeats was to champion, a class which the younger poet criticized for its 'obsolete bravado' and 'insidious bonhomie'.[6] Indeed, it has been suggested by Peter MacDonald that MacNeice operated in some ways as the inverse of Yeats with regard to Ireland: that if 'Yeats used Ireland to construct a dominant myth of the self, MacNeice undermined the self to complicate and qualify the myth of "Ireland"'.[7] The poetic profits and losses of MacNeice's hyphenated identity have been well documented by critics, particularly in his relationship to Ireland.[8] Living in this deracinated state gave him the freedom to clarify or read deeply into the Irish condition, to feel both affection and revulsion, to flaunt both his sentimentality and his sarcasm. It is the purpose of this essay to examine how MacNeice's outsider status affected his transactions with the group of Auden-inspired

English poets of the 1930s, with which he has been misleadingly aligned in the past, and to understand how his childhood in Ireland fostered and determined an instinct which was sceptical of doctrinaire political slogans and wary of totalizing political thought.

From a very early age, MacNeice was exposed to the conflicted and potentially lethal nature of politics in Ireland in the early twentieth century. In his long poem, *Autumn Journal* (1939), he recounts his experience of growing up in 'Darkest Ulster':

> And I remember, when I was little, the fear
> Bandied among the servants
> That Casement would land at the pier
> With a sword and a horde of rebels;
> And how we used to expect, at a later date,
> When the wind blew from the west, the noise of shooting
> Starting in the evening at eight
> In Belfast in the York street district;
> And the voodoo of the Orange bands
> Drawing an iron net across darkest Ulster
> Flailing limbo lands ... [9]

As a child sitting in his walled garden in Carrickfergus, MacNeice must have felt a certain sense of vulnerability both to the strange, atavistic drumming of Ulster's Orangemen that could often be heard in the distance and the latent threat of violent Republican attacks from the nearby seashore. He would have felt, too, the opposing unionist and nationalist sentiments within Ulster from inside his own home as channelled through Annie, the Catholic cook, and Miss Craig, his Protestant nanny, who both had a marked influence on his early upbringing. Even the West of Ireland, which he associated with his mother and her romantic perception of it, was tinged with threat. MacNeice's father forbade visits there due to the activities of the Republican movement and, as MacNeice states in his posthumously published autobiography, *The Strings are False* (1965), it was not until he was nearly an adult that he first ventured to the south of Ireland: 'In late September (for my seventeenth birthday) we went to Donegal, my first holiday in the "South" ... my father in spite of his nationalism had said, "How can you mix with people who might be murderers without knowing it?" '[10]

The poem 'Carrickfergus' (1937) further emphasizes MacNeice's sensitivity to the political and social disunity of the region in which he spent his childhood:

The Norman walled his town against the country
 To stop his ears to the yelping of his slave
And built a church in the form of a cross but denoting
 The list of Christ on the cross in the angle of the nave.

I was a rector's son, born to the Anglican order,
 Banned forever from the candles of the Irish poor;
The Chichesters knelt in marble at the end of a transept
 With ruffs about their necks, their portion sure.

The War came and a huge camp of soldiers
 Grew from the ground in sight of our house with long
Dummies hanging from gibbets for bayonet practice
 And the sentry's challenge echoing all day long;

A Yorkshire terrier ran in and out by the gate-lodge
 Barred to civilians, yapping as if taking affront:
Marching at ease and singing 'Who killed Cock Robin?'
 The troops went out by the lodge and off to the Front.[11]

As Longley notes of this poem, the 'quatrains cover oppression and war in Ulster from the Normans to dynasties like the Chichesters (a Major Chichester-Clark was Stormont Prime Minister in the early 1970s), to the First World War'.[12] The images of murder or maiming, of boundaries, barriers and sieges underline MacNeice's childhood awareness of a province in disunity and the potential violence germinating under the surface. The phrase 'Born to an Anglican order' underlines MacNeice's membership of the once established Church of Ireland. Membership of this faith, however, meant MacNeice was largely cut off from the Roman Catholic community on the one hand, and to a lesser extent the Presbyterian one on the other. Yet the solace and solidarity gained from belonging to one side of the political divide was not afforded MacNeice. His father was a nationalist rector, who ministered a Protestant community, which was bound in its political stance by religion. As a child, therefore, MacNeice experienced the tension of conflicting loyalties that his position as a son of a nationalist rector in the north of Ireland involved.

If MacNeice felt constricted and hemmed in by the political and social context of his Irish childhood, the nature of the local climate and the surrounding landscape was to have more liberating effects. For MacNeice, the ever changing vistas of his surroundings – the sometimes highly variegated and vivid world of shifting light, rain, cloud and pattern – provided an escape and release from the restricting atmosphere of his familial home and the tensions close at hand. The qualities of light in particular were to have a profoundly positive impact on his perception, as the poet makes clear: 'An Irish landscape is capable of pantomimic transformation scenes; one moment it will be desolate, dead, unrelieved monotone, the next it will be an indescribably shifting pattern of prismatic light. The light effects of Ireland make other landscapes seem stodgy.'[13] Throughout MacNeice's poetry light is a positive symbol and it is often associated with shifting patterns which achieve momentary syntheses. In 'Train to Dublin' (1934) MacNeice attempts to describe the landscape as seen from a moving train. Light pervades the passing country-side, as the poet describes it:

> The vivid chequer of the Antrim hills, the trough of dark
> Golden water for cart-horses, the brass
> Belt of serene sun upon the lough.[14]

The experience of travelling through the countryside at speed is the occasion for MacNeice to reinterpret his country through its land-scape. He offers up his own version of life away from the rigidities of truculent politics and doctrinaire thinking:

> But I will not give you any idol or idea, creed or king,
> I give you the incidental things which pass
> Outward through space exactly as each was
>
> …
>
> I give you the toy Liffey and the vast gulls,
> I give you fuschia hedges and whitewashed walls,
>
> I give you the smell of Norman stone, the squelch
> Of bog beneath your boots, the red bog grass
>
> …
>
> And I give you the faces, not the permanent masks
> But the faces balanced on the toppling wave … [15]

The poem concludes with the poet wanting to give more but admitting: 'I cannot hold this stuff within my hands.' Yet MacNeice is not being merely flippant here; he is asking profound metaphysical and political questions. How can pattern be achieved without stasis? How can one subscribe to ideologies which will falsely and inevitably systematize the world? What MacNeice is encouraging is an elasticity of thought which at least attempts to do justice to the world's flux and which does not negate the individual or the particular in theoretical abstraction or obtuse dogma.

MacNeice seeks to transcend the destructive binaries of politics in Ireland where:

> One read black where the other read white, his hope
>   The other man's damnation:
> Up the Rebels, To Hell with the Pope,
>   And God save – as you prefer – the King or Ireland.[16]

One of the consequences of sectarianism and narrow-minded tribalism is that people lose a sense of individuality, becoming subsumed into a destructive, inhibiting and monistic world view. MacNeice makes this clear in his satire of the Orange-day parades in *Autumn Journal*:

> King William is riding his white horse back
> To the Boyne on a banner.
> Thousands of banners, thousands of white
> Horses, thousands of Williams
> Waving thousands of swords and ready to fight
> Till the blue sea turns orange.
> Such was my country ... [17]

MacNeice, then, had developed a deep sensitivity to the nefariousness of totalizing thought and he applied this awareness to the philosophical underpinning of much of the poetry written by his English contemporaries in the 1930s.

Of all the prominent poets of the period, MacNeice was probably closest to W.H. Auden. A close bond was formed between the poets when MacNeice began living and lecturing in Birmingham, Auden's home city. They strengthened their poetic alliance when they toured Iceland together in 1936, which resulted in the publication of a book of poems and travel writings, *Letters from Iceland* (1937), which they wrote together. Auden was seen as the literary leader of his generation after his first collection, *Poems*, was published in 1930. In this volume, Auden carefully avoided Yeatsian romantic self-expression – the poems were short, untitled and intriguingly cryptic. He was also a central voice in the epoch-making anthologies *New Signatures* (1932) and *New Country* (1933) and showed interest in Marx and Freud, quickly gaining a reputation as a leftist intellectual. His was a dissenting voice and he a counterculture poet whose individualistic disaffection was focused on the public-school ethos so prized by the previous generation. His perspective widened to include the whole condition of England at a period when the Great Depression and European fascism were having profound social and political effects. Auden's influence on other writers was strong and his modes of oratory were converted into manifestos by poets like Cecil Day Lewis and Stephen Spender, Spender's *Forward from Liberalism* (1937) representing a zenith of belief in the writer's obligation to align himself with the communist position.

MacNeice, however, was more independent of Auden's influence and never took him seriously as the quasi-messiah figure as projected by some of his followers. In his book *Modern Poetry*, MacNeice emphasizes the artistic fruitfulness of Auden's approach, not its political usefulness: 'Auden has the advantage of seeing the world both in terms of psycho-analysis and of a Marxian doctrine of progress. Thereby nearly all the detail in the world becomes significant for him.'[18] However, MacNeice is clear about the potential dangers of this approach and makes strong distinctions between poetry and propaganda:

> Poetry today should steer a middle course between pure enter-tainment ('escape poetry') and propaganda. Propaganda, the extreme development of 'critical' poetry, is also the defeat of criticism. And the mere slogan-poet contradicts his name – *poietes*, a 'maker'. The poet is a maker, not a retail trader. The writer today should be not so much the mouthpiece of a community (for then he will only tell what it knows already) as its conscience, its critical faculty, its generous instinct.[19]

One feels that in the poem 'To a Communist' (1933), MacNeice is act-ing very much with his critical faculty on high alert as he points out his instinctive sense of the inherent problems of the communist position:

> Your thoughts make shape like snow; in one night only
> The gawky earth grows breasts,
> Snow's unity engrosses
> Particular pettiness of stones and grasses.
> But before you proclaim the millennium, my dear,
> Consult the barometer –
> This poise is perfect but maintained
> For one day only.[20]

MacNeice implies, through his central symbol, snow, the shape and structure of communist doctrine. Yet he denies the permanence of that shape, predicting, as Orwell did, that its fragile unity will hold only fleetingly before life's particulars impinge and disrupt the ideal. But to whom is the poem directed? Jon Stallworthy, in his biography of MacNeice, proposes Auden as the intended target, citing the phrase 'my dear' as a reference to Auden's homosexuality.[21] This argument seems plausible, particularly when it is taken into account that the title satirically recalls Auden's poem 'A Communist to Others'. However, his description of Oxford in the late 1920s reveals that he saw 'my dear' as a general marker of homosexuality rather than as the private property of Auden: 'the air was full of the pansy phrase "my dear". I discovered that in Oxford homosexuality and "intelligence", heterosexuality and brawn were almost inexorably paired. This left me out in the cold and I took to drink.'[22] So it would seem that it is just as possible that the poem is directed at Spender, who was as openly homosexual as Auden and, indeed, more definitively communist. If this is the case, as Richard Brown has astutely observed,[23] the poem could be seen, therefore, as a response to Spender's poem 'After they have tired of the brilliance of cities', which is centred on the image of snow and its implications of universality and clarity:

> We have come at last to a country
> Where light equal, like the shine from snow, strikes all faces,
> Here you may wonder
> How it was that works, money, interest, building, could ever hide
> The palpable and obvious love of man for man.[24]

Spender's poem, a lyrical anticipation of a communist revolution, anticipates rather naively that the radical changes in society will occur as a seamless development of human consciousness. It seems highly plausible that MacNeice found much that was incongruent with his poetic and political cast of mind in this poem. The overly optimistic political vision couched in romantic rhetoric must have jarred with MacNeice's more sceptical world view. Yet it is perhaps Spender's figurative use of snow and light to imply the alleged unity of a communist Utopia which triggered a more subtle resistance in MacNeice's poetic imagination. As we have seen, light as an image in MacNeice's poems, while often positive, implies only momentary synthesis. But it is that quality of unpredictability and transience which gives it value. In MacNeice's poem 'Snow' (1935), the incongruous juxtaposition of 'snow and pink roses' prompts metaphysical reflection on 'The drunkenness of things being various'.[25] In MacNeiceian topos, then, these images resonated with different effect and in 'To a Communist' MacNeice debunks the metaphor of snow-shine as a permanent state, revealing its ultimate fragility.

Whether directed at Auden or Spender or indeed both, 'To a Communist' typifies MacNeice's aversion to poetry as a mere conveyor belt of overt political creed. This is confirmed by his essay 'Poetry To-day', published in September 1935, which states: 'I have no patience with those who think poetry will become merely a handmaid of communism. Christianity, in the time of the Fathers, made the same threats; all poetry but hymns was bogus, no one was to write anything but hymns.'[26] MacNeice makes a link here between extreme socialism and extreme religiosity, seeing both as totalizing ideologies and drawing parallels between the restrictive religious ideologies that he would have experienced as a child and the present political ideology of Marx and Lenin.

With regard to both the idols and creeds preached by both sides in Ireland and the Utopias and dreams of some English poets of the period, MacNeice often takes up the role of demythologizer. Samuel Hynes finds MacNeice a fertile source of demythologizing comments on his contemporaries, proving that on both sides of the Irish Sea MacNeice functioned critically between attachment and detachment, always eager to test any universal or utopia against his own particular lived experience. His own voice had been developed in a different culture to that of many of his contemporaries, as Edna Longley points out: 'Coming from the "wilds" of a more primitively politicized culture, MacNeice understood where literature ends and real politics begins.'[27]

Unwilling or unable to muster the faith required for full immersion in religious or political dogma, MacNeice had to go his own way. Yet through many of his poems in the 1930s he did engage critically and artistically with his contemporaries without subscribing wholeheartedly to their doctrine. MacNeice's summary of the role of the 1890s aesthetic movement in Yeats's career could easily be applied to his relation to the other 'Thirties' poets: 'He was at the same time of them and not of them; some of their doctrine persisted in his mind to the end but he always applied it his own way.'[28] Indeed, as Auden was recanting his belief, announced at the beginning of the decade, that poetry had the power to bring profound change, MacNeice was showing more stamina. In reaction to Virginia Woolf's attack on the 'Thirties' writers, 'The Leaning Tower' (1941), MacNeice, in his article 'The Tower that Once' (1942), sought to salvage something of value from what Auden had termed that 'low, dishonest decade':

> Recantation is becoming too fashionable; I am sorry to see so much self-flagellation, so many *Peccavis*, going on the literary Left. We may not have done all we could but we did do something ... we were right to advocate social reconstruction and we were even right – in our more lyrical work – to give personal expression to our feelings of anxiety and despair (for even despair can be fertile). As for the Leaning Tower, if Galileo had not had one at Pisa, he would not have discovered the truth about falling weights. We learned something of the sort from our tower too.[29]

REFERENCES

Brown, R.D., 'Neutrality and Commitment: MacNeice, Yeats, Ireland and the Second World War', *Journal of Modern Literature*, 28, 3 (2005), pp.109–29.

Brown, R.D., ' "Your Thoughts Make Shape Like Snow": Louis MacNeice on Stephen Spender', *Twentieth-Century Literature*, 48, 3 (2002), pp.292–323.

Brown, T., *Louis MacNeice: Sceptical Vision* (Dublin: Gill & MacMillan, 1975).

Brown, T., 'MacNeice's Ireland', in T. Brown and N. Greene (eds), *Tradition and Influence in Anglo-Irish Poetry* (London: Macmillan, 1989), pp.79–96.

Hynes, S., *The Auden Generation: Literature and Politics in England in the 1930s* (London: Bodley Head, 1976).

Longley, E., *Louis MacNeice: A Critical Study* (London: Faber, 1988).

McDonald, P., *Louis MacNeice: The Poet in his Contexts* (Oxford: Clarendon Press, 1991).

MacNeice, L., *Modern Poetry: A Personal Essay* (Oxford: Oxford University Press, 1938).

MacNeice, L., *The Poetry of W.B. Yeats* (London: Oxford University Press, 1941).

MacNeice, L., *The Strings are False: An Unfinished Autobiography* (London: Faber, 1965).

MacNeice, L., 'Poetry Today', in A. Heuser (ed.), *Selected Literary Criticism of Louis MacNeice* (Oxford: Clarendon Press, 1987), pp.10–43.

MacNeice, L., 'The Tower that Once', in A. Heuser (ed.), *Selected Literary Criticism of Louis MacNeice* (Oxford: Clarendon Press, 1987), pp.19–24.

MacNeice, L., *Collected Poems*, ed. P. McDonald (London: Faber, 2007).

Spender, S., *Collected Poems 1928–1953* (London: Faber, 1955), pp.47–8.

Stallworthy, J., *Louis MacNeice* (London: Faber, 1996).

NOTES

1. See, for example, R.D. Brown, 'Neutrality and Commitment: MacNeice, Yeats, Ireland and the Second World War', *Journal of Modern Literature*, 28, 3 (2005), pp.109–29.

2. S. Hynes, *The Auden Generation: Literature and Politics in England in the 1930s* (London: Bodley Head, 1976), p.334.

3. P. McDonald, *Louis MacNeice: The Poet in his Contexts* (Oxford: Clarendon Press, 1991), p.8.

4. T. Brown, *Louis MacNeice: Sceptical Vision* (Dublin: Gill & Macmillan, 1975), p.13.

5. McDonald, *Louis MacNeice*, p.8.

6. L. MacNeice, *The Poetry of W.B. Yeats* (London: Oxford University Press, 1941), p.217.

7. McDonald, *Louis MacNeice*, pp.227–8.

8. See, for example, E. Longley, *Louis MacNeice: A Critical Study* (London: Faber, 1988), pp.1–34; T. Brown, 'MacNeice's Ireland', in T. Brown and N. Greene (eds), *Tradition and Influence in Anglo-Irish Poetry* (London: Macmillan, 1989), pp.79–96; McDonald, *Louis MacNeice*, pp.203–29.
9. L. MacNeice, *Collected Poems*, ed. P. McDonald (London: Faber, 2007), p.138.
10. L. MacNeice, *The Strings are False: An Unfinished Autobiography* (London: Faber, 1965), p.226.
11. MacNeice, *Collected Poems*, p.55.
12. Longley, *Louis MacNeice*, p.18.
13. MacNeice, *Poetry of W.B. Yeats*, p.50.
14. MacNeice, *Collected Poems*, p.18.
15. Ibid., pp.17–18.
16. Ibid., p.138.
17. Ibid., p.139.
18. L. MacNeice, *Modern Poetry: A Personal Essay* (Oxford: Oxford University Press, 1938), p.25.
19. Quoted in Longley, *Louis MacNeice*, pp.38–9.
20. MacNeice, *Collected Poems*, p.22.
21. J. Stallworthy, *Louis MacNeice* (London: Faber, 1996), p.154.
22. MacNeice, *Strings*, p.103.
23. R. Danson Brown, ' "Your Thoughts Make Shape Like Snow": Louis MacNeice on Stephen Spender', *Twentieth-Century Literature*, 48, 3 (2002), pp.309–12.
24. S. Spender, *Collected Poems 1928–1953* (London: Faber, 1955), pp.47–8.
25. MacNeice, *Collected Poems*, p.24.
26. L. MacNeice, 'Poetry Today', in A. Heuser (ed.), *Selected Literary Criticism of Louis MacNeice* (Oxford: Clarendon Press, 1987), p.25.
27. Longley, *Louis MacNeice*, p.42.
28. MacNeice, *Poetry of W.B. Yeats*, p.32.
29. L. MacNeice, 'The Tower that Once', in Heuser (ed.), *Selected Literary Criticism*, pp.123–4.

PART 2
DISSENT ON STAGE

6

Tribunal Theatre and the Voice of Dissent as seen in *Bloody Sunday: Scenes from the Saville Inquiry*

Sheila McCormick

Verbatim theatre is any form of theatre that uses actual documents in its production. These documents can range in type from edited court transcripts to recorded conversational material. The study of verbatim theatre can examine the form both theatrically, as a growing genre in theatre production, and politically, as a system of public address. Ultimately, research in the area also questions the so-called performance of reality, its mediation of events as an artistic construction and its increasing popularity in contemporary theatre production.

This paper addresses the notion of performance-provided 'healing', a word often used in relation to the verbatim play. The paper asks if tribunal verbatim theatre, which as a system of public address has the ability to challenge dominant forces and therefore voice dissent, can be seen as a mode for cathartic witness-bearing or simply a means of solidifying the mythification of historical events. To explore this argument, I make particular reference to Richard Norton-Taylor's 2005 work, *Bloody Sunday: Scenes from the Saville Inquiry*.

The Saville Inquiry was announced on 29 January 1998 by then British Prime Minister Tony Blair. It followed over two decades of campaigning by the families of those killed on Bloody Sunday to reopen an investigation into the events of that day. Staged in 2005, five years before the conclusion of the inquiry, the verbatim theatre production by the Tricycle Theatre Company, London, *Bloody Sunday: Scenes from the Saville Inquiry*, can be read as an attempt to bear witness to historical trauma, rather than an effort at disclosing truth. Indeed, many tribunal theatre texts (a phrase coined by the company to denote verbatim productions that specifically use court transcripts) are produced with an already assumed outcome, indicating that the people most profoundly affected by such inquiries are not waiting for the truth to be determined, but instead for the truth to be told.

Verbatim productions such as *Bloody Sunday* do not wait for bureaucratic guidance before addressing their audience. Rather than recount the official line, *Bloody Sunday* and similar productions allow a witnessing of events to occur which might have otherwise gone unwitnessed, performed for an audience presupposed to be capable of forming an opinion without official guidance. Because of its content and timing of production, one can argue verbatim theatre of this nature voices dissent. It dissents from the principle that society must await official guidance before commenting on a traumatic event. By doing so, it also dissents from the notion that a traumatized group is marked irrevocably by the trauma it experiences. Verbatim theatre dissents from the idea that identity is solid and unchanging. Its performance allows the traumatized group to address its trauma and reclaim its identity according to its own wishes and beliefs.

As Derek Paget argues, the power of this theatrical form lies in the audience's confrontation with the verbatim texts, revealing that this power remains conditional upon the ability of audiences to 'accommodate such confrontation'.[1] If, through its performance of trauma, verbatim theatre provides a necessary witness to traumatic events, where does this performance end and what happens when the events considered solidify through re-enactment, thus becoming unchallengeable?

Often theatre criticism discusses verbatim theatre in relation to the incident each production reflects. The Tricycle Theatre, London embraces its relationship to specific events, entitling several of its productions with both the name of the tribunal and the situation it addresses. Indeed, the decision to do so can be seen in the aforementioned *Bloody Sunday: Scenes from the Saville Inquiry*, as well as the less recent productions *The Colour of Justice: The Stephen Lawrence Inquiry* (1999) and *Justifying War: Scenes from the Hutton Inquiry* (2003). All three titles of the self-styled tribunal theatre plays produced by the Tricycle Theatre Company emphasize the relationship the verbatim production has, not only to the present, but also to the experience of the past. Indeed, this relationship has the potential to solidify past traumatic events in such a way as to mythify their presence both in the present and in the future.

When discussing reconciliation and the Northern Ireland conflict, clinical psychologist and Honorary Fellow of the United Nations Research Centre for the Study of Conflict at the University of Ulster,

Brandon Hamber, explores the assertion that truth recovery and the expression of guilt promotes healing in the traumatized individual.[2] Trauma theory appears to suggest that the engagement by the survivors of trauma with their experience and their development of that traumatic event into a narrative form can help to produce meaning and prevent the trauma from becoming the individual's defining feature. The development of a narrative and the willingness on the part of others to bear witness to the trauma allows that burden to be shared and can help those who have suffered to reclaim ownership over the past and thus facilitate their assimilation into the present.

Bloody Sunday, like other tribunal verbatim plays, can be read as an attempt by its author, Norton-Taylor, to infuse the public arena with private information. The Saville Inquiry is now completed and its official findings are widely known. However, while its documents were always technically available through its website, throughout the inquiry's duration calls to have it televised were ignored. Subsequently, for its duration the inquiry remained inaccessible. By revealing information from the inquiry while it was still in session, Norton-Taylor allowed a public examination both of the events of the day in question and of the institution erected to provide supposed justice. In this way, the playwright's dissenting voice addresses a need for institutional disclosure and acknowledges the presence of a democratic deficiency within contemporary society.

Through his choice of excerpts from the 434-day inquiry, edited to create a theatrical production, Norton-Taylor provides his impression of the Saville Inquiry. Because of the sheer volume of testimony, it is only possible for a small section of the entire tribunal to be represented; thus the act of choosing and omitting material becomes extremely relevant and negates any claim the author might have to impartiality. Despite the fact that the sources used in verbatim tribunal theatre are often official, the playwright's ability to edit the material in such a way as to expose underlying injustices inherent in official structures allows the material to become a means through which to voice dissent.

Verbatim theatre, by its very nature, is subjective and, as such, like other art or media forms, produces a biased construction of an event. However, where *Bloody Sunday* and other verbatim tribunal plays differ from most forms of media production is in their ability to activate the text. Here, its audience controls the outcome of the verbatim play. In a way, completely dissimilar to the actual tribunal, the audience of the verbatim tribunal affects, through their reception of it, the play's success or failure.

This symbiotic relationship between the verbatim play and its audience was most obvious at the post-show discussion that followed the Abbey Theatre staging of *Bloody Sunday* during the 2006 Dublin Theatre Festival. Here a dialogue was encouraged between the makers of the production, its audience and several speakers, some of whom were originally from Northern Ireland and were directly involved in or affected by the events of Bloody Sunday itself. As well as tackling the political implications of the play, the panel discussed the rising interest in the genre of verbatim theatre and its theatricality or lack thereof. John Kelly, the brother of Michael Kelly who at 17 years of age was murdered on Bloody Sunday, discussed with interest the accuracy of the theatrical production compared to the actual tribunal. Kelly noted the reactions from the audiences to *Bloody Sunday* in two of its four main venues, Derry and London, as having correlated to those witnessing the tribunal in both cities. The audience's responses in each theatre connected to the response of the people receiving the actual or real event in the Court Gallery of the Guildhall, Derry, and the Central Hall, London. This correlation in responses proposes a relationship between the reality of the tribunal and its representation, which suggests that verbatim theatre has the ability to appropriate the emotional response of the actual event.

Also addressed at the post-show discussion was the potential for verbatim theatre to be used as a system of public address, a form of production which would allow otherwise unseen events to be observed and experienced and, therefore, recount for the masses an experience that would otherwise only have been observed by the few. Those invested in the Saville Inquiry did not wait for its duration to see what the truth would be; instead, they waited to see if the truth would in fact be told. Verbatim productions of this kind can therefore fulfil a role that is more about bearing witness than discovering truth; often that truth is already widely known, though not publicly or officially announced. What they allow, then, is a testament to what has occurred, a witnessing of something that may have otherwise gone unwitnessed.

Audience members attending *Bloody Sunday* did so in a similar way to the audience of the inquiry. Artistic choices that encouraged this similarity included director Nicholas Kent's choice to leave the houselights up for the entire play, and designer Clare Spooner's attention to detail in relation to the appropriating of the set to match the actual tribunal. These and other choices, such as the absence of a curtain call, further enhanced the idea of the audience actively bearing witness rather than being passively entertained. This action of bearing witness promotes a level of alienation from the emotions attached to the subject matter, thus allowing an examination of both the tribunal's institutional process and the information offered, an intention aided by the production's weighty programme, itself a document containing documents, including pictures and copies of testimonies from the tribunal.

As Baz Kershaw explains, performances of this kind show that 'history can be rescued from the reign of nostalgia by the performance of the past as a reclamation of its radical instability in the present'.[3] As well as revisiting the events of the tribunal, *Bloody Sunday*, like other verbatim productions, offers its audience members the opportunity to relive, however differently, the event of Bloody Sunday itself. What these individuals experience then as a general audience, through the theatrical event, allows them to revisit their actual experience of Bloody Sunday, whether that experience occurred in person, as is the case of the individuals involved, or as a mass audience through the immediate television and newspaper coverage of the event.

Revisiting, rather than reliving, these past events and moments can draw attention to areas of distress in the present. As Nicholas Abercrombie and Brian Longhurst note:

> The theory exists that audience members attend a performance in order to concentrate their energies, emotions and thoughts on that performance and distil some form of meaning. The effectiveness of this is that it relates to involvement, which in turn relates to effect. The more involved an audience is in a performance the greater the intellectual and emotional impact.[4]

The re-witnessing of events during a verbatim play allows the audience to recall their own memories both of the tribunal and of the day in question, the culmination of both leading to a higher degree of involvement in the subject matter.

In 2007, a public forum entitled 'Making Peace with The Past' – The Healing through Remembering Organization was held in Derry. Twenty-five years after Bloody Sunday, this cross-community project made up of a range of individuals holding a variety of political perspectives gave its executive summary. The public forum was held during the annual Bloody Sunday memorial weekend in Pilot's Row, Rossville Street, a community centre situated in the heart of the Bogside. Here, the executive summary detailed options for truth recovery and rehabilitation in Northern Ireland.

Before opening to the floor, the eclectic group of delegates, which included an ex-army officer, a spokesperson for convicted republican paramilitaries and a cross-community worker, explained their plans for reconciliation. In the course of the discussion, several members mentioned 'the myth of blamelessness' and its hindrance to the recovery process. The forum appeared to suggest that for reconciliation to occur, there needs to be an acceptance that blamelessness does not exist and that all members involved or implicated in the troubles have suffered in some form or another.

This opinion, unsurprisingly, received a strong reaction from several members of the public attending the forum. A family member of one of the victims of Bloody Sunday best articulated her reaction by suggesting that while the balance of power remains unequal, blamelessness, and therefore recovery, is almost impossible. She also suggested that the notion of victimhood removed autonomy, that survivor terminology should be used instead to explain her and others' experience where violence was enacted upon them without provocation. The terminology used to describe those affected by the Troubles, specifically Bloody Sunday, became a heated and obviously personal debate, suggesting that the definition used and the personal identity of those in question was intrinsically linked. As Wendy Brown suggests, identity and history are difficult to separate. Because of this 'the past cannot be redeemed unless the identity ceases to be invested in it, and it cannot cease to be invested in it without giving up its identity as such, thus giving up the economy of avenging and at the same time perpetuating its hurt'.[5] Trauma and its attachments have the possibility, then, to perpetuate a singular definition of those it affects, de-historicizing those who have suffered, removing any past other than the defining spectacle of aggression that was enacted upon them.

As Graham Dawson notes, certain societies and individuals in Northern Ireland 'challenge ... official memory, through the articulation of an oppositional narrative, or counter-memory, that asserts the innocence of the victims and denounces both the violence and injustice inherent in the British military occupation of Ireland'.[6] Pilot's Row, where this public forum took place, is directly across from the site of the old Rossville flats, the area where most of the murders took place on Bloody Sunday. New council house buildings now replace the long-torn-down flats. Beside Pilot's Row sits the Bloody Sunday memorial. Within eye line is the Free Derry monument and several of the Bogside's famous murals. Also within yards is the Bloody Sunday museum, newly erected and officially opened that same memorial weekend. Displaying personal and communal artefacts, the museum, set up by the Bloody Sunday Trust, educates outside the official line in a way that one could only presume would be difficult to allow in a state-assisted museum. Each of these devices suggests an intention within the community of the Bogside to dissent from the official explanation of Bloody Sunday and define its own identity.

During the 2007 memorial weekend, visitors to the Bogside photographed these commemorative devices and visited the museum while around them a still underprivileged and marginalized community awaited the outcome of the Saville Inquiry. For the survivors of Bloody Sunday, these sites are not only frozen in memory but remain geographical disturbances to the development of new memories. Prior to the opening of the Saville Inquiry and the publication of its findings, perhaps the only way to address the legacy of trauma was through the commemoration seen in the murals positioned at the heart of the landscape where the trauma took place. This commemoration provided, as Dawson continues, a 'political counter-memory of injustice and resistance ... [and] ... a symbolic reclaiming and "detoxifying" of the site of the atrocity – a contaminated space of trauma and death – by and for the local community'.[7]

The production of *Bloody Sunday: Scenes from the Saville Inquiry* by the Tricycle Theatre Company, regardless of the inquiry's outcome, had a similar effect. Each performance reasserted a political counter-memory of injustice and resistance by exposing the obvious innocence of those lives taken and the institutional injustices that occurred prior to, during and after the event. The production acknowledged the demand by the community for political recognition and subsequent redefinition. By acknowledging the significance of Bloody Sunday as an historical moment, the production attempted to divest the violence that occurred on that day of its defining power, thus removing the classification of victim from those who survived.

There are those who may not be satisfied with the level of political recognition found in the now published Saville report. This lack of satisfaction in the official outcome may delay the psychological healing of those who had been traumatized. However, if the findings of the Saville Inquiry do not provide significant recognition, productions like *Bloody Sunday* allow a public recognition, not only of the events of the day but also of the institutional injustice that occurred following those events. Perhaps more importantly, they publicly expose the inadequacies of official institutions such as the Saville Inquiry and allow for the communal acknowledgement that, whatever the outcome of the tribunal, the truth regarding Bloody Sunday was understood and already widely known.

REFERENCES

Abercrombie, N. and Longhurst, B., *Audiences: A Social Theory of Performance and Imagination* (London: SAGE, 1998).

Brown, W., *States of Injury: Power and Freedom in Late Modernity* (Princeton, NJ: Princeton University Press, 1995).

Dawson, G., 'Trauma, Place and the Politics of Memory', *Historical Workshop Journal*, 59 (2005), pp.151–178.

Hamber, B., 'Rights and Reasons: Challenges for Truth Recovery in South Africa and Northern Ireland', *Fordham International Law Journal*, 26, 4 (2003), pp.1074–94.

Kershaw, B., *The Politics of Performance: Radical Theatre as Cultural Intervention* (London: Routledge, 1992).

Paget, D., *True Stories? Documentary Drama on Radio, Screen and Stage* (Manchester and New York: Manchester University Press, 1990).

NOTES

1. D. Paget, *True Stories? Documentary Drama on Radio, Screen and Stage* (Manchester and New York: Manchester University Press, 1990), p.48.
2. B. Hamber, 'Rights and Reasons: Challenges for Truth Recovery in South Africa and Northern Ireland', *Fordham International Law Journal*, 26, 4 (2003), pp.1074–94.
3. B. Kershaw, *The Politics of Performance: Radical Theatre as Cultural Intervention* (London: Routledge, 1992), p.24.
4. N. Abercrombie and B. Longhurst, *Audiences: A Social Theory of Performance and Imagination* (London: SAGE, 1998).
5. W. Brown, *States of Injury: Power and Freedom in Late Modernity* (Princeton, NJ: Princeton University Press, 1995), p.73.
6. G. Dawson, 'Trauma, Place and the Politics of Memory', *Historical Workshop Journal*, 59 (2005), p.152.
7. Ibid., p.165.

Exploding the Kitchen Comedy: Maurice Meldon's
Purple Path to the Poppy Field

Ian Walsh

The 1950s have been described as 'a sort of Dark Ages'[1] in which Irish society had 'its eyes shut tight'[2] and for many scholars the only theatrical brilliance of the time radiated from the flames of the fire that burnt down the old Abbey Theatre in 1951. The age is denigrated largely for the faults of The Abbey Theatre[3] and the policies pursued by its director, Ernest Blythe.[4] Hugh Hunt, in his study of the theatre, wrote that 'In fairness to the playwrights of the time … the leadership of the Abbey offered little to inspire them and there was little to encourage experiment with new forms or ideas.'[5] The forms of drama that remained dominant in the Abbey repertoire were farce, comedy and tragicomedy exclusively. These plays became the signature of the Abbey 'peasant style', labelled as 'kitchen comedies' and 'parlour tragedies' due to their rarely escaping the setting of a country cottage or urban tenement and their respective kitchens or parlours.[6] Such plays were presented in a realistic style but were not works of 'gritty realism';[7] rather, they were 'idealized representations of the life felt to be expressive of the very core of the nation'.[8] D.E.S. Maxwell described this form as 'self-enclosing realism', a style that was 'prosaic, documentary, taking place on a stage whose curtains open on a measurable world, quite precisely fitted to the world which it is modelling'.[9] The world that the plays were 'modelling' has itself been much maligned and is seen to be one characterized by conservatism and artistic stagnation. Due to its isolated position as a neutral country in the Second World War, Ireland entered 'a period of internalization, a period marked by ever-increasing uniformity in matters of morals and political outlook'.[10] Consequently it was not in the dominant state-run or commercial theatres that the dissenting voices of this age were to be found. It was instead, as Augustine Martin writes, 'left to the smaller, less organized groups to break away from the confining naturalism of the Abbey and restore poetry to its place in the theatre'.[11] One such 'smaller, less organized group' was the '37' Theatre Club. Set up by actors Barry Cassin and Nora Lever in 1951, this small theatre was located firstly in the basement of a Georgian house in Baggot Street, Dublin, and then later over the Swiss Gem Company in O'Connell Street. This theatre, in the three short years of its existence, helped 'lay the foundations for the new post-war theatre and a new generation of Irish actors',[12] inspiring Alan Simpson and Carolyn Swift to set up the now notorious Pike Theatre[13] and producing one of Ireland's most unique, innovative and neglected playwrights, Maurice Meldon.

It is the aim of this article to reintroduce the dissenting voice of Maurice Meldon through an examination of his play, *Purple Path to the Poppy Field*. I argue that Meldon's play in its disruption of the dominant realist form upsets the received wisdom that the drama of the 1950s was solely of a conservative kind, 'committed to the notion of a consensual Irish identity'.[14]

As the play and playwright in question are now relatively obscure, I will provide the reader with a brief biography of the author and a short synopsis of the play. Maurice Meldon was born in Dundalk in 1926 but lived and worked in Dublin as a civil servant. His debut play, *Song of the Parakeet*, won the Radio Eireann prize in 1948 and his first staged play, an allegorical piece about the decline of an Anglo-Irish family entitled *House under Green Shadows*, was performed at the Abbey Theatre in 1951. His next drama, *Aisling*, was an expressionistic work and was staged by Cassin/Lever productions at the '37' Theatre Club in 1953 and was later revived for the Gate Theatre. *Purple Path to the Poppy Field* was Meldon's last play and the only one to be published in his lifetime. It was also staged by Cassin/Lever Productions in the '37' Theatre Club. Meldon trained as an actor under Ria Mooney at the Gaiety School of Acting and appeared in many plays under the pseudonym Art O'Phelan, his most famous appearance being in the premiere of Brendan Behan's *The Quare Fellow* staged in the Pike Theatre. Meldon died tragically on 11 September 1958 in a road accident. He was only 32. Robert Hogan writes that 'In Meldon the Irish theatre lost the boldest experimental talent it had seen in twenty years; it lost a symbolist, a satirist, and an allegorist, a tragic-comic writer capable of wit and poignance, a potential master.'[15]

The Purple Path to the Poppy Field, subtitled *A New Legend*, takes the structure of a long one-act play with eight scenes. It is a symbolic satire which, despite an auctorial disclaimer, could be read as an allegory of Ireland and its deadly obsession with tradition. It is set on an island with an old dying population who are superstitious in the extreme. These islanders rely for their livelihood on the trading of potheen, the secret of which was given to them by the ancient mythical Daghdha, who founded their island community.[16] At the opening of the play, in a graveyard scene, we learn that there are only two young people left on the island now that Finbar MacTarbh is being buried. These two are the dreamy Bridgeen Lua and feckless Meehawl MacTarbh. On the day on which Bridgeen is due to leave the island, the quay, which facilitates traffic to and from the mainland, is destroyed and she is unable to make her journey. In the face of this isolation from the mainland, the future of the island rests with Meehawl and Bridgeen and their future offspring who could perhaps turn to the land, rather than trade potheen, and make a self-sufficient future for the island. However, this is not to be, as Meehawl blows himself up when showing off his brother's grenades to Bridgeen. After his death the myth-making deluded community canonizes Meehawl as a hero, despite the fact that his death means the decimation of their race. Bridgeen reports that upon his death, the field in which Meehawl exploded is filled with red poppies. The image is one of an open space filled with blood, death and forgetfulness all signified in the opiate poppy flower. The island itself transforms into that which was its undoing – it becomes myth.

In an ironic note on his play, Meldon writes that it is 'wholly a work of fiction. No reference is intended to any person, place or time. Any resemblance between the island of the story and modern Ireland is purely coincidental.'[17] With the play being of no particular time or place, Meldon is clearly stating that his dramatic space is to be without any specific signification. What is established in this note is that his stage is to be an island. We are presented, therefore, with what Stanley Vincent Longman in his taxonomy of stage space calls 'a floating stage'.[18] That is where 'the stage is used as encapsulating a generalized locale and several places within it'.[19] He elaborates that this floating stage allows for both the extremes of what he terms a fixed stage, where the action occurs in a fixed place, and a fluid stage, which is a constantly changing, fluid place. The play is always situated in the fixed place of the island but as the eight scenes of the piece are played out the space is constantly changing. We move from graveyard to 'a fragment of a cottage'[20] to 'a height on a hill'[21] to a schoolhouse, and in the short final scene we move from 'within a cottage'[22] to an illusory field of flowering red poppies.

This final presented space is the conclusion to the ongoing conflict between what Michael Issacharof terms the mimetic space – the visible space onstage – and the diegetic space – the imaginative space of the character's dialogue.[23] Traditionally, the diegetic space is offstage but in Meldon's drama it threatens to dominate the mimetic space and with Meehawl MacTarbh's transcendent sacrifice in the last scene of the play it arguably does. Henri Hubert and Marcel Mauss write in *Sacrifice: Its Nature and Function* that sacrifice is 'a means of communication between the sacred and the profane worlds through the mediation of a victim'.[24] Meehawl's earlier boasts that he could 'be versed in ways OUTSIDE of this world' is prophetic, as in his death he becomes that very interloper between the two worlds;[25] after he unwittingly blows himself up with a grenade his death is celebrated as that of a sacrificial hero by the community. 'There was great glory in it; glory beyond the power of this world. Glory beyond all,' Bridgeen reports dreamily of his death.[26]

Meldon's intentions are clear at this point; he wishes to demystify the cult of martyrdom and self-sacrifice which has plagued the Irish nation. Claudia Harris writes: 'Cloaked in allusiveness, charged with emotion, martyrdom passes beneath Irish consciousness to that cultural value of a type of death which gives meaning to life. Martyrdom has become an Irish "cultural root paradigm".'[27] The playwright through his construction of warring spaces is warning of the deadly dangers of nationalistic myth-making. Meehawl becomes the caustic 'New Legend' alluded to in the subtitle of the play. Aspasia Velissariou writes in her article entitled 'The Dialectics of Space in Synge's *In the Shadow of the Glen*' that for Synge's heroes and heroines:

> Departure and the acceptance of death are presented as the only premises for their inscription into legend ... these two endings ... represent the protagonists' final transformation from mimetic into diegetic characters, and especially into legendary figures who, by virtue of their discursive position, overwhelm time. Legend, or rather the prospect of being talked about, is offered as the symbolic surpassing of the constraints of the mimetic, signaling defeat by the diegetic.[28]

Reading Meldon's play in light of this illumination from Synge, we can consider Meehawl as a character who through his death moves from the mimetic to the diegetic. He becomes what he has earlier claimed, the 'equal of the Daghdha',[29] but in his death he also changes the landscape. Bridgeen cries out, 'Meehawl, Meehawl, awhile ago you were tied to one place and to one shape. But, now you're everywhere; in everything.'[30] She then describes what is happening to the landscape 'The field. It's – it's springing with poppies ... a glittering splatter of poppies ... you kept your word. A field full of poppies.'[31] If mythical Meehawl is 'everywhere in everything', he is now the field and the flowering poppies. The landscape, through Meehawl's actions and Bridgeen's language, has now become myth. A stage direction alerts us that Bridgeen delivers these lines while the community gathers in the 'fading twilight'.[32] It is clear that the mimetic space onstage is giving way to a dreamy 'twilight' space in which the imaginative can dominate the real. We end the play therefore in a diegetic space that exists only in the mind's eye of the islanders and the audience. The field full of poppies is a field of dreams signified by the poppy flower – the emblem of the Greek god Morpheus, the god of dreams.

In *Purple Path to the Poppy Field* we are presented with several outside spaces as well as indoor spaces. All of these are liminal (threshold) spaces with permeable boundaries. These spaces are for Victor Turner in *From Ritual to Theatre* 'an instant of pure potentiality when everything hangs in the balance'.[33] Throughout the discourse of the characters and in the physical spaces described on stage, a violent natural world from outside is invading the inside spaces onstage. This is similar to what Velissariou writes of *The Shadow of the Glen*: 'The topology of the play is simple: the mimetic (represented) space is identified with the inside, whereas the diegetic is identified with the outside, which is never seen but reported.'[34] I wish at this point to focus on the permeable setting of scene two (which is also repeated in scenes seven and eight) in this regard.

The setting is described as 'A fragment of a cottage interior. A hearth on the left-hand side and a door on the right.'[35] The cottage interior with a hearth and half-door was a familiar setting in the theatre of the 1950s. As previously mentioned, it was associated with the genre of the realistic peasant play at the Abbey Theatre that came to be known as the kitchen comedy. Anthony Roche writes:

> In symbolic terms the kitchen had been foregrounded in the plays staged at the Abbey Theatre as 'the hearth' or the site of a pastoral ideal which was used to oppose urban, materialistic values of a surrounding foreign (usually English, increasingly

American) culture. As such, the kitchen had acquired archetypal status in Irish terms as the locale of any drama claiming to be national. By the 1950s it had become a cliché, an increasingly archaic myth in the negative sense.[36]

In Meldon's play the cottage kitchen with its hearth and half-door is not presented to us in its entirety; he presents us with 'A fragment of a cottage'.[37] If the cottage interior represents 'a pastoral ideal' of 'the nation' as Roche claims then Meldon is clearly saying that his nation is a fragmented and split place. It has no clear boundaries and resists idealization. The audience is empowered to imaginatively build the walls of the cottage/nation for themselves. The nation is placed in a liminal space of potential, in between the outside and inside, the diegetic and mimetic. In this Meldon's drama points towards what Richard Kearney has termed 'Postnationalist Ireland' where ' "No Surrender" and "Ourselves alone" are cat cries of the past.'[38] As Richard Kearney suggests, 'Every nation is a hybrid construct, an "imagined" community which can be reimagined again in alternative versions. The ultimate challenge is to acknowledge this process of ongoing hybridization from which we derive and to which we are constantly subject.'[39] It is important to recognize that Kearney's postnationalism is described as a 'process of hybridization' and, as such, is fluid and changing. This is contrary to Benedict Anderson's concept of the nation as an 'imagined community' that is both fixed and sovereign.

This notion of the in-between or hybrid is embodied in the character of Bridgeen. If Meehawl can be read as the 'poppy field' of the title then Bridgeen is the 'purple path'. As her name suggests, she is 'the bridge' linking the mythical and the material, youth and age, the island and the mainland. In scene three, on 'a remote height of the island' Bridgeen is established as a visionary who is moved by her own dreams and walks the island with her eyes closed. Where Meehawl hears the sounds of the sea, Bridgeen hears 'the whispering of the Daghdha'.[40] She connects the mythical to the material as she speaks of the legendary Daghdha always in terms of the natural landscape. When she claims to be the reincarnated 'Boann, Queen of the Daghdha'[41] she tells Meehawl how she remembers the past glory of the island's fabled founders just in these terms:

> The sun was dressed in gold and red. And the Daghdha was the sun. And down below, the cloak of the Daghdha was the ollamh's cloak in sea and sky. And the path going down was green awhile and gold awhile and red awhile. And after that, it was purple.[42]

After hearing this, Meehawl questions how a path could be so many colours, to which Bridgeen replies that it was four paths and many colours but yet it was still 'One path' with 'as many ways of walking it, as there were colours one by one in turn'.[43] What Bridgeen is alluding to here could be read in many different ways but is itself an apt image of the theatrical space, where the diegetic path goes in many directions and has many colours, and can exist in conjunction with a mimetic physical path on stage. Theatre can provide the 'One path' of many significations, a characteristic that makes it ideal for effective resistance to essentialist discourse.

However, Bridgeen is a character who never transcends her own space. She is forever caught in-between. She is both Bridgeen of the bridge and Queen Boann of the River Boyne.[44] When the quay is reported to have collapsed in scene six, her fate on the island is sealed. She will never connect to the mainland as she desires. Indeed, in her dual nature as ancient mythical queen and young girl she is easily read as a satire of Cathleen Ni Houlihan who in Yeats and Gregory's play transforms from 'old hag' to 'a young girl with the walk of a queen'.[45] In Bridgeen's speeches to Meehawl on the immortality of great deeds she mimics Yeats and Gregory's heroine, telling how 'no one of greatness ever dies for good'[46] and how when the Daghdha returns she will be 'reigning in glory forever and ever'.[47] Unlike Cathleen Ni Houlihan, however, who inspires or bewitches the young men of Ireland to fight for her future and freedom, Bridgeen coaxes Meehawl into playing with a grenade, resulting in him needlessly blowing himself up. With Meehawl dead she guarantees her entrapment on the island and leaves it no hope for the future. Her poetic dedication to myth and tradition blinds her of any vision for the future except the nightmare of an apocalypse. Here, Meldon, who has been happy to give us an abundance of hybridized and fragmented images, warns against the power of the imagination and its ability to reinforce essentialist discourse through the creation of destructive shibboleths. He questions a fixed and absolute notion of identity as represented by the self-enclosing realist form but he also questions the over-abstraction of identity as was often presented in the symbolist plays of Yeats and Lady Gregory.

This is most evident in the character of Uabhas MacCoo, the unelected leader of the community. He matches Bridgeen's poetic devotion to the Daghdha with his pious perseverance of the same. He leads the congregation in a prayer 'giving thanks for our immortal past … For providing the present in which to contemplate it' and 'withholding the future for the enlargement of that contemplation'.[48] His piety for the past is the paralysis of the present and future of the island. He and his congregation are living in that space that Stewart Parker characterized as 'Ireland's continuous past'.[49] The play's cyclical spatial structure also reflects this sense of continuity and return. The final space of the poppy field is also the graveyard from which we began the play. In his explosion of himself Meehawl digs his own burial place and makes earth of himself, just as his brother, Finbar, is represented as a mound of earth onstage at the opening of the play. In the *Purple Path to the Poppy Field*, the time/space cycle moves from the mimetic to the diegetic signified in the two brothers' deaths and can thus be read as a process of decolonization. However, this is problematic as the cyclical space is one of doom for the islanders; blinded by their mythical ideology they gain no insight and end the play as they began it – heralding their own deaths.

The Master is the only voice of dissent that rallies against the inaction of Uabhas and the community to free themselves from this future. He tells them how they are 'moon-mad fools' who should till the land now that they can no longer trade potheen.[50] His wisdom is ignored, as he is given the status of outsider in only marrying onto the island and is described as not having 'the pure faith' of the rest of the people.[51] His outside status links him to a diegetic space and it is to him and not Bridgeen that the future demise of the island reveals itself. But the diegetic is a destructive space to occupy. The Master, like the island, is destroyed by it. His role of outsider places him as 'round the bend'; he is made mad in his isolation and rendered as pathetic and as inert as the rest of the doomed islanders. He is the Master who is rendered masterless, due to his not being of the indigenous people of the Island. This points to the problems of adopting a nationalist identity based on difference. The decolonizing discourse or the Irish-Ireland element of the free state was exclusive of many of the peoples of Ireland, having its basis in Gaelic-speaking and Catholicism. Those of the Protestant faith as well as those who did not speak the native language were to be viewed as less Irish. The problems of this mode of decolonization are further complicated by the partition of Ireland into North and South, with the North having a majority population of Protestants. In choosing the Master as that character to whom the demise of the island reveals itself, Meldon is emphasizing the need for an inclusive hybrid discourse if the island/Ireland is to have any progressive future.

To conclude, Maurice Meldon in *Purple Path to the Poppy Field* creates a drama that questions the concept of a homogenized national identity. I have shown this to be realized by the use of dramatic strategies that disrupt the form of realist drama such as the use of a floating stage space, the refiguring of myth and the disruption of linear time. As a fantastical cautionary tale against essentialist ideology and in its evocation of a more inclusive hybridized future this forgotten play is as relevant to a multicultural contemporary Ireland as it ever was in its own time period and deserves ultimately to be not only reread but re-performed.

REFERENCES

Counsell, C. and Wolf, L. (eds), *Performance Analysis* (London: Routledge, 2001).

D'Arcy, M., *Loose Theatre, Memoirs of a Guerilla Theatre Activist* (Victoria, BC: Trafford Publishing, 2005).

Fitz-Simon, C., *The Irish Theatre* (London: Thames & Hudson, 1983).

Harris, C., 'The Martyr-wish in Contemporary Irish Dramatic Literature', in M. Kenneally (ed.), *Cultural Contexts and Literary Idioms in Contemporary Irish Literature* (Gerrards Cross: Colin Smythe, 1988), pp.251–68.

Hogan, R., *After the Renaissance: A Critical History of Irish Drama since 'The Plough and the Stars'* (London: Macmillan, 1968).

Hubert H. and Mauss, M. (eds), *Sacrifice: Its Nature and Function* (Chicago, IL: University of Chicago, 1964).

Hunt, H., *The Abbey 1904–1978* (Dublin: Gill & Macmillan, 1979).

Issacharoff, M., 'Space and Reference in Drama', *Poetics Today*, 2, 3 (1981), pp.211–24.

Kearney, R., *Postnationalist Ireland: Politics, Culture, Philosophy* (London: Routledge, 1997).

Kenneally, M. (ed.), *Cultural Contexts and Literary Idioms in Contemporary Irish Literature* (Gerrards Cross: Colin Smythe, 1988).

Longman, S., 'Fixed, Fluid and Floating Stages', in J. Redmond (ed.), *The Theatrical Space: Themes on Drama 9* (Cambridge: Cambridge University Press, 1987), pp.151–60.

Martin, A., 'Literature and Society 1938–1951', in K. Nowlan and T. Williams (eds), *Ireland in the War Years and After, 1939–51* (Dublin: Gill & Macmillan, 1969), pp.167–84.

Maxwell, D.E.S., *Modern Irish Drama* (Cambridge: Cambridge University Press, 1984).

Meldon, M., *Purple Path to the Poppy Field*, in *New World Writing, Fifth Mentor Selection* (New York: New American Library, 1954), pp.146–79.

Murray, C., *Mirror up to Nation: Twentieth Century Irish Drama* (Manchester: Manchester University Press, 1997).

Nowlan, K. and Williams, T. (eds), *Ireland in the War Years and After, 1939–51* (Dublin: Gill & Macmillan, 1969).

Parker, S., *Plays 2* (London: Methuen, 2000).

Pilkington, L., 'The Abbey Theatre and the Irish State', in S. Richards (ed.), *The Cambridge Companion to Twentieth-Century Irish Drama* (Cambridge: Cambridge University Press, 2004), pp.231–43.

Redmond, J. (ed.), *The Theatrical Space: Themes on Drama 9* (Cambridge: Cambridge University Press, 1987).

Richards, S. (ed.), *The Cambridge Companion to Twentieth-Century Irish Drama* (Cambridge: Cambridge University Press, 2004).

Richards, S., 'Plays of (Ever) Changing Ireland', in S. Richards (ed.), *The Cambridge Companion to Twentieth-Century Irish Drama* (Cambridge: Cambridge University Press, 2004), pp.1–17.

Roche, A., *Contemporary Irish Drama: From Beckett to McGuinness* (Dublin: Gill & Macmillan, 1994).

Smyth, G., *Decolonisation and Criticism* (London: Pluto, 1998).

Swift, C., *Stage by Stage* (Dublin: Poolbeg, 1986).

Velissariou, A., 'The Dialectics of Space in Synge's *In the Shadow of the Glen'*, *Modern Drama*, 36, 3 (1993), pp.409–19.

Welch, R., *The Abbey Theatre 1899–1999* (Oxford: Oxford University Press, 1999).

Yeats, W.B., *The Major Works* (Oxford: Oxford University Press, 1997).

NOTES

1. G. Smyth, *Decolonisation and Criticism* (London: Pluto, 1998), p.1.
2. C. Murray, *Mirror up to Nation: Twentieth Century Irish Drama* (Manchester: Manchester University Press, 1997), p.10.
3. Being the only state-subsidized theatre in the Republic of Ireland until 1971 and due to its association with such international figures as W.B. Yeats, J.M Synge and Sean O'Casey, most theatrical histories of Irish drama in the twentieth century have made the mistake of equating Irish Drama with Abbey Drama. The achievements of the Gate are rarely acknowledged (except by C. Fitz-Simon) and the small theatre clubs are forgotten.
4. As Minister for Finance in 1925, Ernest Blythe, both a nationalist and an admirer of the Abbey Theatre, was instrumental in securing the government grant for the theatre; he was to become a director in 1935 and managing director from 1941 to 1972. He implemented his Gaelic policy in 1942. This insisted that all members of the company should be bilingual and capable of playing in the Irish language. The policy was subsequently blamed for decreasing standards of production, as actors were hired for their knowledge of Gaelic rather than their ability.
5. H. Hunt, *The Abbey 1904–1978* (Dublin: Gill & Macmillan, 1979), p.165.
6. C. Fitz-Simon, *The Irish Theatre* (London: Thames & Hudson, 1983), p.160.
7. S. Richards, 'Plays of (Ever) Changing Ireland', in S. Richards (ed.), *The Cambridge Companion to Twentieth-Century Irish Drama* (Cambridge: Cambridge University Press, 2004), p.5.
8. Ibid., p.5.
9. D.E.S. Maxwell, *Modern Irish Drama* (Cambridge: Cambridge University Press, 1984), p.140.
10. R. Welch, *The Abbey Theatre 1899–1999* (Oxford: Oxford University Press, 1999), p.138.
11. A. Martin, 'Literature and Society 1938–1951', in K. Nowlan and T. Williams (eds), *Ireland in the War Years and After, 1939–51* (Dublin: Gill & Macmillan, 1969), p.177.
12. M. D'Arcy, *Loose Theatre: Memoirs of a Guerilla Theatre Activist* (Victoria, BC: Trafford Publishing, 2005), p.169.
13. C. Swift, *Stage by Stage* (Dublin: Poolbeg 1986), p.98.
14. L. Pilkington, 'The Abbey Theatre and the Irish State', in Richards (ed.), *The Cambridge Companion to Twentieth-Century Irish Drama*, p.5.
15. R. Hogan, *After the Renaissance: A Critical History of Irish Drama since 'The Plough and the Stars'* (London: Macmillan, 1968), p.229.
16. The Daghdha was a leading mythic character in Irish Literature, one of the *Tuatha De Danann*, who was demonstrably the principle deity in ancient times. He is usually referred to with the definite article, namely *'an Daghdha'* (the Daghda).
17. M. Meldon, *Purple Path to the Poppy Field*, in *New World Writing, Fifth Mentor Selection* (New York: New American Library, 1954), p.146.
18. S. Longman, 'Fixed, Fluid and Floating Stages', in J. Redmond (ed.), *The Theatrical Space: Themes on Drama 9* (Cambridge: Cambridge University Press, 1987), p.152.
19. Ibid.
20. Meldon, *Purple Path to the Poppy Field*, p.154.
21. Ibid., p.157.
22. Ibid., p.161.
23. M. Issacharoff, 'Space and Reference in Drama', *Poetics Today*, 2, 3 (1981), p.212.
24. H. Hubert and M. Mauss (eds), *Sacrifice: Its Nature and Function* (Chicago, IL: University of Chicago, 1964), p.97.
25. Meldon, *Purple Path to the Poppy Field*, p.171.
26. Ibid., p.178.
27. C. Harris, 'The Martyr-Wish in Contemporary Irish Dramatic Literature', in M. Kenneally (ed.), *Cultural Contexts and Literary Idioms in Contemporary Irish Literature* (Gerrards Cross: Colin Smythe, 1988), p.251.

28. A. Velissariou, 'The Dialectics of Space in Synge's *In the Shadow of the Glen*', *Modern Drama*, 36, 3 (1993), p.411.
29. Meldon, *Purple Path to the Poppy Field*, p.171.
30. Ibid., p.179.
31. Ibid.
32. Ibid.
33 Quoted in C. Counsell and L. Wolf (eds), *Performance Analysis* (London: Routledge, 2001), p.206.
34. Velissariou, 'Dialectics of Space', p.411.
35. Meldon, *Purple Path to the Poppy Field*, p.154.
36. A. Roche, *Contemporary Irish Drama: From Beckett to McGuinness* (Dublin: Gill & Macmillan, 1994), p.80.
37. Meldon, *Purple Path to the Poppy Field*, p.154.
38. R. Kearney, *Postnationalist Ireland: Politics, Culture, Philosophy* (London: Routledge, 1997), p.179.
39. Kearney, *Postnationalist Ireland*, p.188.
40. Meldon, *Purple Path to the Poppy Field*, p.158.
41. Ibid.
42. Ibid., p.159.
43. Ibid.
44. Meldon writes a note of general references at the beginning of the play-text in which he writes of queen 'Boann', 'Known as the wife of the Daghdha. Her name survives in the river Boyne.' Ibid., p.146.
45. W.B. Yeats, *The Major Works* (Oxford: Oxford University Press, 1997), p.220.
46. Meldon, *Purple Path to the Poppy Field*, p.158.
47. Cathleen sings: 'They shall be remembered forever/They shall be alive for ever/They shall be speaking for ever/The people shall hear them forever', in Yeats, *Major Works*, p.219.
48. Meldon, *Purple Path to the Poppy Field*, p.164.
49. S. Parker, *Plays 2* (London: Methuen, 2000) p.3.
50. Meldon, *Purple Path to the Poppy Field*, p.164.
51. Ibid.

8

A Brief Consideration of Dissent in Two Reformation Moralities: *Love Feigned and Unfeigned* and *Three Laws*

Brian Gourley

Dissent was rarely a simple or straightforward matter in the English or European Reformations. From the very moment that Martin Luther nailed his 95 theses to the door of the Castle Church in Wittenberg in 1517, dissent blossomed across Europe like Mao Zedong's thousand flowers. Within the critical decade of the 1520s, the unity of Western Latin Christendom fragmented into a diverse and squabbling plurality of denominations which opposed the Roman Catholic Church and each other. In the shifting and turbulent confessional landscape of the sixteenth century, reformers and counter-reformers alike made use of long-standing dramatic forms and popular festivity (as well as the emergent print economy) to forward their own particular agendas. Reformation England and elsewhere in Europe bore eloquent and frequently controversial witness to the continued use of pre-existing cultural forms to promote cultural change.[1]

This article will consider the expression of dissent from religious orthodoxies in two very different Reformation-era plays based on the medieval tradition of the morality play: the ex-Carmelite turned zealous reformer John Bale's most accomplished play, *Three Laws* (1538), and a fragment from c. 1547 provisionally entitled *Love Feigned and Unfeigned*, whose thematic concerns indicate a likely Anabaptist provenance.[2] Both plays advocate religious reform, but *dissenting reform* that departs not only from prevailing doctrinal orthodoxy and popular religious practice in pre-Reformation England, but also from the officially sanctioned policies of both the Henrician and Edwardian Reformations.

Written with strikingly different purposes in mind, they exemplify the sheer plurality and dissonance of voices in the European Reformations. When considered in combination, they amply refute the notion of the Reformation as the monolithic whole of popular historical imagination, and illustrate how reforming voices rarely spoke in unison. Although it may be tempting to try and find some common ground and some unifying aesthetic and doctrinal purpose in a joint analysis of *Three Laws* and *Love Feigned and Unfeigned*, one has to acknowledge that in the fractured denominational landscape that arose in the Reformation's wake, both mid-sixteenth-century drama and polemic inevitably reflect a fissile atmosphere where dissent could just as easily be against the idea of dissent per se as against orthodoxy. Dissenting voices were in frequent conflict about the form that religious and political reform could take in the diversity of confessional viewpoints that emerged across Europe from the early 1520s onwards.

As such, reformers saw in the established popular dramatic forms such as the festive morality play and carnival folk play genres such as the *farce du Pastis* of French origin ready and serviceable vehicles for the communication of pro-reform agendas. As Paul Whitfield White and Diarmaid MacCulloch, amongst others, have explored in detail, the already existing patterns of pre-Reformation festive and popular culture allowed for the open expression of dissent and a Dionysian challenging of the old order.[3] Often as not, there was a very carnivalesque flavour to the incidents of iconoclasm that erupted across Europe in the 1520s and 1530s, as witnessed by the fiery destruction of the popular object of devotion, the Boxley Rood, at Smithfield during the 1538 campaign of iconoclasm orchestrated by Henry VIII's chief minister, Thomas Cromwell.[4] The festive traditions of household drama and outdoor playing associated with Corpus Christi and other religious holidays could be easily adapted and appropriated for the purposes of reformers across Europe.

Playing and players, either local or as part of a visiting troupe, were thus intrinsically linked with festive occasions in late medieval and early-modern English and continental culture. Peter Burke notes how plays were a 'recurrent element in Carnival'.[5] In Mikhail Bakhtin's famous conception of carnival (albeit within a somewhat naive and limited understanding of its full implications) there is always a contested degree of licence and permission to transgress the limits and boundaries of everyday existence, where prevailing social hierarchies and orthodoxies are challenged and upturned, and where human life becomes freer and more authentic. Indeed, in his seminal work, *Rabelais and His World*, first published in 1965, Bakhtin talks of carnival as 'the people's second life, organized on the basis of laughter'.[6] Carnival is that temporal festive period of time during which 'there is no other life outside it', and 'life is subject to its own laws, that is, the laws of its own freedom'.[7]

Thus dramas performed within the context of the Bakhtinian model of carnival as a 'temporary' world of disorder generated by popular festivity, even with the explicit sanction of secular and ecclesiastical authorities, could theoretically serve as a vehicle for the expression of social and political dissent. The model of carnival as an unofficial open forum in turn unlocks the potential for the expression of polyphony. Bakhtin defines polyphony – multi-voicedness or counterpoint – as 'a plurality of independent and unmerged voices and consciousnesses'.[8] This reveals polyphony's central dilemma and inherent contradiction: it is inescapably a problem of voice. We never really know who is speaking in much late medieval and early Reformation drama.

The problem of subversion and dissent is acute in *Three Laws* and *Love Feigned and Unfeigned* because of their generic affinity and questioning of the orthodoxy of pre-Reformation Christianity. As very late examples of the medieval morality play genre adopted to facilitate very early Protestant agendas, they stand out as examples of the subtly conflicting paths that dissent took during the Reformation, adapting the conventions of the genre to show very conflicting readings of Scripture and Revelation exegesis. The interpretation of Revelation and the coming of the End Times in light of current events acquired a rabid and virtually unstoppable momentum in the 1520s and 1530s as observers felt that Luther's defiance of the Pope inaugurated the seventh and final stage of history as it was conceived in the Book of Revelation.[9] Written as responses to and further interpretations of the fevered atmosphere of millenarianism that flowered in the wake of the Reformation, they illustrate how the ostensibly democratizing exercises of print and reading gave rise to the variegated continuum of doctrine and belief that characterizes Western Christendom to this very day.

Both *Three Laws* and *Love Feigned and Unfeigned* indicate adherence to conventions of dramatic performance within the framework of the popular festive occasion, and continue within the morality play traditions of the fourteenth and fifteenth centuries, i.e. *psychomachia* (the battle between good and evil within the individual soul), allegorical characters and the dramatization of the Christian message of initial grace, Fall and final redemption.[10] They follow in the tradition of earlier morality plays of monastic provenance, such as the late-fifteenth-century *Mankind,* in which a group (usually a trio) of vice characters tempt an initially naive and apparently gullible protagonist. The locus of temptation is always to be found in the problematics of sexual vice, more specifically the fleshly corruption of the protagonist by the assorted vices. In the conventional late medieval morality play, governing hierarchies are, on the surface at least, reinforced and propagated rather than challenged and subverted.

On first consideration, *Three Laws* and *Love Feigned and Unfeigned* make rather unlikely bedfellows for joint analysis, given the frequent antipathy that John Bale articulated towards Anabaptists during his career as a polemicist and playwright. On the surface, Bale's career and central participation in the official campaign orchestrated by Henry VIII's Chief Secretary Thomas Cromwell, in favour of the largely structural reformation of the English Church following the king's break with Rome, seems to place him firmly in the mainstream vanguard of the early Protestant reformers. However, closer analysis of his doctrinal position, in particular concerning the vexatious question of clerical marriage and enforced celibacy, shows him to be very much at variance with the theological and doctrinal orthodoxy of Henry VIII himself. Bale was recruited in 1537 by Cromwell to lead a troupe of players to perform dramas across England in support of the Henrician Reformation, and with all the zeal of a convert, he set about promoting reformed doctrine to largely sceptical audiences.

Of the twenty-four or so dramas attributed to Bale, only five are currently extant: a Biblical trilogy of plays (*John the Baptist's Preaching, The Temptation of Christ* and *God's Promises*), the historical work *King Johan* and the festive morality play *Three Laws.* Structured around a tri-partite psychomachia and rooted in a millenarian eschatology, *Three Laws* presents the successive corruption of the laws of historic Nature, Moses and Christ by three pairs of vice characters led by a head vice or fool, namely Infidelity. It seems to have been composed with perform-ance in a large playing-space such as the Great Hall of an aristocratic household as its intended aim, and to have been written specifically to appeal to a broad cross section of spectators. Its framework, grounded as it is in morality convention and a Revelation exegesis, is juxtaposed with bawdy, scatological language and carnivalesque slapstick. Perhaps the most conclusive evidence pointing towards the composi-tion of *Three Laws* specifically for staging on festive occasions is to be found in Bale's own description of his clash with a French Breton priest of orthodox temperament during his tenure as the rector of the Hampshire parish of Bishopstoke in the early 1550s. In *An Expostulation Or Complaynte Agaynste The Blasphemyes of A Franticke Papyst of Hamshyre*, Bale derides his papist opponent, 'In the weke before Christmas last past', for having called a servant of his household 'heretyke and knave, because he had begonne to studie a parte in suche a comedie, as myghtely rebuked the abhomynacyons and fowle filthie occupienges of the Bishopp of Rome'. The comedy in question was 'A Comedie concerning iii lawes of nature, moses & Christ, etc'.[11]

It goes without saying that *Three Laws*, as a scatological and scurrilously anti-Papal play, is in itself an act of dissent. However, not only does it dissent from the old religion, which continued to enjoy widespread public support in 1530s England, but it is also a problematic form of deviation from the official line of the Henrician Reformation by virtue of its open advocacy of doctrinal reform and sacerdotal marriage. What I intend to briefly explore here is how it uses the inherently subversive possibilities of the theatrical performance itself to articulate its own unique form of dissent. It opens with Infidelity's degradation of the Law of Nature accomplished through the moral and physical pollution perpetrated by the twin vices of Sodomy and Idolatry.[12] Upon first meeting them, Infidelity tells them both that 'At Christmas and Paske/Ye maye daunce the devyll a maske/Whyls hys great cawdron plawe', and at the beginning of the second act he playfully teases the Law of Nature with the greeting, 'And the holyman saynt Steven/Sende ye a good newe yeare.'[13] *Three Laws* dissents from medieval Catholic orthodoxy, but it articulates its dissent more forcefully through the carnivalesque and corporeal transgression of the effeminized character of Idolatry which is created as an allegorical representation of the corrupt Roman Church. And the veneration of the female image and of the flesh is both 'vanyte' and 'slyppernesse', because it is the curse of Baal, and a false submission to the 'worshyppynge' of 'ydolles'.[14] That idolatry corrupts the body through fixation with beauty and the projection of the vanity of the self through appearance and onto created objects, is what makes it lustful, and, given Bale's characteristic looseness of terminology, potentially sodomitical. Hence Idolatry is paired with Sodomy as a vice whose 'sedes … the lawe of nature begyle'.[15] Garrett Epp describes Idolatry as a 'worldly, effeminate and effeminating desire that substitutes flesh for God, serving "the creature more than the Creatour" and one who plays "the submissive partner in sodomitical relationships" '.[16] Such a judgement of the Idolatry–Sodomy pairing sorely neglects the dynamic interplay that exists in the relationship between the two vices, and the magical power that is very much an inherent characteristic of a body that is both Ovidian and Dionysian in essence, and to use a loose, if arguably apt cliché, gender-bending. The socially and biologically constructed blurring of masculinity and femininity underlines what Judith Butler calls 'the categorical confusion of dissident sexuality and gender roles'.[17]

Idolatry's body resists easy classification, and indicates how the act(s) of theatrical disguise and embodiment are in themselves forms of dissent, especially if the body becomes in the act of performance a vehicle for the expression of dissidence. From Idolatry's inception, it is clear that the issue of gender transition and metamorphosis is determined by the character's ability to operate as an independent agency with the aid of diabolic magic and witchcraft. Idolatry's gender mutability is a form of emblematic hermaphroditism, which presages his/her participation together with Sodomy in the cuckold-ing and rape of the Law of Nature. Analysing early modern hermaphroditism, Ruth Gilbert notes that amongst other guises, 'The hermaphrodite [is] variously figured as a girl, a monster ... a man, a woman, a transvestite, a sodomite.'[18] Idolatry occupies what Marjorie Garber calls a 'third space' where a plurality of gender(s) can exist beyond the binary of male and female.[19]

Gender transgression becomes the locus of Bale's argument that it is the False Church of the Papacy which strays from Christian truth. Idolatry thus presents the spectator with an image of dissent embodied in physical appearance and corporeal/gender transgres-sion, as an allegorical and emblematic embodiment of the pre-Reformation Church and excessive Marian devotion. Her dissent implicitly masquerades Bale's own tenuous dissent from the official line of the first and very early English Reformation, and popular sentiment which remained predominantly attached to the old religion. For Bale, corporeality and allegorical embodiment are sufficient modes of transgression. In *Three Laws* it is what the vices *signify* rather than what they *say* which becomes the central means of expressing dissent, and in the hierarchical dichotomy that the play establishes between visual and verbal modes of transgression, it is clearly the former which enjoys supremacy. For Idolatry and Sodomy (and indeed for the two other pairs of vices in the play) mere self-definition and costume/masking within the generic conventions of the festive morality play are enough for them to become instruments of dissent.

At the end of the second act, the Law of Nature appears on stage with syphilitic sores and pleads openly for the legalization of clerical marriage as the means by which the Church, religion and the kingdom may be properly restored to full health of body, mind and spirit. The pairing of Sodomy and Idolatry clearly gestures towards Bale's own dissent through his marriage to Dorothy from the state-sponsored form of the Henrician Reformation, and towards the ferocious controversy that the issue of sacerdotal marriage generated in the early stages of the English Reformations. Bale is using sexual and gender dissidence to rebut his doctrinal and clerical dissidence, but his rhetorical strategy only serves to underscore the fragility of his own position as a cleric in direct defiance of a king who retained a strong preference for the celibacy of the clerical estate.

Bale's radical views incited much hostility from audiences largely inclined to attachment to traditional devotional practices, prayer and worship, as witnessed by the controversy surrounding his preaching against the Pilgrimage of Grace in Thornden in Suffolk in 1536. He attracted even greater controversy in relation to his likely staging of plays in Canterbury in 1562 during the last years of his career as prebendary of the cathedral. More often than not, this radicalism may well have led Bale to have been tarred with accusations of being in favour of Anabaptist doctrine. Such accusations may well have been led to the revision of his most important play *King Johan* in order to deflect such charges in light of Elizabeth I's anti-Anabaptist proclamation of 1561. The C-text revisions of the play indicate that it was performed for the Queen during her visit to Ipswich in 1561.

John N. King identifies *Love Feigned and Unfeigned*, which dates from around 1547–49, as being of possible Anabaptist provenance.[20] This short work of fewer than 500 lines remained lost for some 350 years or so until its discovery in the British Museum by the scholar Arundell Esdaile in a copy of Johannes Herolt's *Sermones Discipuli* published in Strasbourg in 1492. Given the relatively controversial nature of its subject matter, it is highly likely that it was composed for covert performance in an upstairs playing-space such as the upper storey of an inn. The play follows the pattern of the conventional morality: the vice characters Falsehood and Love Feigned are confronted by the virtue characters of Love Unfeigned and Fellowship – fellowship or brotherhood being a key concept in the Anabaptists' egalitarian outlook.

In *Love Feigned and Unfeigned*, Love Unfeigned talks of 'feloship', which 'should you love in harte above all other love' in direct contrast to the vice character Falsehood who declares that he 'can speake fare to a man and imbrace hime as my brother whom inwardlie I disdayne and hate above all other'.[21] In Falsehood, one again finds the old morality play convention of corporeal transgression having its seed, so to speak, in the idea of mental or spiritual sin. *Love Feigned and Unfeigned* makes much of the virtue of fraternal love and communitarianism, citing the third epistle of St John with its demand unto the faithful that 'thou doest faithfully whatsoever thou doest to the brethren, and to strangers'.[22] Love Unfeigned declares that 'Saint John in his thyrd epistle me love commendeth. Saint Peter like wyse whose wrytinge unto me greting sendeth the holie prophete salamon in ecclesiastic declareth that eche beaste for his owne passing lye.'[23]

In its broadest sense, this can be interpreted as an expression of belief in the valency of the Gospel message of fraternal love and universal brotherhood. However, the text should be considered in the light of the aftermath of the 1534 Anabaptist seizure of the German city of Münster and in the light of the royal proclamations with their tone of anxiety about the spread of Anabaptist influence in Tudor England, and, more specifically, about the possible influence of radical Anabaptist doctrines advocating radical egalitarianism, the communal ownership of property and the rejection of oaths and allegiance to magistrates. Taken to extremes, the ideal of communal property in Münster had led to polygamy and the sharing of wives as well as other unorthodox sexual practices, which were viewed with deep revulsion across early Reformation Europe. Widespread adoption of Anabaptist beliefs in an England that faced the possibility of invasion by the combined forces of Henry II's France and the Holy Roman Empire of Charles V could prove to be highly destabilizing. The refusal to bear arms or swear oaths to the Tudor monarchy made the task of raising an army to combat foreign threats much more problematic, while sexual and social utopianism questioned the conventional institutions of the household and the family, and threatened to abolish social rank and privilege. Bale's abhorrence of Anabaptism and the Münster Rebellion underscores one of the key aspects of dissent that he fundamentally reads and *mis*reads: that the act of reading and interpretation is in itself a subversive act that is inherently unstable and open to contradiction and challenge. If anything, the open marketplace that the Reformation imposes upon the narrative of Revelation exegesis ultimately de-authorizes and decentres it as a text and turns it into a locus of dissent rather than one which resists it.

There is no definitive evidence to prove that *Love Feigned and Unfeigned* is of Anabaptist provenance: when Falsehood talks of how 'I reigne as an Imperiall magistrate at rome/I ame honoured in all nations whersoe I come/he that hath not my practyse in his conversation/ys tearmed an asse and rude in comunicatyon', he could very easily have expressed a mainstream reformist viewpoint contained within the official antipapal campaign of the late 1530s orchestrated by Thomas Cromwell. The reinvigoration of stridently Lutheran reform under Edward VI encouraged a much more licentious atmosphere where the expression of anti-Papal sentiment mixed with radical social dissent could explode into vigorous life. Falsehood may well have been a mouthpiece for officially sanctioned propaganda, which could point to a provenance for *Love Feigned and Unfeigned* in the mainstream of sixteenth-century English religious reform. However, considering the lack of accompanying evidence regarding the play's authorship and the circumstances of its staging and performance, much of whatever one can say about this brief work remains in the realms of conjecture and speculation. Nonetheless, *Love Feigned and Unfeigned*, as a drama concerned with the propagation of its doctrinal message, challenges and inverts *Three Laws'* hierarchical championing of visual over verbal transgression.

Love Feigned and Unfeigned and *Three Laws*, as Reformation appropriations of the medieval morality play, offer audiences contrasting verbal and visual modes of ideological and cultural dissidence that interrogated pre-Reformation forms of ideological reproduction in the subject. The problematization of dissent has its roots in the political orthodoxy of the 'real' world outside festivity, but the covert disguise of voice within it is what brings this to the fore. The paradox is thus manifest: the medieval and Reformation festive play invites us to read it as the theatrical uncovering of the hidden voice, yet by its context it bewilders the search for its true locus.

REFERENCES

Bakhtin, M., *Rabelais and His World*, trans. H. Iswolsky (Bloomington, IN: Indiana University Press, 1984).
Bakhtin, M., *Problems of Dostoevsky's Poetics*, trans. C. Emerson, intr. W.C. Booth (Minneapolis, MN: University of Minneapolis Press, 1984).
Bale, J., *An Expostulation or Complaynte Agaynste the Blasphemyes of a Franticke Papyst of Hamshyre* (STC 1294) (London: John Day, 1552).

Bale, J., *The Complete Plays of John Bale*, Vols 1 and 2, ed. P. Happé (Woodbridge, Suffolk: Boydell and Brewer, 1986).

Bauckham, P., *Tudor Apocalypse: Sixteenth-Century Apocalypticism, Millenarianism and the English Reformation from John Bale to John Foxe and Thomas Brightman* (Oxford: Sutton Courteney Press, 1978).

Billington, S., *A Social History of the Fool* (Brighton: Harvester Press; New York: St Martin's Press, 1984).

Billington, S., 'The Fool and the Moral in English and Scottish Morality Plays', in F.S. Andersen, J. McGrew, T. Pettitt and R. Schroeder (eds), *Popular Drama in Northern Europe in the Later Middle Ages: A Symposium* (Odense: Odense University Press, 1988), pp.113–33.

Burke, P., *Popular Culture in Early Modern Europe* (London: Temple Smith, 1978).

Butler, J., *Bodies That Matter: On the Discursive Limits of Sex* (London and New York: Routledge, 1993).

Epp, G., ' "Into A Womannys Lyckenes": Bale's Personification of Idolatry: A Response to Alan Stewart', *Medieval English Theatre*, 18 (1996), pp.63–73.

Esdaile, A. (ed.), *The Malone Society Collections Part 1* (Oxford: Oxford University Press, 1907), pp.17–25.

Fairfield, L., *John Bale: Mythmaker for the English Reformation* (West Lafayette, IN: Purdue University Press, 1976).

Firth, K., *The Apocalyptic Tradition in Reformation Britain, 1530–1645* (Oxford: Oxford University Press, 1978).

Garber, M., *Vested Interests: Cross-Dressing & Cultural Anxiety* (London: Routledge, 1997).

Gilbert, R., *Early Modern Hermaphrodites: Sex and Other Stories* (London: Palgrave, 2002).

Happé, P., *John Bale*, Twayne's English Author Series (New York: Twayne, 1996).

King, J.N., *Reformation Literature: The Tudor Origins of the Protestant Tradition* (Princeton, NJ: Princeton University Press, 1982).

MacCulloch, D., *Reformation: Europe's House Divided 1490–1700* (London: Penguin, 2004).

Scragg, L., 'Love Feigned and Unfeigned: A Note on the Rise of Allegory on the Tudor Stage', *English Language Notes*, 3 (1966), pp.248–52.

Scribner, R., 'Reformation, Carnival and the World Turned Upside-Down', *Social History*, 3 (1978), pp.303–29.

Westfall, S., *Patrons and Performance: Early Tudor Household Revels* (Oxford: Clarendon Press, 1990).

White, Paul Whitfield, *Theatre and Reformation: Protestantism, Patronage and Playing in Reformation England* (Cambridge: Cambridge University Press, 1993).

Whitfield White, P., 'Reforming Mysteries' End: Reconsidering Protestant Intervention in English Civic Drama', *Journal of Medieval and Early Modern Studies*, 29, 1 (Winter 1999), pp.122–47.

NOTES

1. This article will touch upon the propaganda impulses of the reform movements in the sixteenth-century German- and English-speaking worlds. For a useful discussion of pro-reform iconoclasm and playing, see, amongst others, R. Scribner, 'Reformation, Carnival and the World Turned Upside-Down', *Social History*, 3 (1978) pp.303–29.

2. J. Bale, *The Complete Plays of John Bale*, Vols 1 and 2, ed. P. Happé (Woodbridge, Suffolk: Boydell & Brewer, 1986). This two-volume edition contains Bale's five extant plays: *Three Laws, King Johan, John the Baptist's Preaching, The Temptation of the Lord* and *God's Promises*. *Love Feigned and Unfeigned* is reprinted by A. Esdaile in *The Malone Society Collections Part 1* (Oxford: Oxford University Press, 1907). Under the auspices of the Malone Society for early English literature, Esdaile edited a reprinted version of *Love Feigned and Unfeigned* in *Collections Part 1: The Malone Society 1907*, pp.17–25. To date, *Love Feigned and Unfeigned* has attracted comparatively little attention despite the interesting questions surrounding its provenance and theological standpoint. See L. Scragg, 'Love Feigned and Unfeigned: A Note on the Rise of Allegory on the Tudor Stage', *English Language Notes*, 3 (1966), pp.248–52.

3. P. Whitfield White, *Theatre and Reformation: Protestantism, Patronage and Playing in Reformation England* (Cambridge: Cambridge University Press, 1993); P. Whitfield White,

'Reforming Mysteries' End: Reconsidering Protestant Intervention in English Civic Drama', *Journal of Medieval and Early Modern Studies*, 29, 1 (Winter 1999), pp.122–47; D. MacCulloch, *Reformation: Europe's House Divided 1490–1700* (London: Penguin, 2004).

4. See P. Burke, *Popular Culture in Early Modern Europe* (London: Temple Smith, 1978) for an excellent introduction and discussion of festive culture in the Reformation period. See Paul Whitfield, *Theatre and Reformation: Protestantism, Patronage and Playing in Reformation England* (Cambridge: Cambridge University Press, 1993), for a comprehensive exploration of the Henrician Reformation's use of drama to promote royal religious policy. For a discussion of the traditions of household drama and festive playing in England, see S. Westfall, *Patrons and Performance: Early Tudor Household Revels* (Oxford: Clarendon Press, 1990).

5. Burke, *Popular Culture in Early Modern Europe*, p.78.

6. M. Bakhtin, *Rabelais and His World*, trans. H. Iswolsky (Bloomington, IN: Indiana University Press, 1984), p.8.

7. Ibid., pp.7–8.

8. M. Bakhtin, *Problems of Dostoevsky's Poetics*, trans. C. Emerson, intr. W.C. Booth (Minneapolis, MN: University of Minneapolis Press, 1984), pp. 6–7.

9. For a brief discussion of the frenetic atmosphere of millennialism that erupted across Europe after 1500, see MacCulloch, *Reformation*, pp.94–7. See P. Bauckham's *Tudor Apocalypse: Sixteenth-Century Apocalypticism, Millenarianism and the English Reformation from John Bale to John Foxe and Thomas Brightman* (Oxford: Sutton Courteney Press, 1978), and K. Firth's *The Apocalyptic Tradition in Reformation Britain, 1530–1645* (Oxford: Oxford University Press, 1978) for analyses of the development of early English Protestant apocalyptic thought and the birth of the Protestant tradition of Revelation exegesis.

10. On this point, the earliest surviving example of a medieval morality play in the English language is the reprinted text fragment *The Pride of Life* which dates from c. 1350 and which originates from a manuscript connected with Christchurch Cathedral, Dublin.

11. *An Expostulation or Complaynte Agaynste The Blasphemyes of A Franticke Papyst of Hamshyre* (STC 1294), C2. The pamphlet was published by John Day at Cheapside in 1552. As both Happé and Fairfield point out, Bale procured his appointment to the rectorship of Bishopstoke, five miles outside Southampton under the authority of John Ponet who had been appointed by Edward VI to the see of Winchester as a replacement for Stephen Gardiner: L. Fairfield, *John Bale: Mythmaker for the English Reformation* (West Lafayette IN: Purdue University Press, 1976), p.90; Happé suggests that *An Expostulation* 'seems to have been an attempt to obtain preferment, and indeed it may have been contributory to his elevation to the episcopacy in the same year'. See Happé, *John Bale*, Twayne's English Author Series (New York: Twayne, 1996), pp.42–3.

12. S. Billington, *A Social History of the Fool* (Brighton: Harvester Press; New York: St Martin's Press, 1984), pp.25–6.

13. J. Bale, *Three Laws*, lines 403–5: B3; lines 182–3: A6, in *Complete Plays of John Bale*, Vol. 2, pp.18, 12.

14. J. Bale, *God's Promises*, line 825: E1v, in *Complete Plays of John Bale*, Vol. 2, p.24.

15. Bale, *Three Laws*, lines 552–4: B6, in *Complete Plays of John Bale*, Vol. 2, p.21.

16. G. Epp, ' "Into A Womannys Lyckenes": Bale's Personification of Idolatry: A Response to Alan Stewart', *Medieval English Theatre*, 18 (1996), p.66.

17. J. Butler, *Bodies That Matter: On the Discursive Limits of Sex* (London and New York: Routledge, 1993), p.2.

18. R. Gilbert, *Early Modern Hermaphrodites: Sex and Other Stories* (London: Palgrave, 2002), p.9.

19. M. Garber, *Vested Interests: Cross-Dressing and Cultural Anxiety* (London: Routledge, 1997), p.11.

20. J.N. King, *Reformation Literature: The Tudor Origins of the Protestant Tradition* (Princeton, NJ: Princeton University Press, 1982), pp.311–12.

21. *Love Feigned and Unfeigned* (D1–2), pp.15–16.

22. 3 John 1:5.

23. *Love Feigned and Unfeigned* (D2), p.16.

In 1915, Padraig Pearse published an essay entitled 'Ghosts' which

9

Irish Nationalist [Mis]readings of Ibsen: Padraig Pearse, Lennox Robinson and Thomas MacDonagh

Irina Ruppo Malone

borrowed the title from Henrik Ibsen's play and revealed Pearse's blatant misunderstanding of its ideas. 'Ghosts are troublesome things in a house or in a family, as we knew even before Ibsen taught us', wrote Pearse; 'There is only one way to appease a ghost. You must do the thing it asks you. The ghosts of a nation sometimes ask very big things; and they must be appeased, whatever the cost.'[1] Ghosts are indeed troublesome in Ibsen's play – they are venereal diseases and incestuous relationships that lurk behind the veneer of Victorian respectability. They are outmoded ideals and stifling conventions that inhibit individual freedom. In his article, Pearse inverted the metaphor. His ghosts are the voices of Wolfe Tone, John Mitchell, Thomas Davis, James Fintan Lalor and Parnell calling Irishmen to arms. Ibsen's *Ghosts* is an exposure of the morbidity of idealism; Pearse's 'Ghosts' is a protest against the decay of ideals in his generation.

Pearse's article indicates the importance of Ibsen for pre-1916 Dublin society. While Ibsen's dramas were only rarely produced in Ireland (there were only sixteen productions between 1894 and 1915), his name was often used in critical debates and theatre reviews. His influence on many Irish playwrights was particularly noticeable (and freely acknowledged) in the case of the Cork Realists – Lennox Robinson, T.C. Murray, R.J. Ray and Seamus Kelly – whose plays dominated the Abbey stage between 1910 and 1915. As Lennox Robinson later recalled, 'We were very young and we shrunk from nothing. We knew our Ibsen and the plays of the Lancashire school, we showed our people as robbers and murderers, guilty of arson, steeped in trickery and jobbery.'[2] Irish realists were frequently criticized by nationalist critics who believed that the business of playwrights was the building of national character, rather than the ridiculing of their countrymen. However, the Irish realists' greater problem was that they considered themselves national writers and attempted to combine their nationalism with Ibsenism, two things which, as Pearse's misreading of *Ghosts* demonstrates, are not easily compatible ideologies.

George Bernard Shaw defined the quintessence of Ibsenism in 1891 as an 'attack on ideals and idealism'.[3] Even though Ibsen's realist plays do not deal specifically with nationalism, his letters reveal a mistrust of the ideals of nationalism: 'I do not believe', Ibsen wrote in 1879, 'that it is our mission to be responsible for the freedom and independence of the State, but rather to awaken individuals to freedom and independence – and as many of them as possible.'[4] The difficulty in reconciling the Ibsenite attack on idealism with nationalist ardour is noticeable in Lennox Robinson's *Patriots*. When produced on 11 April 1912, *Patriots* was remarkably well received. The audience of the Abbey 'listened [to the play] with rapt attention like a class of well behaved children'. *Patriots* was called 'a wonderfully balanced' play and a 'marvellous piece of characterization'. 'And', said one eyewitness, 'the funny part is that no one could be sure what [Robinson]'s politics [were].'[5] Robinson's indebtedness to Ibsen was widely acknowledged, yet none of the reviews mentioned the play's obvious affinity with *John Gabriel Borkman*.

Like John Gabriel Borkman, the protagonist of Robinson's play is an ex-convict. After eighteen years in prison, James Nugent returns home hopeful to continue his armed fight against the British occupation. Upon his return he discovers that his comrades in arms have sunk to drunken complacency while his devoted wife Ann has become an embittered miser. She has turned the shop that was once a safe place for rebels into a successful business. Parliamentarianism is predominant in the New Ireland to which James Nugent returns. In his attempts to rekindle the old spirit of revolution, Nugent is followed only by the representatives of the younger generation: his disabled daughter Rose and her admirer Willie, the only son of his old friend. A confrontation with Ann occurs when Nugent tries to prevent her from evicting Willie's parents for non-payment of rent. When Nugent accuses her of greed and insensitivity, she reminds him that after his arrest she had to provide for their invalid daughter. In the final scene of the play, Ann tells Nugent that it was the shock of his arrest that caused a premature birth and permanently disabled the child. Upon discovering the truth the ex-convict seems to age instantly. He finds the strength only for these words:

I've killed a man, I've crippled a child, I've got myself shut up for eighteen years – God knows what good came out of it all – but ... I meant – I tried ... I know I meant right – and in prison my cell used to be filled with the sad faces of men like me who had given everything for Ireland – they would not have come to me, would they? If I hadn't been of their company. They are here now – I see them all around me – there is Wolfe Tone, and there is ... oh quiet watching faces, I have tried – tried as you tried – and been broken ... [6]

A prisoner's return to freedom, a resentful wife, a squandered family fortune, a woman whose happiness had been destroyed, an ideal for which these sacrifices have been made and which remains beyond the hero's reach – *Patriots* resembles a simplified version of *John Gabriel Borkman*. Like Ibsen's tragedy of a banker of Napoleonic ambitions, *Patriots* explores idealism through the juxtaposition of the impassioned hero and the spiritually impoverished people whose happiness he has destroyed. Both *John Gabriel Borkman* and *Patriots* lead their characters to dead ends. Similar to Gunhild Borkman and her sister Ella, the once passionate and loving Ann Nugent had given in to bitterness and hate. Like the kindly Vilhelm Foldal, who alone believes in Borkman's ability to restore his name and make a fortune, Nugent's friends nurture their passive acceptance of foreign rule with feeble dreams of a better future and memories of their past battles.

The main difference between the two plays lies in the authors' choice of an occupation for their idealist-hero. In Ibsen's play the grandiose notions of self-fulfilment, human charity and divine vocation are exemplified by the unlikely figure of a corrupt banker and would-be millionaire. Only through his powerful rhetoric does John Gabriel convince the audience that his financial schemes represent a glorious and revolutionary ideal. Through his fantastic language, John Gabriel, invests finance with the power and appeal of magic:

I seem to touch them, the prisoned millions; I can see the veins of metal stretch out their winding, branching, luring arms to me. I saw them before my eyes like living shapes, that night when I stood in the strong-room with the candle in my hands. You begged to be liberated and I tried to free you. But my strength failed me; and the treasure sank back into the deep again. [7]

As Borkman recites this love song to his riches, the reader loses sight of the swindler and sees a figure of ancient splendour, a warrior or a prophet. Through his character's language, Ibsen demonstrates that the vitality and power of an ideal is independent of its immediate basis in reality. By contrast, Robinson chooses for his hero an ideal that would be immediately understood by his audiences and whose power has been developed in the real world, outside the bounds of his play. Consequently, James Nugent's speeches do not need to be eloquent. It is enough that his wife remembers his ardent nationalist addresses and the audience will recall the 'James Nugents of history' and believe in the eloquence of Robinson's hero.

The play was interpreted as a homage to revolutionaries and as propaganda for the physical force movement not only by some of the contemporary reviewers but also, more recently, by Christopher Murray:

> Although it is clear that to Robinson Nugent is the real hero, violent though his republicanism is, it is equally clear from the ending of *Patriots* that the majority reject Nugent's dream. The play is thus a study of a social leader passed by and isolated by a change in public mood. The irony of the ending provides a sharp critique of this public mood, and adds as it were, a bold question mark to the play's title.[8]

Surely, while the passionate James Nugent is a more interesting and sympathetic character than his apathetic countrymen, it would be wrong to ignore his guilt for the fate of his daughter. The dreamy, patriotic Rose is an innocent victim, a casual sacrifice to Nugent's patriotism. Her name is important. In the tradition of *aisling* poetry, Rose stands for Ireland – an Ireland disfigured by the violence of her would-be saviours. Neither can one disregard Ann's condemnation of patriotism in the following interchange with Nugent:

> **James:** I am thinking of my country. If patriotism demands –
> **Ann:** Oh don't talk to me of patriotism – I am sick of it. It's made Sullivan a bankrupt; it's made Brennan a drunkard; you a murderer; it's destroyed my happiness; it's made Rose a cripple.[9]

The 'bold question mark' implicit in the play's title refers equally to the slovenly townspeople and to Nugent himself. The former are condemned for their lack of idealism and for their materialistic acceptance of foreign rule, yet the latter is condemned for disregarding the life of those who are dear to him in his fight for freedom. Through the figure of the suffering child, Robinson reveals, as Ibsen does in *Brand*, *Little Eyolf* and *The Wild Duck*, the horror at the heart of idealism, the inhumanity of a philosophy that believes in the supremacy of any cause, however righteous, over a single life. And yet Robinson himself seems to have invited Murray's reading by dedicating the play to 'the James Nugents of history'. The dedication contradicts the play's conclusion. It is as if Ibsen dedicated *The Wild Duck* to Gregers Werle (the idealist who unintentionally causes the suicide of the young heroine of the play). The dedication diverts the reader's attention from the play's Ibsenite condemnation of idealism and focuses it instead on the nationalist sympathies of its author.

Another interesting case is Thomas MacDonagh's *Pagans*, produced by the Irish Theatre on 19–24 April 1915, almost exactly a year before its author, one of the signatories of the Proclamation of Independence, was shot by a British firing squad. 'A Modern Play in Two Conversations', as it was subtitled, *Pagans* depicts three people for whom religion has no significance and who have no regard for the institution of marriage. Transposing the gender roles of *A Doll's House*, MacDonagh's play begins where Ibsen ends. The husband has fled the doll's house to find his freedom and the wife is left to meditate on the failure of their marriage. In a conversation with Helen Noble, an artist who admits to being in love with her husband, Frances Fitzmaurice analyses the reasons for John Fitzmaurice's leaving. Accustomed to the high-society life, she found her friends' condescension to John intolerable; she was even more disappointed by his failure to fit in. As in the case of the Helmers, idealism was partly to blame for the failure of this marriage. 'Can you not understand', Frances says to Helen, 'that one may have an ideal – that one may want another – a husband, say – to be that ideal – that one may see that he could be so – that he is so at times? Is it wrong to wish him to have no other times – no other moods? He may spoil it by being lower than himself.'[10] A feminist and individualist, Helen believes that she would 'have accepted him as he was' while also being able to 'go her way': 'the thing that makes intercourse between people is the free play of individuality. We should let others be just what they are.'[11] This is why, in spite of her forebodings, she did nothing to prevent the Fitzmaurices' marriage. Helen tells Frances that she has recently spotted John staring at the statue of the *Winged Victory of Samothrace* at the Louvre; when she saw him she fled lest John should notice her. She then came back three days later, saw him again, and left Paris to come back to Dublin.

The husband appears in the second act. He did in fact notice

Helen at the Louvre. The shock of having seen her sent him back into the arms of his wife. Like the wild duck in Ibsen's play, the headless *Victory of Samothrace* becomes an image in which all the strands of the play coalesce. John had been reminded of the little copy of the statue in his wife's house. Then he saw Helen, and realized that she might have loved him. Since it was too late to repair the damage to Helen, he returned to Frances. Like Alfred and Rita Allmers at the end of *Little Eyolf*, the couple proceed to discuss the future of their relationship. In spite of her love for John, Frances realizes that their life together would now be intolerable. And so the husband leaves once again, his conscience appeased, and his freedom now restored to him by his wife.

Pagans would be an imitation of Ibsen's plays and a reflection on Ibsenite ideas were it not for the final exchange between John and Helen, which as Feeney observes is foreshadowed 'only by a passing reference to his membership in revolutionary societies'.[12] The symbol of the *Victory of Samothrace* suddenly acquires a different meaning. As Levitas puts it, 'while ... gazing at the Victory of Samothrace [John Fitzmaurice] has been contemplating ... not adultery but the necessity of throwing himself into revolution'.[13] The ending of the play is worth quoting in full:

> **Frances:** Goodbye; you are right in all. I now feel quite free, too. For I, too, have been troubled often by a doubt as to the right-ness of our separation. Now we know better. And I shall be glad to know that you can write your best work again.
> **John:** Frances, I shall do better than write. A man who is a mere author is nothing. If there is anything good in anything I have written, it is the potentiality of adventure in me – the power to do something better than write. My writings have been only the prelude to my other work. Though I have been away from Ireland these three years, Frances, I know the progress of things here better than you do – and I know that the great opportunity is at hand. I have long regretted that I have not in my time had an opportunity of doing something worth while, and now it is here.
> **Frances:** Politics, John? What is the good of your leaving me, in order to free yourself, if you are going to mix yourself up in Irish politics? Half of our trouble was your political ideas.
> **John:** I don't call them politics. Sooner than you think, Frances, politics will be dropped here, and something better will take their place. I am now free to do something to bring the better thing.

Frances: John, you're a queer mixture. What had I to do with these things?

John: You were a hostage that I had given to the other cause – to this life that keeps you here. You are no longer my hostage.

Frances: John, what are you going to do?

John: I am going to live the things that I have before imagined. It is well for a poet that he is double-lived. He has two stores of power. You will not know yourself in the Ireland that we shall make here – when I return to you. (Exit John.)[14]

In one instant, MacDonagh has transformed the play from a study of marriage, which could be set anywhere in Europe, into a play about the Ireland of 1915. The shock is considerable for the reader; it must have been even greater for the audience. The poet Michael Crevequer (who did not even like the play) recalled his state of mind upon seeing it:

> Issuing forth into the lamplit April evening we felt impelled to run down the crowded length of O'Connell Street, talking as we ran, dodging round the pedestrians, and meeting again to continue our conversation, and finally reaching our rooms in a fever to prolong till morning the festive ecstasy *Pagans* aroused among our half-formulated theories of a thousand subjects.[15]

The ending reproduces the effect of unexpected elation that occurs at the end of Ibsen's plays. The wild landscape seen through the window in the settings of most of Ibsen's realistic dramas indicates, as Seamus Deane puts it, 'the struggle between the wildness and closed life of the middle classes and the boundless life of the idealistic spirit'.[16] MacDonagh similarly created an atmosphere of a stifling doll's house. However, instead of gesticulating towards the imaginary outside as the location of freedom, his ending of the play points towards the auditorium as a source of that joy; it throws the doors open to the revolutionary spirit of the real Ireland.

But what of John's suggestion in the final words of the play that he will return to Frances? John here echoes Nora's parting words that should the greatest miracle occur – that is, the transformation of their living together into marriage – she might regain her love for Torvald. But unlike Nora, who does not believe that 'a miracle of miracles' may happen,[17] John believes in the miraculous transformation of Ireland through which his union with Frances will become possible. The collapse of the old order with its restricting social conventions needs to occur before their life together can be resumed.

For all its emotional power, *Pagans*, is not a good play; as Michael Crevequer acknowledged in 1921, it is a 'philosophical statement rather than drama, an essay in dialogue'.[18] Moreover, what makes the ending of *Pagans* exciting is precisely the fact that it does not quite fit in with the rest of the play. Its final scene is a revolt against the constrictions of the writer's craft and a declaration of the author's allegiance to the adventure of real life. Like Robinson's dedication of *Patriots*, or Pearse's misreading of *Ghosts*, Thomas MacDonagh's play demonstrates that Ibsenism did not quite work in the context of an idealistic struggle for independence. Like Pearse, who in his essay apologized 'to the shade of the Norwegian dramatist ... for a plagiaristic but inevitable title',[19] MacDonagh performed an exorcism of the spirit of Ibsen in preparation for the revolution.

REFERENCES

Archer, W. (trans. and ed.), *The Collected Works of Henrik Ibsen*, Vol. 11 (London: Heinemann, [1906–12]).

Deane, S., Carpenter, A. and Williams, J. (eds), *The Field Day Anthology of Irish Writing*, Vol. 2 (Derry: Field Day Theatre Company, 1991).

Feeney, W.J. (ed.), *Lost Plays of the Irish Renaissance, Vol. 2: Edward Martyn's Irish Theatre* (Newark, DE: Proscenium Press, 1979).

Feeney, W.J., *Drama in Hardwicke Street: A History of the Irish Theatre Company* (Rutherford, NJ: Fairleigh Dickinson University Press, 1984).

Hogan, R. and Kilroy, J., *The Rise of the Realists 1910–1915* (Dublin: Dolmen Press, 1979).

Ibsen, H., *Letters and Speeches*, ed. E. Sprinchorn (New York: Hill & Wang, 1964).

Levitas, B., *The Theatre of Nation* (Oxford: Clarendon Press, 2002).

Murray, C. (ed.), *Selected Plays of Lennox Robinson* (Washington, DC: Catholic University of America Press, 1982).

Pearse, P., *Political Writings and Speeches* (Dublin: Phoenix, 1916).

Robinson, L., *Curtain Up: An Autobiography* (London: M. Joseph, 1942).

Shaw, G.B., *Collected Prefaces* (London: Paul Hamlyn, 1965).

NOTES

1. P. Pearse, *Political Writings and Speeches* (Dublin: Phoenix, 1916), p.224.
2. L. Robinson, *Curtain Up: An Autobiography* (London: M. Joseph, 1942), p.22.
3. G.B. Shaw, *Collected Prefaces* (London: Paul Hamlyn, 1965), p.831.
4. Ibsen to Bjornson, 12 July 1879, in H. Ibsen, *Letters and Speeches*, ed. E. Sprinchorn (New York: Hill & Wang, 1964), p.179.
5. A letter to Yeats from a Miss Byrne from London dated 15 April 1912. NLI [National Library of Ireland]MS 18, 722. Cited in R. Hogan and J. Kilroy, *The Rise of the Realists 1910–1915* (Dublin: Dolmen Press, 1979), p.185.
6. C. Murray (ed.), *Selected Plays of Lennox Robinson* (Washington, DC: Catholic University of America Press, 1982), p.62.
7. W. Archer (trans. and ed.), *The Collected Works of Henrik Ibsen*, Vol. 11 (London : Heinemann, [1906–12]), p.318.
8. Murray (ed.), *Selected Plays of Lennox Robinson*, p.13.
9. Ibid., p.60.
10. W.J. Feeney (ed.), *Lost Plays of the Irish Renaissance, Vol. 2: Edward Martyn's Irish Theatre*

(Newark, DE: Proscenium Press, 1979), p.35.

11. Ibid.
12. W.J. Feeney, *Drama in Hardwicke Street: A History of the Irish Theatre Company* (Rutherford, NJ: Fairleigh Dickinson University Press, 1984), p.85.
13. B. Levitas, *The Theatre of Nation* (Oxford: Clarendon Press, 2002), p.216.
14. Feeney (ed.), *Lost Plays of the Irish Renaissance, Vol. 2*, p.53.
15. 'Pagans: A modern play by Thomas MacDonagh reviewed by Michael Crevequer', *Studies*, 10 (June 1921). Cited in Feeney, *Drama in Hardwicke Street*, p.87.
16. S. Deane, A. Carpenter and J. Williams (eds), *The Field Day Anthology of Irish Writing*, Vol. 2 (Derry: Field Day Theatre Company, 1991), p.568.
17. Archer (trans. and ed.), *Collected Works of Henrik Ibsen*, Vol. 7, p.190.
18. Feeney, *Drama in Hardwicke Street*, p.87.
19. Pearse, *Political Writings and Speeches*, p.222.

PART 3
POSTCOLONIALISM AND IRISH IDENTITY

PART 3

10

Murder in the Margin: Descent and Dissent in Patrick McCabe's *Winterwood* and Sherman Alexie's *Indian Killer*

Jessica Dougherty-McMichael

Postcolonial literature, whether viewed within the context of anti-colonialism or after colonialism, finds its strength in rhetorics of empowerment and rejuvenation. As the colonial world has crawled along the precarious road of independence, hedged in on all sides by a litany of 'isms' – colonialism, postcolonialism, neocolonialism, essentialism, modernism, traditionalism, postmodernism – a more complex literature emerges. In this literature, we find a nuanced criticism of the newly founded nation and the neocolonial. Such work is vital to ongoing development in any given culture but it also runs the risk of slipping into a self-deprecating nihilism and losing the political edge that characterizes much postcolonial literature. This awkward balance between dissent and descent makes Irish writer Patrick McCabe's *Winterwood* (2006) and Spokane writer Sherman Alexie's *Indian Killer* (1996) particularly interesting in the space of a changing postcolonial literature. McCabe and Alexie stand out on an international stage for their frenetic merging and discordant combinations of popular culture, canonical literature, music and film. As such, they are also critics of their own literary traditions, drawing as much confusion as they do praise from their readers. Neither author stops with criticism of the colonial but criticizes the neocolonial and questions the very tenets of the postcolonial structure from which they have emerged. They turn their critical insights onto the way that stories are told, extending the familiar trope of the unreliable narrator toward a more radical unreliable structure, context, reality, narrative and, most problematically, an unreliable tradition. In *Winterwood* and *Indian Killer* particularly, this cutting insight focuses on Irish and Native American postcolonial icons. The question becomes whether this is a productive evaluation of the status of postcolonial literature within an ever-globalizing context or a descent into self-referential shock literature. Do these texts work as critiques of the contemporary state of 'postcolonial' contexts? Or, rather, do they appease the neocolonial reader?

Through a comparison of these two different authors from separate traditions, I seek to highlight the problematic area of dissent from and within the amorphous category of postcolonial literature. It is the critique of that increasingly thin line between postcolonial icons of 'true' culture and a neocolonial co-optation of culture via these often fossilized icons that maintains the novels' force of dissent rather than allowing the novels to descend into literary madness. In this manner, *Winterwood* and *Indian Killer* are critiques simultaneously of the colonial/neocolonial and the postcolonial. Their use of madness, crime and the gothic enables these critiques but also complicates the critiques to such a degree that a certain amount of effectiveness and readability is lost. What is compelling about these novels is just this juxtaposition of madness and the gothic with the detective novel/crime thriller. Madness and the gothic are frequently used as forms of dissent, particularly regarding marginalized groups. The detective/crime novel is not; rather, it is a genre of control, of explaining and rationalizing violence so that, in the reader's mind, it can be prevented. As we shall see, the so-called return of the repressed ravages the crime-solving structure of the novels. Vital to this shift are the commodity cultures and commodification of culture in contemporary Dublin and Seattle, respectively. Before moving on with this point, I will give a short synopsis of each text. I will then address similar preoccupations of the texts and their dissent to the postcolonial tradition.

Winterwood is narrated by Red or Redmond Hatch over a period of twenty-five years, from the 1980s to 2006. Hatch, like most McCabe characters, is unable to escape the past despite his economically viable future. The novel opens with his meeting Ned or Edmund Strange, a mountain storyteller from Slievenageeha, Hatch's home area. Hatch writes a series of articles on Strange, with such success that Strange becomes a much sought-after icon of traditional Irish culture, holding ceilidhs and giving music lessons to the local children whose parents are hoping to acquaint their children with 'Irishness'. To his later horror, Hatch discovers that Strange has molested and killed a young boy and later committed suicide himself. Between this and the disintegration of Hatch's family, which ends in divorce and the loss of custody of his daughter, Hatch begins to fall apart. He fakes his suicide and stalks his ex-wife and daughter – all the while having ghostly visitations from Strange. This culminates in his murder of his daughter Imogen and later of his ex-wife Catherine. Hatch's obsession is more with Imogen, to whom he tells of his invented Winterwood. This winter place is coded throughout the text as death and is a place where Hatch can supposedly maintain control over an ever-changing world.

The novel blurs Hatch and Strange. Their first names, Redmond and Edmund, are both visually and audibly similar. And of their respective last names, Hatch and Strange, a language lesson from Strange reveals that Hatch is from the Irish *ait* for odd or strange.[1] Through a series of intimate relationships, infidelities and murders, the novel also establishes a behavioural pattern that links the two men. Strange, although the narrative enables other possibilities, had been cuckolded by two women who both meet gruesome ends. The second murder, when considering when and how it happened, could almost have been committed by Hatch and not Strange. Hatch is married twice and both marriages end with his wives' affairs. Hatch murders Catherine after his second marriage ends. Each of the four relationships, and, for the most part, each of the murders, occur at twenty-year intervals. This blurs the two men and inevitably undermines the reader looking for victim and criminal. Hatch is aware of the blurring and spends most of the text attempting to escape the legacy of the mountain, to escape being a 'pathetic mountain mongrel'.[2] However, towards the end of his life, he slips more and more into a performance of the legacy.

By the end of the story, the reader is fairly certain that Strange is actually Hatch's Uncle Florian, who sexually molested him as a child. This is confirmed, as much as it can be, when the narrator shifts from Hatch to Strange who waits for him in the graveyard. As Hatch dies he '[realizes] just who his companion was, as I flashed my incisors and drew him towards me: Little Red ... '[3] Strange refers to Hatch with Florian's nickname for him in this vampiric conclusion. *Winterwood*'s conclusion also further blurs the two characters as it shifts from Hatch's to Strange's voice and the two are reunited in death. This shift is necessary, for as Strange tells the reader:

> Nothing would give me greater pleasure than to allow Redmond Hatch to conclude his own story. Regrettably, however, that is impossible. There are times, it has to be acknowledged, when he will make the most valiant efforts. But somehow he never seems to transcend a certain point.[4]

And this is Hatch's problem: he never manages to 'transcend a certain point'. For all our sympathy for Hatch, he is unable to escape his hell; there is no redemption through the modern or the traditional.

Where *Winterwood* leaves the reader with a relatively limited amount of possible readings, *Indian Killer* leaves the reader with so many possible readings that s/he is unable to form a stable hypothesis. Even the title itself refuses to mean something tangible, as *Indian Killer* refers both to a serial killer in the text who is assumed to be an Indian, and to killers of Indians. The crimes around which the novel is based are a series of murders of white men and the kidnapping of a white boy that are performed in a seemingly ceremonial fashion. As readers, we witness the murders and know that the killer considers his actions to be part of Native American ceremony. The extent to which the killer is acting within a specific cultural context or simply acting what he thinks is a cultural context assures that the reader cannot even narrow the killer's identity down to possible race.

One of the focal characters, John Smith, is compelling in part because of his desire to kill the 'white man who had done the most harm to the world'.[5] He was born to a young Native American woman, of whom he knows nothing, and was adopted by a white couple, Daniel and Olivia Smith. The novel opens with an imagining of this event in a chapter titled 'Mythology', and it becomes John's creation myth as he attempts to find some connection with his biological mother. The Smiths mean well but are incapable of understanding John's lived experience. After all, they name their son John Smith, a generic 'white' name and the name of the early colonizer of Pocahontas fame. During one of Daniel's searches for John, an Indian man is astonished on hearing his son's name and responds: 'You adopted an Indian kid and named him John Smith? No wonder he talks to himself ... ' and continues, 'Hey, Daniel, I've got to say I don't know one Indian named John Smith ... You must have dreamed him up.'[6] John embodies both the colonizing white American and the colonized Native America. With this split mind and split identity, John is a classic schizophrenic, and as a literary character he illustrates the problematic space between Native America and non-native America. While critics such as Christie Stuart, in his article 'Renaissance Man: the Tribal "Schizophrenic" in Sherman Alexie's *Indian Killer*',[7] criticize this appropriation of schizophrenia in literature, we are necessarily reminded of the tradition of madness in colonial and postcolonial literature. John's condition is a criticism of the world he is in as well as a dissent from this world. Unfortunately, his schizophrenia also makes him the prime suspect in *Indian Killer*.

Like the reader's inability to decipher where Hatch stops and Strange begins, John's existence is constantly called into question. Not only does Daniel encounter doubt at the very mention of his son's name, John is constantly being compared to fictional characters. One of these fictional characters is actually found in Alexie's fictional detective novelist Jack Wilson's Shilshomish detective, Little Hawk. Upon seeing John, Wilson is struck by the similarity between John and his created character Little Hawk and, moreover, 'felt as if he'd brought Little Hawk to life through some kind of magic'.[8] Wilson later writes a book on the murders called *Indian Killer* where John becomes the killer. In Alexie's novel, John is a construction of competing narratives.

What becomes apparent in these summaries is a handful of similar preoccupations. For McCabe's Hatch and Alexie's John there are distinct possibilities for economic success but they are unable to take full advantage of these opportunities. This economic positioning highlights criticism of what we might consider the neocolonial, particularly for McCabe, or the threat of assimilation for Alexie. There is also the longing for family, particularly for a mother figure. The juxtaposition of family and a prospering middle class establishes the commodity culture that the novels criticize and undermine through Hatch's and John's inability to access that culture.

Both *Winterwood* and *Indian Killer* critique the commodification of 'traditional' culture which occurs when culture is experienced as a class or an event only, rather than as an integrated and normal aspect of the home life. In these novels, this type of culture is a bottled culture with unequal parts: colonial and postcolonial versions of a supposedly original and traditional culture. Returning to an idea of culture is not the same as a living culture. The cultures that the middle-class characters in these novels send their children to experience are idealized, fossilized conceptions and not integrated, lived culture. The children sent to Strange live this Irish culture only when they are with him, and while John's parents mean the best when they send him to powwows or encourage his connections to Native cultures, these links are only with the outside; they are not in the home. As these cultural locations are idealized they are too sacred to incorporate into everyday life and are too 'authentic' to question. In the case of *Winterwood*, the cultural cache Strange is given allows him to successfully prey upon his students for years. In the case of *Indian Killer*, John is split between his home life and the 'authentic' Indian world; as an ideal, he can never truly access this identity that he is meant to strive for (a goal supported by his parents). Here commodification becomes more problematic as this bottled culture enables writers and scholars like Professor Mathers and Jack Wilson to assume Native American voices at the expense of actual Native Americans. Or, as Marie Polatkin observes when Wilson's book shows up on Mather's course syllabus rather than works by native authors such as Simon Ortiz, Luci Tapahonso or Elizabeth Woody, 'It's like his books are killing Indian books.'[9]

A further preoccupation for the novels is madness, a fertile literary trope in Irish and postcolonial literatures. The logic behind this is clear; if the colonial power is the power that develops the parameters of sanity, the colonized will necessarily fall to the margins of this created sanity as well as political and economic margins. In his book, *The Novel and the Nation*, Gerry Smyth highlights the obsession with madness in Irish literature, locating it both in an indigenous occupation with fantasy, dreams and the absurd, and in a colonial tradition with which Fanon and Nandy are concerned.[10] It is telling, after all, that Fanon, one of the founding figures of postcolonial theory, was a psychiatrist. Madness becomes a real effect of the colonial and decolonizing state as well as a way by which to subvert and dissent from the colonial, from the sane.

While challenging normative definitions of sanity, both *Winterwood* and *Indian Killer* also make direct forays into similar genres: detective, mystery, thriller, psychological, gothic. McCabe has claimed *Winterwood* as his first real attempt at gothic[11] and, as James Richard Giles points out in his *The Spaces of Violence*, '*Indian Killer* is, in part, about the ghosts of Native Americans returning in order to obtain some long-deferred revenge.'[12] Neither text is limited to the gothic, and both novels force the reader to see through the eyes of a detective. As we wade through the texts we must speculate about who has committed which crime. McCabe is particularly adept at undermining a tradition of the 'true crime' type of novel in the Irish tradition. Whereas texts such as Banville's *The Book of Evidence* and Eoin McNamee's *Resurrection Man* explore traumatic events and enable control over the horrors committed, McCabe's unpredictable and even sympathetic characters spin so far out of control that they inevitably reveal their capacities for violence and the social structures that created them. The ambiguity in *Winterwood's* characters, events, structure and genre prevents containment of the novel's violence and the reader is incapable of leaving it securely between the covers of the novel. Likewise, Alexie's *Indian Killer* promises the reader a crime thriller and even interweaves crime novels – from John Grisham to Tony Hillerman – into the text. And yet, for all the insight into the mind of the killer, for all the crimes witnessed and the breakdown of Seattle society, the reader is left with no resolution, no satisfaction that racially motivated crime and mob mentality are contained and resolvable.

This use of madness and genre becomes a vehicle for social criticism. Part of this criticism addresses the binary relationship that postcolonialism perpetuates – that of colonizer/colonized. In his *Deconstructing Ireland: Identity, Theory, Culture,* Colin Graham emphasizes the need to move away from this binary.[13] *Winterwood* and *Indian Killer* attempt to do this in their criticism of neo and post colonialisms. Dissent in these two novels focuses on a challenge to icons of postcolonial literary traditions. For McCabe this is centered on the storyteller, challenging the Irish postcolonial through his own perverse storytellers, both Strange and Hatch. The storyteller has long been placed on high as the propagator of true Irish tradition, *teanga* and all. McCabe is not the first to challenge this fixation; however, he challenges it in a way that only McCabe can. Strange is not simply a teller of tales, who has an absurd side, or who, beneath all the revival and Free State finery, is human – rather, Strange is a gothic monster, a paedophile, who trains Hatch not in 'traditional Irish stories' but in wife and child murdering. He controls Hatch's access to Irish tradition, filtering song and story through his own perverse objectives. The traditional storyteller and relic of Irish language deploys his knowledge of 'tradition' to perpetuate the terrors he has committed.

Alexie also undermines the storyteller; however, for *Indian Killer* storytelling is already suspect and any teller of stories is probably a teller of lies. The main brunt of dissent from postcolonial readings is focused on Native American renaissance literature. Perhaps the passage with the most overt reference to the Native American canon focuses on Daniel's search for John. The reader is told that:

> [he] never found anybody, white or Indian, who had ever heard of an Indian named John Smith, though they all knew a dozen homeless Indian men.
> 'Yeah, there's that Blackfoot guy. Loney.'
> 'Oh, yeah, enit? And that Laguna guy, what's his name? Tayo?'
> 'And Abel, that Kiowa.'[14]

The references here are to three seminal works: James Welch's *The Death of Jim Loney*,[15] Leslie Marmon Silko's *Ceremony*[16] and N. Scott Momaday's *House Made of Dawn*.[17] All three authors are preoccupied with the intersection of trauma and traditional methods of healing. Welch's Loney is most like John. Tayo and Abel, however, are significantly different from John. War veterans Tayo and Abel return home only to find themselves unable to reintegrate themselves into society, but through the help of members of the traditional community they are finally able to heal and rejoin the community and bring with them the possibility of cultural rejuvenation. Each of these works focuses on the traditional ceremonies of the character's respective tribe, which draws heavy criticism from Alexie. In an interview with John Purdy shortly after the publication of *Indian Killer*, Alexie asserted: 'We shouldn't be writing about our traditions, we shouldn't be writing about our spiritual practices. Not in the ways which some people are doing it.'[18] But it is more than just writing tradition; rather, it is a question of Native American writers writing their lives, not what their lives are expected to be. Alexie says: 'Momaday – he's not a traditional man. And there's nothing wrong with that, I'm not either, but this adherence to the expected idea, the bear and all this imagery. I think it is dangerous, and detrimental.'[19] He continues: 'I want to take Indian lit *away* from that, and away from the people who own it now.'[20] Not mentioned here is Silko, whose work relies on traditional Pueblo forms and practices. It is Silko's *Ceremony* that *Indian Killer* most directly challenges.

In Silko's novel, the title, *Ceremony*, refers both to the ceremony that will heal Tayo and the world and to the ceremony that will destroy everything. Tayo is the deciding factor between the ceremonies and it is his refusal of violent action that enables the completion of the healing ceremony. Alexie borrows from Silko the characters whose violence Tayo refuses: Emo, Leroy, Pinkie and Harley are echoed as Reggie, Ty and Harley in *Indian Killer*. Reggie's violence parallels the Indian Killer's ceremonial violence and both share similarities with the ceremony of destruction in Silko's work. Alexie's killer understands his ceremony as the beginning of a new world order and the final chapter is entitled 'A Creation Story'. Here, as the Indian Killer dances and sings, other Indians are drawn to him and perform this ceremony of violent intent. This is far removed from Silko's healing ceremony and Alexie further complicates this with reference to the Ghost dance. In the end, Alexie refuses the return to traditionalism as a way to address contemporary social

problems. As we have seen, he hopes to take Native American literature in new directions. However, is this violence then a way forward?

McCabe has commented on the lack of redemption in
Winterwood, saying: 'It's like redemption is the *deus ex machina* that
you're dragging in because you still believe. And I don't think I do
still believe in it.'[21] This impossibility of redemption and the violence
implicated at the end of *Indian Killer* do not offer the empowerment
or rejuvenation found in much postcolonial literature. What they do
offer, however, is the ability to critique the postcolonial while not
standing in opposition to it. These works subvert the binary that
postcolonial literature and theory are often reduced to and
commodified as. With their critical focus on the postcolonial and
neocolonial, these novels enable a realm of engaged dissent applicable
to the multiple readings in the novels.

REFERENCES

Alexie, S., *Indian Killer* (New York: Grove Press, 1996).
Giles, J.R., *The Spaces of Violence* (Tuscaloosa, AL: University of Alabama Press, 2006).
Graham, C., *Deconstructing Ireland: Identity, Theory, Culture* (Edinburgh: Edinburgh University
    Press, 2001).
Heaney, M., 'Ireland: Patrick McCabe', *Times Online*, 12 November 2006,
    http://entertainment.timesonline.co.uk/tol/arts_and_entertainment/article630954.ece,
    accessed 15 January 2007.
McCabe, P., *Winterwood* (London: Bloomsbury, 2006).
Momaday, N.S., *House Made of Dawn* (New York: Harper & Row, 1968).
Murphy, P., 'Dance McCabre: Interview with Patrick McCabe', *New Review*, 22 December 2006,
    http://www.laurahird.com/newreview/patrickmccabeinterview.html, accessed 12 January
    2007.
Purdy, J., 'Crossroads: An Interview with Sherman Alexie', *Studies in American Indian
    Literatures*, 9, 4 (1998) pp.1–18.
Silko, L.M., *Ceremony* (New York: Viking Press, 1977).
Smyth, G., *The Novel and the Nation: Studies in the New Irish Fiction* (Chicago, IL: Pluto Press,
    1996).
Stuart, C., 'Renaissance Man: The Tribal "Schizophrenic" in Sherman Alexie's *Indian Killer*',
    American Indian Culture and Research Journal, 25, 4 (2001), pp.1–19.
Welch, J., *The Death of Jim Loney* (New York: Harper & Row, 1979).

NOTES

1. P. McCabe, *Winterwood* (London: Bloomsbury, 2006), p.129.
2. Ibid., p.136.
3. Ibid., p.242.
4. Ibid., p.239.
5. S. Alexie, *Indian Killer* (New York: Grove Press, 1996), p.27.
6. Ibid., p.219.
7. C. Stuart, 'Renaissance Man: The Tribal "Schizophrenic" in Sherman Alexie's *Indian Killer*',
    American Indian Culture and Research Journal, 25, 4 (2001), pp.1–19.

8. Ibid., p.268.
9. Ibid., pp.67–8.
10. G. Smyth, *The Novel and the Nation: Studies in the New Irish Fiction* (Chicago, IL: Pluto Press, 1996).
11. P. Murphy, 'Dance McCabre: Interview with Patrick McCabe', *New Review*, 22 December 2006, http://www.laurahird.com/newreview/patrickmccabeinterview.html, accessed 12 January 2007.
12. J.R. Giles, *The Spaces of Violence* (Tuscaloosa, AL: University of Alabama Press, 2006), p.135.
13. C. Graham, *Deconstructing Ireland: Identity, Theory, Culture* (Edinburgh: Edinburgh University Press, 2001).
14. Alexie, *Indian Killer*, p.220.
15. J. Welch, *The Death of Jim Loney* (New York: Harper & Row, 1979).
16. L.M. Silko, *Ceremony* (New York: Viking Press, 1977).
17. N.S. Momaday, *House Made of Dawn* (New York: Harper & Row, 1968).
18. J. Purdy, 'Crossroads: An Interview with Sherman Alexie', *Studies in American Indian Literatures*, 9, 4 (1998), p.15.
19. Ibid., p.8.
20. Ibid.
21. M. Heaney, 'Ireland: Patrick McCabe', *Times Online*, 12 November 2006, http://entertainment.timesonline.co.uk/tol/arts_and_entertainment/article630954.ece, accessed 15 January 2007.

11

Serious Fancy: Oscar Wilde, Charles Dickens and the Literary Fairy Tale in Colonial Discourse

Katherine O'Keefe

The literary fairy tale is a form that has been a contested space for nearly the length of its existence. It is a hybrid form, descended from oral folklore but influenced by both oral and literary traditions and it is often marginalized as 'not serious' or a 'paraliterary genre', as it blithely ignores the strictures of realism and its traditional literary responses. In the mid to late nineteenth century, the fairy tale often acted as a nexus in which discourses of colonialism, nationalism and questions of oral tradition vs written literature intersected. The line between the folk tale and the literary fairy tale is often blurred. The literary fairy tale enjoyed great popularity throughout the latter half of the nineteenth century, following the translation of the Jacob and Wilhelm Grimm's *Kinder- und Hausmärchen* and, subsequently, the stories of Hans Christian Andersen. Authors such as John Ruskin, George MacDonald, William Makepeace Thackeray and Charles Dickens all made use of the 'fairy tale' form to different effects, while collectors interested in English folklore, such as Andrew Lang, published their own literary fairy tales alongside collected and edited folklore. Oscar Wilde's later contributions to the genre take particular advantage of the ambiguities and the hybrid nature of the form, using it for social and artistic critique as well as critiquing colonial discourse.

Dickens's influential voice stands as a representative of dominant arguments and expectations, which Wilde in turn subverts. In many ways, Dickens exemplifies Wilde's opposite with regard to the fairy tale. He denies the indigenous oral-folk origins of the fairy tale, instead linking it to primitive (or savage) nursery version of civilized adult literacy. The restriction of the fairy tale to the nursery and childhood development feeds strongly into the imagery of colonial discourse, as the fairy tale represents the marginalization and subordination of indigenous culture to the realm of the nursery and the 'childhood' of civilization.

Jack Zipes creates a distinction between 'folk tales', which he describes as indigenous and subversive (oral) tales, and 'fairy tales', which are fixed written texts that preserve the status quo. However, the fairy tale is still associated with the 'primitive' and 'fancy,' or the imaginative, and childlike credulity. As a form associated with the 'primitive' and 'imagination', authors such as Charles Dickens championed the purity of the fairy tale, arguing that 'In an utilitarian age, of all other times, it is a matter of grave importance that fairy tales should be respected.'[1]

Folk tales, collected and changed again to suit the purposes of the collectors, became texts whose purity should not be tampered with, but also became a contested space in which authors like Charles Dickens debated the value of 'fancy' and the non-utilitarian. As U.C. Knoepflmacher suggests, 'Only those prone to identify fairy tales with an untainted innocence have repeatedly tried to defend fairy tales from their presumed corruption.'[2] Dickens's essay 'Frauds on the Fairies', an impassioned argument against modification of 'classic' fairy tales, exemplifies this emphasis on the 'purity' of the fairy tale as text, as he states that 'the little books themselves, nurseries of fancy as they are, should be preserved ... in their simplicity, and purity, and innocent extravagance, as if they were actual fact',[3] as any alteration of the 'text' for any purpose is seen as a step on the slippery slope to complete loss of artistic integrity.

Dickens praises the fairy tale's ability to 'captivat[e] a million of young fancies' while praising its moral benefits: 'many such good things have been first nourished in the child's heart by this powerful aid'. But he also characterizes them as a sanctuary of sorts for adults: 'It has greatly helped to keep us, in some sense, ever young, by preserving through our worldly ways one slender track not over-grown with weeds, where we may walk with children, sharing their delights.'[4]

Knoepflmacher highlights a certain sexual anxiety in Dickens's essay, drawing attention to Dickens's fears that a male beast, a 'Hog of unwieldy dimensions', might intrude and 'root' (and hence also rut) 'among the roses' of the virginal 'fairy flower garden'.[5] This anxiety, with its contrast of a virginal rose garden under threat from an unmannerly beast, suggests strong resonance with the sexualized imagery within colonial discourse. As (contrary to Dickens's sugges-tion of a pure text) the fairy tale's origins in an oral culture's folk tale is not far removed at all, the simultaneous re-imaging of the tale as a pure hyper-feminine text needing protection from the defilement of the savage, with the image of the 'phallic' 'rooting hog' (which is linked to the changing of the text or the fluid nature of folk tale in oral tradition) bears a strong parallel to the political caricatures of Hibernia needing protection from a savage, simian Paddy in its mix of strongly sexualized imagery.[6]

Critics such as Jacqueline Rose have noted the strong links between children's literature and colonial discourse in the mixing of the idea of the noble savage and the idea of the 'primitive' as a state of humanity in childhood. Rose states:

> Childhood is seen as the place where an older form of culture is preserved (nature or oral tradition), but the effect of this in turn is that this same form of culture is *infantilized*. At this level, children's fiction has a set of long-established links with the colonialism which identified the new world with the infantile state of man.[7]

This link is strengthened and complicated by the general banishment of the folk tale and fairy tale to the nursery. As the 'primitive' is equated with the infantile and the oral with the pre-literate, the fairy tale, whether collected and sanitized folk tale or literary stylistic imitation, would only be fit fare for adults if looked at with nostalgia for the innocence of childhood or pre-civilization. The emphasis on the folk tale and more particularly its literary counterpart, the fairy tale, may also be linked to the Celticism of Matthew Arnold, who proposed the study of Celtic literatures as the 'sentimental' (note the similarity to 'fancy') part of the 'composite English genius'.[8]

One of Dickens's own fairy tales, contained within his serialized story *Holiday Romance*, carries the infantilization of the fairy tale even further, and also places it in a subordinate role to the ideal of social justice. The fairy tale of 'The Magic Fishbone' is the second in a four-part story and the only section of it presented as a fairy tale. Dickens plays with several conventions in the series, presenting a child's narration of societal conventions, the fairy tale, boys' adventure novels and domestic fiction. The first section, an 'Introductory Romance from the pen of William Tinkling Esquire (Aged eight)', sets the tone for the following three. Dickens firmly sets the stories and their narrators within the realm of play-acting, which is emphasized by the mention of William's cousin, Bob Redforth, who 'want[s] to be the editor' though he 'has no idea of being an editor', and who undermines William's authority by 'shaking the table as I write'.[9] Dickens imbues the narrative with a childlike belief in the great importance of grown-up words, narrating the stories with a whimsical humour that emphasizes the difference between the innocence of childhood and the sophistication of adult culture. Notably, the framing device of the narrative puts great emphasis on the act of writing down the stories as giving them legitimacy. Not only are the stories from the 'pen' of various writers, but they also require an editor. To make a play on the title of one of Nathanial Hawthorne's books, these are not 'Twice Told Tales', these tales are 'Twice Written'.

The fairy tale itself is firmly set in the context of the nursery as a story 'from the pen of Miss Alice Rainbird (aged 7)'.[10] The tale of the magic fishbone is a didactic tale of an impoverished family of an overworked father, an invalid mother and several children, seen through the fairy tale imaginings of Alice, or 'Princess Alicia'. Princess Alicia's father, 'King Watkins the first', is accosted by the good Fairy Grandmarina while at the fishmonger's; she tells him how Alicia may find the magic fishbone, which is 'a magic present which can only be used once; but that it will bring her, that once, whatever she wishes for, provided she wishes for it at the right time'.[11] The Fairy Grandmarina, whose gift provides the impetus for the narrative, is linked quite strongly to childish irrationality, opposed to 'you grown-up persons'. As a fairy, she is presented as opposed to reason both in the opposition to norms of reality and at the narrative level of explaining herself: 'The reason for this, and the reason for that, indeed! You are always wanting the reason. No reason. There! Hoity toity me! I am sick of your grown-up reasons.'[12]

The narrator, 'Miss Alice Rainbird', is transparently linked to the 'Princess Alicia'. Similarly, the fairy tale device is transparently stretched over domestic reality. Dickens's ironic employment of layered narrative and play-acting suggest that for an adult the fairy tale form lacks depth or misrepresents reality. The child narrator's translation of real problems into 'fairy tale' terms, while helping a young child cope with a difficult situation, fails to fully portray the situation in a way that a more adult form such as the novel would. From a didactic standpoint, Alicia is rewarded for self amelioration, not asking for help until she has no power to help herself or others. From a critical standpoint, the fairy godmother *deus ex machina* steps in when social justice fails. While overtly using conventions linked to classic fairy tales, Dickens simultaneously undermines them of any value apart from their psychological use as a coping mechanism. The 'virginal integrity and childlike innocence' that Dickens assigns to fairy tale narration links it irrevocably to children telling themselves stories while wishing to be old enough to be taken seriously by adults, as do the children in his *Holiday Romance*.[13] Dickens's fairy tales are subordinate, necessary to the psychological development of the child, but nothing more than artefacts of childhood, not serious art for adults or civilized culture. Although Dickens was a vocal proponent of social justice, his treatment of the fairy tale remains within an imperialist framework that further marginalizes oral cultures.

As an Irish writer of literary fairy tales, Wilde subverted the colonial hierarchical understanding of the place of orality and of folk culture by publishing highly-polished stories that had their origins in oral culture, treating them with the gravity of high art. Wilde's famous quip about Dickens's writing, that 'one must have a heart of stone to read the death of Little Nell without laughing',[14] sets him firmly in opposition to Dickens's ethos of purity and sentimentality even while he uses the death of the innocent in his own stories. Contrary to the patronizing tones often taken by authors such as Dickens, Wilde's stories have a self-consciously artistic style, recognized by aesthetic critics such as Walter Pater, who called them 'gems' and 'genuine little poems in prose'.[15]

Each of Wilde's stories is a discrete work of art, manifesting serious artistic expression no matter who the audience. If Wilde found his tales (suitably edited) fit fare for his sons, they were refined, at the same time, in the audience of aesthetically aware adults more able to navigate their subtleties. The first record of 'The Happy Prince' is as a story told in 1885 to a group of Cambridge undergraduates.[16] In contrast to the 'innocent rose garden' of Dickens's imagining, Wilde's fairy tales are often quite sophisticated and sensual, and critics such as Naomi Wood have noted homosexual undercurrents in the texts, particularly 'The Happy Prince'.[17]

In the case of 'The Devoted Friend', Wilde creates an embedded narrative that emphasizes orality – not in a folksy or primitive setting, but instead in society. The animals of the framing narrative are transparent caricatures of types of figures in society. In contrast to the 'twice written' tales of Dickens's *Holiday Romance*, 'The Devoted Friend' is 'twice told'. 'The Devoted Friend' lends itself to a political reading. The story of Little Hans and Big Hugh the Miller plays a witty riff on a style of folk tale relatively common in northern Europe. This style of folk tale may be represented by Hans Christian

Andersen's literary version, *Big Klaus and Little Klaus*. Indeed, Wilde emphasizes the oral quality of the tale by framing it with an oral setting. In fact, this is the story in which the idea of morals in story-telling is emphasized, as Mary Shine Thompson points out, by the story of little Hans being 'presented to us at two removes, embedded in two Chinese narrative boxes'.[18] Thompson reads the double framing as a *caveat lector*, a warning to distrust the idea of authenticity in narrative. This gives another meaning to the mysterious narrator who chimes in at the end, agreeing that the danger of telling stories with morals arises if one considers the 'danger' of telling a tale with a political moral. A moral is indeed dangerous if it might incite rebellion.

The narrative takes on a particular poignancy if read as a coded critique of Anglo-Irish relations. Read allegorically, the story becomes biting criticism 'safely' encoded in stories which Wilde claimed were 'meant partly for children, and partly for those who have kept the childlike faculties of wonder and joy and, and who find in simplicity a subtle strangeness'.[19] Little Hans – or Ireland – is represented as a simple, agricultural type, close to a state of nature, his garden the loveliest in the country. The larger, more powerful nation, Hans's devoted friend, the prosperous Big Hugh the Miller, was so devoted that 'he would never go by his garden without lean-ing over the wall and plucking a large nosegay, or a handful of sweet herbs, or filling his pockets with plums and cherries if it was the fruit season'.[20] Big Hugh's mill, cows and sheep seem a nod to major English products of the time. While the products are, on the one hand, somewhat generic agrarian goods, wool had long been a major English product and the mill, while a simple grain mill in the context of the tale, evokes the image of another type of mill prominent in the post-Industrial Revolution context – the textile mills that so influenced the urban life of nineteenth-century England. The picture of colonial relations is strengthened by Big Hugh's 'noble ideas' about how 'real friends should have everything in common', despite the completely one-sided sharing in actual practice.

Indeed, little Hans falls to the same famine situation as Ireland in the mid-nineteenth century:

> ... when the winter came, and he had no fruit or flowers to bring to the market, he suffered a good deal from cold and hunger, and often had to go to bed without any supper but a few dried pears or some hard nuts. In the winter, also, he was extremely lonely, as the miller never came to see him then.[21]

Big Hugh's statement that 'when people are in trouble they should be left alone and not be bothered by visitors'[22] bears a close similarity to John Stuart Mill's statement: 'We must give over telling the Irish that it is our business to find food for them. We must tell them, now and forever, that it is *their* business.'[23] While English responses to the famine were complex and multifarious, Big Hugh's attitude sums up laissez-faire economics in response to the Famine, which allowed a comfortably self-righteous non-response. Wilde gives a nod to the desire to help expressed by the private charities that sent aid, and the debate within the press about how to handle the Irish problem, with the miller's youngest son's desire to help. The youngest son is perfectly willing to give half his porridge to little Hans and to 'show him [his] white rabbits', but Hugh scoffs at such generosity as leading Hans into temptation, particularly the temptation to ask for some flour on credit. For 'flour is one thing, and friendship is another and they should not be confused'.[24] Hugh's selfish attitude is compounded with accusations of laziness when Hans is too weak from hunger to work – an accusation similar to the typical critique of the sloth of Irish peasants, and a nod to tenant–landlord relations – when Hans is unable to work in his garden due to spending so much time mending Hugh's roof.[25] Ultimately, little Hans falls into a ditch and dies, after fetching the doctor for big Hugh's son on a stormy night, and is chiefly mourned by Hugh because he has lost a way to get rid of his broken wheelbarrow.

In the sense of the framing narrative, the water rat to whom the story is told sees nothing wrong with the bitter portrait, is quite glad to identify with Big Hugh and sees no point in the telling of stories with a moral. Also, the duck attempting to get her children into society is perfectly happy to associate with the water rat, thus by association with Hugh or with colonizing England. Additionally, as Thompson notes, the double framing serves to remove the reader from little Hans, preventing sympathy for the character.[26] This layered form of critique is not unique to 'The Devoted Friend'. Each of Wilde's fairy tales carries its own complex of symbols and critiques, varying from caricatures of current debates in art and aesthetics, social critique or intertextual commentary on other complexes of motifs and images. Using traditional forms famous for simplicity and transparency, Wilde deliberately wrote layered works with multiple symbolic possibilities. As he said in a letter to Thomas Hutchinson, 'I did not start with an idea and clothe it in form, but began with a form and strove to make it beautiful enough to have many secrets and many answers.'[27]

Wilde refused to define his fairy tales as specifically for children or for adults by denying the idea that intended audience was of import at all. He scoffed at the idea, responding to a reviewer's suggestion that his prose should have any relation to 'the extremely limited vocabulary at the disposal of the British child' by saying, 'I had about as much intention of pleasing the British child as I had of pleasing the British public.'[28] While this particular response may be mooted as a sidestepping of the question of whether or not his fairy tales succeeded as children's literature, the thrust of his response enters into a broader debate, as Wilde proposed that his fairy tales were art for art's sake. This argument is unsurprising in the context of a flâneur, but it is notable that the question of artistic value and the need for moral value in literature is one that holds particular resonance in the case of the fairy tale. The fairy tale was in fact an ideal form for such dialogue. According to M.O. Grenby, 'fairy tales were caught up in a sort of "turf war" that had engulfed all of children's literature in the later eighteenth century'.[29] As such, Wilde's fairy tales obliquely enter into political and artistic dialogue regarding the question of value and place for a uniquely national folk culture by nature of their form.

REFERENCES

Arnold, M., *On the Study of Celtic Literature; and on Translating Homer* (Edinburgh: Macmillan & Co., 1895).

Curtis, L.P., *Apes and Angels: The Irishman in Victorian Caricature* (Newton Abbot: David & Charles, 1971).

DeNie, M., *The Eternal Paddy: Irish Identity and the British Press, 1798–1882* (Madison, WI: University of Wisconsin Press, 2004).

Dickens, C., 'Frauds on the Fairies', *Household Words: A Weekly Journal*, 8, 184 (1 October 1853), pp.97–100.

Dickens, C., 'Holiday Romance' (1868), *Charles Dickens Literature*, http://www.dickens-literature.com/Holiday_Romance/0.html, accessed 10 February 2008.

Ellmann, R., *Oscar Wilde* (Harmondsworth: Penguin, 1988).

Grenby, M.O., 'Tame Fairies Make Good Teachers: The Popularity of Early British Fairy Tales', *Lion and the Unicorn*, 30, 1 (2006), pp.1–24.

Knoepflmacher, U.C., 'Literary Fairy Tales and the Value of Impurity', *Marvels & Tales: Journal of Fairy-Tale Studies*, 17, 1 (2003), pp.15–36.

Lebow, R.N. (ed.), *John Stuart Mill on Ireland, with an Essay by Richard Ned Lebow* (Philadelphia, PA: Institute for the Study of Human Issues, 1979).

Mason, S., *Bibliography of Oscar Wilde* (London: Rota, 1967).

Rose, J., *The Case of Peter Pan or the Impossibility of Children's Fiction* (Basingstoke: Macmillan, 1994).

Shine Thompson, M., 'Surface and Symbol: Oscar Wilde's Fairy Tales', in *Change and Renewal in Children's Literature*, International Research Society for Children's Literature 15th Biennial Congress, http://www.childlit.org.za/irsclpapthompson.html, accessed 10 February 2008.

Wilde, O., 'The Devoted Friend', in O. Wilde, *Collins Complete Works of Oscar Wilde*, 5th edn (Glasgow: HarperCollins, 2003).

Wilde, O., *Complete Letters*, ed. M. Holland and R. Hart-Davies (New York: H. Holt, 2000).

Wood, N., 'Creating the Sensual Child: Paterian Aesthetics, Pederasty and Oscar Wilde's Fairy Tales', *Marvels & Tales: Journal of Fairy-Tale Studies*, 16, 2 (2002), pp.156–170.

NOTES

1. C. Dickens, 'Frauds on the Fairies', *Household Words: A Weekly Journal*, 8, 184 (1 October 1853), pp.97–100.
2. U.C. Knoepflmacher, 'Literary Fairy Tales and the Value of Impurity', *Marvels & Tales: Journal of Fairy-Tale Studies*, 17, 1 (2003), pp.15–36.
3. Dickens, 'Frauds on the Fairies', p.97.
4. Ibid.
5. Knoepflmacher, 'Literary Fairy Tales', p.17.
6. This visual rhetoric has been extensively documented by L. Perry Curtis and M. DeNie, in L.P. Curtis, *Apes and Angels: The Irishman in Victorian Caricature* (Newton Abbot: David & Charles, 1971), and in M. DeNie, *The Eternal Paddy: Irish Identity and the British Press, 1798–1882* (Madison, WI: University of Wisconsin Press, 2004).
7. J. Rose, *The Case of Peter Pan or the Impossibility of Children's Fiction* (Basingstoke: Macmillan, 1994), p.50.
8. M. Arnold, *On the Study of Celtic Literature; and on Translating Homer* (Edinburgh: Macmillan & Co., 1895), p.87.
9. C. Dickens, 'Holiday Romance' (1868), *Charles Dickens Literature*, http://www.dickens-literature.com/Holiday_Romance/0.html, accessed 10 February 2008.
10. Ibid.
11. Ibid.
12. Ibid.
13. Knoepflmacher, 'Literary Fairy Tales', p.17.
14. R. Ellmann, *Oscar Wilde* (Harmondsworth: Penguin, 1988), p.441.
15. O. Wilde, *Complete Letters*, ed. Merlin Holland and Rupert Hart-Davies (New York: H. Holt, 2000), p.351n.
16. Ellmann, *Oscar Wilde*, p.253.
17. N. Wood, 'Creating the Sensual Child: Paterian Aesthetics, Pederasty and Oscar Wilde's Fairy Tales', *Marvels & Tales: Journal of Fairy-Tale Studies*, 16, 2 (2002), pp.156–170.
18. M. Shine Thompson 'Surface and Symbol: Oscar Wilde's Fairy Tales', in *Change and Renewal in Children's Literature*, International Research Society for Children's Literature 15th Biennial Congress, http://www.childlit.org.za/irsclpapthompson.html, accessed 10 February 2008.
19. Quoted in S. Mason, *Bibliography of Oscar Wilde* (London: Rota, 1967) p.335.
20. O. Wilde, 'The Devoted Friend', in O. Wilde, *Collins Complete Works of Oscar Wilde*, 5th edn (Glasgow: HarperCollins, 2003), p.287.
21. Ibid.
22. Ibid.
23. *Morning Chronicle*, 7 December 1846, quoted in R.N. Lebow (ed.), *John Stuart Mill on Ireland, with an Essay by Richard Ned Lebow* (Philadelphia, PA: Institute for the Study of Human Issues, 1979), p.35.
24. Wilde, *Complete Works*, p.288.
25. Ibid., pp.287–9.
26. Shine Thompson, 'Surface and Symbol'.
27. Wilde, *Complete Letters*, p.354.
28. Mason, *Bibliography of Oscar Wilde*, pp.367–8.
29. M.O. Grenby, 'Tame Fairies Make Good Teachers: The Popularity of Early British Fairy Tales', *Lion and the Unicorn*, 30, 1 (2006), pp.1–24.

12

The Bell Magazine: A Dissenting Vision of Irish Identity

Kelly Matthews

The *Irish Times* series 'Changing places' concluded in June 2007 with the question, 'Are the new Irish part of us? And if so, who are we now?'[1] In the early 1940s, Irish people were asking a similar question. Ireland had been independent of British rule for only eighteen years. The Irish government had recently declared neutrality in the Second World War, a decision that would reverberate for decades. For many people, the question lingered: if Ireland was no longer part of Britain, and was not joining the war in Europe, then who were they now?

Eamon De Valera had an answer. On St Patrick's Day 1943, the Taoiseach made a radio address to the people of Ireland, articulating a vision that had been in popular currency for years – his dream of a self-sufficient, rural Irish republic, in what has since become one of his best-known speeches:

> The ideal Ireland that we would have, the Ireland that we dreamed of, would be the home of a people who valued material wealth only as a basis of right living, of a people who were satisfied with frugal comfort and devoted their leisure to the things of the spirit; a land whose countryside would be bright with cosy homesteads, whose fields and villages would be joyous with the sounds of industry, the romping of sturdy children, the contests of athletic youths, the laughter of happy maidens; whose firesides would be forums of the wisdom of serene old age: the home, in short, of a people living the life that God desires that men should live.[2]

This 'economic nationalism', as Terence Brown has described it,[3] went hand in hand with a version of Irish identity that was homogeneous, Gaelic-speaking and resolutely Catholic, and De Valera's insistence on these attributes was not only widely accepted by most of the Irish popular media of the time, but also bolstered by influential groups such as the Gaelic League and the Censorship Board.

It is striking, then, to consider the cultural project of *The Bell* magazine, at the time edited by Seán O'Faoláin, as it endeavoured to widen the spectrum of accepted Irish identity in the 1940s. From its inception, *The Bell* tried to describe and define Irishness in all its various forms. In *The Bell*'s opening editorial, titled 'This is your magazine', O'Faoláin declared that 'this is not so much a magazine as a bit of Life itself, and we believe in Life, and leave it to Life to shape us after her own image and likeness'.[4] *The Bell*'s mission was both to represent and to transform Irish culture in the post-revolutionary era, a time of tremendous social, economic and political change.

Time and again *The Bell* published accounts of various aspects of Irish life that complicated and contradicted De Valera's vision, and challenged the prevailing imagery of Gaelic, Catholic, self-sufficient Ireland. The magazine's editors invited submissions from anyone and everyone with an interest in expressing his or her own experience of life in Ireland:

> You who read this know intimately some corner of life that nobody else can know ... You know a turn of the road, an old gateway somewhere, a well-field, a street-corner, a wood, a handful of quiet life, a triangle of sea and rock, something that means Ireland to you ... Write about your gateway, your well-field, your street-corner, your girl, your boat-slip, pubs, books, pictures, dogs, horses, river, tractor, anything at all that has a hold on you.[5]

Initially, *The Bell*'s version of Irish identity took the form of documentary articles from writers across a broad cross section of Irish society. There were articles by farmers, to be sure, describing the seasonal particulars of turf cutting, threshing and haymaking, but there were also short stories that exposed the harsher economic realities of De Valera's rural republic: for example, Desmond Clarke's story 'Flight', published in February 1941, describing the torment of a young couple's decision to leave their unprofitable farm and seek factory work in England.[6] And there were urban realities to consider as well: for example, the Dublin father of five sharing a house with fifty-six people, one water tap and one lavatory between them, with no means for cooking but an open fire, described in a recorded monologue entitled 'I Live in a Slum', published in November 1940.[7]

The Bell also paid attention to a wide range of Irish identities in its theme issues dedicated to Ulster writers. The first of these appeared in July 1941; the second, in July 1942, attracted so many contributors that it had to be extended over two issues, into August of that year. These Ulster issues attempted to draw a true picture of life in the North, for both Catholics and Protestants, rural farmers and city-dwellers. In one, an unnamed 'Ulster Protestant', whom Terence Brown, among others, has identified as W.R. Rodgers,[8] confesses himself to be 'startled by the lack of any intelligent presentation of the case for the Protestant North'.[9] And in April 1943, *The Bell* printed an article entitled 'Speaking as an Orangeman', whose author was named only as 'One of them', who confessed his fear that southern nationalists might try to force the authority of their church on him if ever the border were dissolved.[10] In these and other articles, *The Bell* gave expression to the minority voices of De Valera's Ireland, and challenged the idea that Irish identity was monolithic.

As *The Bell*'s editors gained experience and solidified their readership, they commissioned two groups of articles that explicitly examined the diversity inherent in Irish culture: the 'Five Strains' symposium, which explored the cultural legacies of the past, and the 'Credo' series, which described religious diversity in the present. The 'Five Strains' symposium appeared in *The Bell* in September 1941, at the end of the magazine's first year of publication. The editors recruited five well-known historians to name the influences of five different cultural heritages on present-day Irish life: the Gaelic influence, the Classical influence, the Norman stream, the Anglo-Irish strain and the English strain. A month later, historian James J. Auchmuty sent in an angry letter about the overlooked Scottish strain, so important in Northern life, and his description was subsequently appended to the symposium.

The editorial note which headed the symposium explained *The Bell*'s motivation for commissioning it:

> In the business of building up a native mode of life agreeable to the natural genius of our people we are always searching, consciously or unconsciously, for a guiding line ... and perhaps the only line acknowledged on all sides is the Gaelic one. This interesting symposium enlarges that rather elementary picture. Yet, we *have* been considerably influenced by the English tradition ... and there have been several other strains – the Norman strain, the Classical strain, and that mixed strain which we call Anglo-Irish. They have all gone to the building of this Ireland.[11]

Each historian in the symposium focused on the key contributions of each strain to contemporary Ireland. Gaelic heritage headed the list, and its influence was still to be found in craft traditions, social attitudes and linguistic speech patterns, according to historian Gerard Murphy, who noted that both English and Irish speakers still used Gaelic forms of expression. The so-called 'Classical influence' was next, and was described by Patrick Browne as the filtering of Latin and Greek forms of thought and written language through the Roman Catholic Church. In this context, it seems ironic that the Catholic orthodoxy favoured by De Valera could trace its roots to a foreign cultural invasion. The Norman stream was credited with bringing business sense and architectural solidity to Ireland, and the Anglo-Irish strain, according to J.M. Hone, was responsible for many of the most powerful ideas of Irish nationalism. W. Bedell Stanford traced the English strain's growing influence after the Act of Union, thanking the English of that time period for 'a measure of peace, wealth, education and good plumbing'.[12] And James J. Auchmuty's late addition described the Scottish contribution to Northern industry, and an independent-mindedness that opposed what he called 'a single, Irish, Gaelic and Roman Catholic nationalism'.[13]

The overall tone of the symposium is detached, factual and academic, a de-romanticized critique of Irish history from the perspective of established scholars. The effect is a set of articles that departs from the personal tone of address that earlier *Bell* articles had established, in order to achieve a more authoritative tone, one which readers would be hard pressed to question. In this symposium *The Bell* seems to be lecturing its readers, chiding them not to forget the multiple heritages on which their Irish identity was based. As O'Faoláin concluded in his introductory note: 'This symposium should serve to remind us of the danger of oversimplifying history.'[14]

But *The Bell* was not finished. One year after De Valera's St Patrick's Day radio speech, as if in answer to his government's overwhelmingly pro-Catholic policies, the magazine set out to publish a series on the various religions of contemporary Ireland. This was the 'Credo' series, a sequence of articles written by individual members of each religion, both clergy and laypeople. The editorial note that preceded the first article in July 1944 declared:

> It is part of the regular policy of THE BELL to open as many windows as possible on the lives of as many people as possible, so that we may form a full and varied picture of modern

Ireland. In this short series a number of contributors set out to show how their creeds affect their daily lives.[15]

Auchmuty's earlier complaints against the Scottish strain's exclusion must have been heard, because this time the Presbyterians got to go first, with an article by the Reverend Matthew Bailey titled 'What it means to be a Presbyterian'. In the following months, *The Bell* printed articles titled 'Why I am "Church of Ireland" ', 'What it means to be a Catholic', 'What it means to be a Unitarian', 'What it means to be a Quaker', and finally, in June 1945, after the end of the war and the end of wartime censorship, 'What it means to be a Jew', A.J. Leventhal's poignant memoir of growing up in the Jewish community of Dublin's Oakfield Place, and his description of the movement to establish a Jewish homeland in what was then Palestine. It is surely not an accident that the article on Catholicism is tucked away in the middle of the series, flanked by articles on Protestant churches whose congregations were much smaller in number. It is as if *The Bell* were sending a message, both to its readers and to the powers that be, that the non-Catholic denominations of Ireland should not be relegated to second-best status.

The 'Credo' articles vary in tone, from preacherly to personal. Although the editor's introduction promises to show how the writers' creeds affect their daily lives, some authors, especially the two who are ministers, maintain a cerebral, theological style throughout their writing, as if they are sermonizing from the pulpit. However, as with much of the earlier material in *The Bell*, the most powerful pieces are those that attempt to document their authors' individual experiences. So, for example, T.W.T. Dillon's article, 'What it means to be a Catholic', though it expounds on the virtues of Catholicism's 'transcendental humanism', most effectively touches the reader when it conveys the author's 'recurrent experience of sharing a bench outside the confessional on Saturday night with all classes and conditions of men and women'.[16] Likewise, Leventhal's account of the street taunts sung by warring Christian and Jewish children in the streets of Dublin serves to illustrate his recollection that as a child his identity was tied up entirely in his religion, and that the neighbouring children were seen not as Irish, but only as *goyim*, or non-Jewish. One need not belabour the point that Leventhal's description of Jewish and Christian children throwing stones at one another in the streets of Dublin paints a striking contrast to De Valera's landscape of cosy cottages and happy maidens.

Not only was *The Bell*'s description of 1940s Ireland different from

De Valera's Gaelic, Catholic, rural republic, it was markedly different from earlier assessments of Irish identity. In 1931, when Daniel Corkery published his book on Synge and Anglo-Irish literature, he described Irish identity as 'a quaking sod': 'Everywhere in the mentality of the Irish people are flux and uncertainty. Our national consciousness may be described, in a native phrase, as a quaking sod. It gives no footing. It is not English, nor Irish, nor Anglo-Irish.'[17] Corkery clearly saw Irish identity as a *lack* of identity, based on an uncertainty that he warned would lead only to mediocrity in education and in national literature. But *The Bell* encouraged its readers to embrace the complexity of Irish identity, and to find strength in the diversity of traditions that gave rise to twentieth-century Irish culture. One can imagine the magazine's editors rewriting Corkery's statement to say that Irish identity *is* English *and* Irish *and* Anglo-Irish, and Norman and Roman and Scottish besides – not to mention Jewish and Quaker and Catholic and Unitarian and Presbyterian.

In the 'Five Strains' symposium and 'Credo' series of articles, and in others like them, *The Bell* reveals its transformative agenda. As O'Faoláin wrote in his introduction to the first 'Credo' article, *The Bell*'s stated intent was explicitly representational: 'to open as many windows as possible on the lives of as many people as possible', so that readers could peer in and glimpse a broad variety of the lived experiences of contemporary Ireland.[18] In practice, however, the choices made by the magazine's editors as to which windows to open, on which people, demonstrate that *The Bell* deliberately attempted to undermine the oversimplified version of Irish identity put forward by De Valera and supported by many of the most popular print media outlets and by government institutions. In his 1996 book *Transformations in Irish Culture*, Luke Gibbons asserts that the act of cultural representation can work as a transformative force on society, not merely as an aesthetic reflection: 'Cultural representations do not simply come after the event, "reflecting" experience or embellishing it with aesthetic form, but significantly alter and shape the ways we make sense of our lives.'[19] Anecdotal accounts of *The Bell*'s influence on Irish readers during the mid-twentieth century are many and vivid, with county librarians and booksellers often passing single copies on to multiple readers, so that the magazine's circulation probably far exceeded its initial print run of 3,000 copies. It is clear that in attempting to widen the spectrum of Irish identity, the magazine was fulfilling a need for Irish readers of the time, and struggling against the homogenizing cultural dictates of mainstream Irish culture. It may be helpful to bear in mind O'Faoláin's warning against 'the danger of oversimplifying history' as we contemplate the increasing multiplicity of Irish identities in the present day.

REFERENCES

Anonymous, 'I live in a slum', *The Bell*, 1, 2 (November 1940), pp.46–8.
Anonymous, 'Conversation Piece: An Ulster Protestant', *The Bell*, 4, 5 (August 1942), pp.305–14.
Anonymous, 'Speaking as an Orangeman, by One of them', *The Bell*, 6, 1 (April 1943), pp.19–27.
Auchmuty, J.J., 'Public Opinion: The Scottish Strain', *The Bell*, 3, 1 (October 1941), pp.79–82.
Bailey, Revd M., 'What it means to be a Presbyterian: Credo – 1', *The Bell*, 8, 4 (July 1944), pp.298–305.
Brown, T., *Northern Voices: Poets from Ulster* (Dublin: Gill & Macmillan, 1975).
Brown, T., *Ireland: A Social and Cultural History 1922–2002* (London: Harper Collins, 2004).
Clarke, D., 'Flight', *The Bell*, 1, 5 (February 1941), pp.56–60.
Corkery, D., *Synge and Anglo-Irish Literature* (Cork: Cork University Press, 1931).
De Valera, E., 'Address by Mr De Valera, 17 March 1943', RTÉ Archives, www.rte.ie/laweb/ll/ll_t09b.html, accessed 28 April 2008 (audio clip 5 of 9).
Dillon, T.W.T., 'What it means to be a Catholic', *The Bell*, 9, 1 (October 1944), pp.12–19.
Gibbons, L., *Transformations in Irish Culture* (Cork: Cork University Press, 1996).
Hone, J., Stanford, W.B., Curtis, E., Brown, Revd P. and Murphy, G., 'The Five Strains: A Symposium', *The Bell*, 2, 6 (September 1941), pp.13–30.
Mac Cormaic, R., 'We need vision of who we are and what we want to make migration work', *The Irish Times*, 27 June 2007, pp.1, 11.
O'Faoláin, S., 'This is your magazine', *The Bell*, 1, 1 (October 1940), pp.5–8.

NOTES

1. R. Mac Cormaic, 'We need vision of who we are and what we want to make migration work', *The Irish Times*, 27 June 2007.
2. E. De Valera, 'Address by Mr De Valera, 17 March 1943', RTÉ Archives, http://www.rte.ie/laweb/ll/ll_t09b.html, accessed 28 April 2008.
3. T. Brown, *Ireland: A Social and Cultural History 1922–2002* (London: Harper Collins, 2004), p.147.
4. S. O'Faoláin, 'This is your magazine', *The Bell*, 1, 1 (October 1940), p.5.
5. Ibid., p.7.
6. D. Clarke, 'Flight', *The Bell*, 1, 5 (February 1941), pp.56–60.
7. Anonymous, 'I live in a slum', *The Bell*, 1, 2 (November 1940), pp.46–8.
8. T. Brown, *Northern Voices: Poets from Ulster* (Dublin: Gill & Macmillan, 1975), p.232.
9. Anonymous, 'Conversation Piece: An Ulster Protestant', *The Bell*, 4, 5 (August 1942), pp.305–14.
10. Anonymous, 'Speaking as an Orangeman, by One of them', *The Bell*, 6, 1 (April 1943), pp.19–27.
11. Note preceding J. Hone, W.B. Stanford, E. Curtis, Revd P. Brown and G. Murphy, 'The Five Strains: A Symposium', *The Bell*, 2, 6 (September 1941), p.13.
12. Hone et al., 'The Five Strains', p.29.
13. J.J. Auchmuty, 'Public Opinion: The Scottish Strain', *The Bell*, 3, 1 (October 1941), p.79.
14. Note preceding Hone et al., 'The Five Strains', p.13.
15. Note preceding Revd M. Bailey, 'What it means to be a Presbyterian: Credo – 1', *The Bell*, 8, 4 (July 1944), p.298.
16. T.W.T. Dillon, 'What it means to be a Catholic', *The Bell*, 9, 1 (October 1944), p.13.
17. D. Corkery, *Synge and Anglo-Irish Literature* (Cork: Cork University Press, 1931), p.14.
18. Note preceding Bailey, 'What it means to be a Presbyterian', p.298.
19. L. Gibbons, *Transformations in Irish Culture* (Cork: Cork University Press,1996), p.8.

13

Postcolonial Trauma – Postmodern Recovery?[1]
Gender, Nation and Trauma in Contemporary Irish and Scottish Fiction

Stefanie Lehner

This chapter proposes a cross-archipelagic framework for reading issues of subalternity, in particular female traumas, in contemporary Irish and Scottish fiction. Examinations of the cross-currents between Scotland and Ireland emphasize, as Marilyn Reizbaum contends, 'their status as minority cultures' with 'comparable "colonial" histories with respect to England'.[2] The predominance of questions of identity that traverse Irish and Scottish studies shows the tendency to prioritize issues of nationality over other sectional interests such as class and gender. I argue that it is these concerns that allow the establishing of affiliations between writers who remain notably critical of masculinist narratives of national as well as of postmodern liberation.

In 1882, Ernest Renan famously postulated that nations are forged by the shared experience of suffering. However, he also emphasized the necessity 'to forget' this foundational trauma, as it 'brings to light deeds of violence which took place at the origin of all political formations'.[3] In an indirect echo to Renan, Leela Gandhi defines the postcolonial nation state by its 'will-to-forget' the colonial past. This postcolonial amnesia, Gandhi notes, 'is symptomatic of the urge for historical self-invention or the need to make a new start – to erase painful memories of colonial subordination'.[4] But as several postcolonial thinkers point out, this 'new start' is rather far from constituting a definite departure from what preceded it.[5] It was especially through the critique of the Subaltern Studies Group in India that the postcolonial nation has been exposed as recuperating colonial forms of oppression.[6] The term 'subaltern' derives from the Italian Marxist, Antonio Gramsci, and describes social groups that have been subjugated and excluded by the dominant classes, in particular the working classes, but also women and other minority groups. By foregrounding how class intersects with other marginalized identity categories, such as gender, sexuality and race, Subaltern Studies contests the notion that a resurgent national culture ever works as a panacea capable of recovering from the traumatic experience of disempowerment and utter objectification.[7] For example, the founding document of the Irish Republic, the 1937 Constitution, effectively re-inscribes the subaltern status of women. The reality of nationalistic politics often meant for subaltern groups, and I will focus here explicitly on women, the continued marginalization of their concerns. The Scottish writer, Janice Galloway, whose work will be discussed later, addresses the ensuing difficulties for female authors:

> Scottish women have their own particular complications with writing and definition, complications which arrive from the general problems of being a colonized nation. Then, that wee touch extra. Their sex. There is coping with that guilt of taking time off the concerns of national politics to get concerned with the sexual sort: that creeping fear it's somehow self-indulgent to be more concerned for one's womanness instead of one's Scottishness ... Guilt here comes strong from the notion that we're not backing up our menfolk and their 'real' concerns. Female concerns, like meat on the mother's plate, are extras after the man and the weans have been served.[8]

Galloway illustrates this marginalized, meagre space of womanhood in her novel, *The Trick is to Keep Breathing*, in the typographical marginalization of her protagonist's inner thoughts and fears, as also her anorexia.

It seems the inclination, if not indeed the imperative, of the national to encompass and eclipse gender issues, not least by constructing cultural discourses which render women silent and invisible while simultaneously appropriating the feminine as a representational category for national definition. In 'The Floozie in the Jacuzzi', Ailbhe Smyth criticizes this codification of woman as 'sign and symbol', which she says functions as a 'pompous denial of woman's right to self-definition'.[9] In her tellingly entitled 'Reality 2', Smyth addresses the implications of this subaltern double bind for the positioning of women in Irish history:

> Irish women are twice dispossessed.
> Dismembered. Unremembered.

Nobody, so to speak.
No past to speak of.
Unremembering our history
of absence, sign of our existence.[10]

She sums up by quoting Julia Kristeva: 'As everyone knows every negation is a definition.'[11] For Smyth, the definition of Irish and, I may add, Scottish women is, thus, seemingly paradoxically constituted by their discursive absence. Forgotten and erased from the official history of the nation, women's unremembered herstories yet continue to subsist in their silence. Scottish author A.L. Kennedy's short story, 'The Role of Notable Silences in Scottish History', describes this as 'the sound of nothingness ... the huge, invisible, silent roar of all the people who are too small to record'.[12] Resisting wholesale erasure, these roaring silences constitute what David Lloyd calls a 'subalternity effect' which disrupts the celebratory proclamation of national success.[13]

While Ireland's and Scotland's historical development seemed previously collapsed into what Joep Leerssen terms a subaltern 'traumatic paradigm' of history,[14] the Republic's boom as the Celtic Tiger and the devolutionary processes in Scotland and Northern Ireland relocate them into the linear and progressive time of history. This changed political climate seems also to have contributed to the proliferation of women writers. Discussing 'the symbolic prominence' given to female authors in recent Irish anthologies, Anne Fogarty points to the striking irony of using women's previously neglected work to generate 'a metacommentary about the present state of Irish society'.[15] While images of the feminine stood before as a muted analogue for the nation's postcolonial trauma, women's writings function nowadays to allegorize their postmodern recovery.

It is in this context that I want to discuss three contemporary Irish and Scottish novels, published between 1989 and 1996: Galloway's *The Trick is to Keep Breathing*, Jennifer Johnston's *The Invisible Worm* and Roddy Doyle's *The Woman Who Walked into Doors*.[16] Rather than attesting to the success narrative of a fundamental postmodern transition, these rather different literary creations all address the continuous traumatic experiences of women in the Atlantic archipelago. Johnston's protagonist, Laura Quilan, was raped by her father as a teenager; Doyle's Paula Spenser suffered seventeen years of domestic abuse by her husband; and Galloway's Joy Stone suffers a nervous breakdown after the accidental death of her lover. In their formal structure, all three novels capture the repetitive time of trauma: the insistent return of flashbacks and memories lacerates not only the text itself but also the narrative consciousness of the protagonist. In this, they textually perform what Edna O'Brien describes in her incest narrative about the X-case, *Down By the River*, as 'a re-enactment of a petrified time'.[17] As Judith Herman notes, 'It is as if time stops at the moment of trauma.'[18] However, as Freud suggests, repetition must be also seen as an attempt to recognize and ultimately to proclaim the horrible and unspeakable that happened. In this respect, Cathy Caruth emphasizes that

> If PTSD [post-traumatic stress disorder] must be understood as a pathological symptom, then it is not so much a symptom of the unconscious, as it is a symptom of history. The traumatized, we might say, carry an impossible history within them, or they become themselves the symptom of a history they cannot entirely possess.[19]

It is this dispossession, the silencing and denial of their personal her-stories, that the women in all three novels confront, which is reflected through the temporal and spatial entrapment of the heroine.

All three women's herstories seem collapsed in a traumatic paradigm. For Paula and Laura, this constitutes to some extent a re-enactment of what Michelle Massé terms the 'marital gothic'.[20] Both women enter marriage to escape their abusive fathers, only to be confronted with the renewed denial of their identity and agency. But while Laura's class position as an ascendancy heiress allows her to retain some power, the violation and abuse Paula suffers in her marriage reinforce her place of utter powerlessness in terms of class. Significantly, it is her husband's attempt to perpetuate the abuse of patriarchal rights by going after her daughter that triggers Paula's agency. Joy becomes similarly convinced of the seeming inevitability of her fate through her maternal heritage when she tries to kill herself after reflecting on the suicidal tendencies of the women in her family.

It is furthermore significant that all three novels are narrated from a domestic setting: Laura's past and present are contained in her inherited Big House; Paula reflects on her past from the limited space of her marital home in a suburb of Dublin; and Joy narrates from the house she used to share with her lover, Michael, in Glasgow. In what they call home, all three women experience the traumatic negation of their subjectivity by being violently reduced to their sexuality, in a manner that Margot Backus says 'mimics both the Catholic Church's and the Irish Constitution's reduction of women'.[21] However, she seems to forget the gendered pattern of colonial-national iconography. Consequently, arguing that 'Laura's [Catholic] father re-enacts [through the rape of his Protestant daughter] the dispossession by which Anglo-Irish society originally came into being', Backus reads 'Laura as a figure for Ireland'.[22]

Laura seems indeed detained in the muted and invisible place of the national trope. But Johnston's novel resists such a reductive reading by critically examining the ethical and political implications that underpin such appropriations. Denying his responsibility for the rape, Laura's father not only accuses her for seducing him, but also blames her for her mother's subsequent suicide, imposing a coercive silence over both. This silence covers the 'dark secret' that, like the 'invisible worm' of William Blake's poem – which makes out the epigraph to Johnston's book – has destroyed her life. It is represented by the overgrown summerhouse in which the rape happened, symbolic of the inaccessibility of her trauma. Laura experiences this dispossession through dissociation; she feels like 'an empty skin' and is haunted by the figure of a running woman:

> I stand by the window and I watch the woman running.
> Is it Laura?
> I wonder that, as I watch her flickering like brown leaves through the trees.
> I am Laura.[23]

Her trauma is embodied in the image of this fleeing woman as it is she who carries Laura's impossible history within her – a herstory that she is not allowed to acknowledge and cannot possess.

For Paula, her entrapment in the patriarchal home of her husband Charlo means being exposed to ceaseless domestic abuse. Like Laura's father, Charlo denies all responsibility for his deeds. At first, Paula embraces his disavowal; she notes: 'I couldn't have coped with it then, the fact that he'd hit me, plain and simple ... It had been a mistake.'[24] Paula starts blaming herself in order to repress the traumatic experience of male violence that threatens not only the institutions of marriage and the family, but also her own existence. But she eventually realizes that his repeated claims of ignorance are merely a trial of her submissiveness to him and his version of reality. After having injured her again, Charlo innocently asks:

> – Where'd you get that?
> – What?

– The eye.

It was a test. I was thumping inside. He was playing with me.
There was only one right answer.

– I walked into the door.

– Is that right?

– Yeah.

– Looks sore. ...

He was messing with me, playing. Like a cat with an injured
bird ... Keeping me on my toes, keeping me in my place.[25]

His coercive implementation of a misogynistic ideology is designed
for her to accept the fact that 'He was everything and I was nothing.'[26]
Prohibited from acknowledging the real cause of her pain and
injuries, when she attempts to narrate her suffering Paula performs,
similarly to Laura, a linguistic split: 'I'm nothing ... Someone's in
pain. Someone's crying. It isn't me yet.'[27] In the disgrace that her
marriage brings to the self-image of Irish society, Paula notices that
everybody deliberately ignores what is happening. In public, Paula
confronts her final erasure: 'I didn't exist. I was a ghost. I walked
around in emptiness. People looked away; I wasn't there. They
stared at the bruises for a split second, then away ... they couldn't
see me. The woman who wasn't there.'[28]

As for the two other women, no place of safety or belonging is
available for Joy. Her inhabitation of the council house that still
bears her lover's name, and the rent for which she can hardly
afford, reflects her dispossession in terms of class and gender. Like
both of the other women, in her house Joy experiences her own self
dissociated from her abject body: she begins her account by noting,
'I watch myself from the corner of the room.'[29] The bathroom
mirror only 'shows a kneeling torso, head chopped off', and rather
than affording a process of identification, Joy feels 'like looking
through a window at someone else'.[30] For Joy, the house becomes
threatening not only by inflicting 'domestic wounds'[31] but also
because it is constantly prone to intrusion. It is in her own bedroom
in which Joy is raped by her boss, Tony, for which she reproaches
herself: 'It's not Tony's fault. It must be me.'[32] Similarly to both other
novels, Joy's essential homelessness indicates her inability to
possess her own herstory. In her position as a mistress rather than
a wife, Joy is denied a place to mourn the death of her lover. The
memorial service for him effectively erases her existence; Joy
recalls:

1. The Rev Dogsbody had chosen this service to perform a miracle.
2. He'd run time backwards, cleansed, absolved and got rid of the ground-in stain.
3. And the stain was me.

I didn't exist. The miracle had wiped me out.[33]

Joy repeats this self-effacement through her anorexia. However, it also becomes a means to resist stereotypical definitions of femininity and womanhood: while her masculine physicality challenges her allocated gender-role, her reproductive role as a mother is similarly undermined by her body's refusal to menstruate. Assuming at first she is pregnant, she undergoes a scan: 'I looked. I was still there. A black hole among the green stars. Empty space. I had nothing inside me.'[34] In *The Modern Scottish Novel*, Cairns Craig claims Joy's body as a symbol for pre-devolution Scotland: 'That "black hole" ', he states, 'is the image not only of a woman negated by a patriarchal society but of a society aware of itself only as an absence [in] its failure to be reborn.'[35] Craig's reading therewith repeats the dispossession and annihilation of female experiences that is addressed in all three novels.

Evoking Smyth's seemingly paradoxical observation, the existence of all three women consists in their absence and dismemberment. In a way, they exemplify Jacques Lacan's statement that 'woman does not exist'; as Slavoj Žižek explains, 'Woman does *not* exist, she *insists*.'[36] As embodiments of Lacan's neologism *sinthome*,[37] Laura's dissociation, Paula's injured body and Joy's anorexic body are the symptoms of a patriarchal social order that not just condones but actually sanctions violation, rape and abuse. The Blakeian resonance of Johnston's title and the deliberate delusion of Doyle's illustrate that it is through the official silence and denial of those crimes that society at large is not only complicit but actively contributes to their re-enactment. They furthermore insinuate the disavowed responsibility by the actual perpetrator: for it is neither an invisible worm nor a 'walk into a door' that caused the injury. Laura notes her husband's 'curious notion that most men have, that in some inexplicable way women are responsible for the terrible violent things like [rape] that happen to them'.[38] It is significant that recent criticism seems inclined to concur with this notion. Discussing *The Trick*, Douglas Gifford reproaches Joy for 'externaliz[ing]' guilt that she, in his view, rightly feels, but wrongly allocates to others.[39] In a remarkably similar fashion, Linden Peach, speaking of Doyle's novel, criticizes Paula in that she 'projected on to Charlo the consequences of everything which she has had to keep hidden: the violence of her home life; the difficulty of being a young woman in the kind of neighbourhood where she was living; and anxieties about her sexual identity'.[40] Suggesting that it is really the women who are to blame since it is they who falsely project blame onto others, these masculinist judgements engender a 'rhetoric of blame' that Edward Said identifies as responsible for the continuing violence in postcolonial societies;[41] as Joy puts it, 'apportion blame that ye have not blame apportioned unto you'.[42] In contrast to this cyclic moralism, all three novels identify guilt as specifically gendered, produced and abused by men in power. In her introduction to *Meantime*, Galloway notes, 'The need to keep women feeling guilty goes deep, obviously. The fear of losing the unfair system that operates in male favour likewise. It is still something for women to bear in mind, something to consciously resist.'[43]

The challenge that all three women have to confront is what I wish to term, with regard to Smyth, an 'Unremembering [of their] history of absence'. This consists not in forgetting an unavoidable reality but asserts what Žižek calls 'a radical ethical attitude of uncompromising insistence'.[44] They must reclaim their repressed experience of oppression and blame. For all three women this means, first of all, identifying with their symptoms – that is, recognizing themselves in their dismembered, unremembered traumas. In *The Invisible Worm*, Laura identifies her own absent self in the figure of the running woman: 'I am no one ... I only see this woman running. I see myself running.'[45] According to Caruth, it is important that Laura relates her trauma not only 'to the very identity of her own self' and to her friend Dominic as the listener of her story, but that she also reveals it as a reality and truth beyond that of a singular case.[46] The indeterminate age of the running woman makes her a representative for 'All ages. All women' who have 'nowhere to run'[47]. Similarly, as Paula comes to accept that the 'someone in pain' is her own suffering self, she notices in hospital that 'There were always other women when I was there, waiting their turn like me, wounded women. I never once thought that I wasn't the only one who'd been put there by her husband.'[48] Joy also seeks to relate her traumatic experiences to that of others, and wonders 'how they manage'.[49] Like both other women, Joy must acknowledge that the 'disembodied glass voice' that talks about her trauma is her very own: 'I suddenly remembered what I was saying wasn't a story. It wasn't the furniture breathing it was me. What I was saying was true.'[50]

This recognition precipitates an ethical awakening to the real that expresses an imperative to act. When Paula notices that Charlo attempts to repeat the cycle of male abuse on her daughter, she reclaims the agency that for seventeen years she had not been able to assert: she hits him with a frying pan and throws him out of the house. While this incident is part of Paula's memorial account, Laura must actually revisit her past. Exhuming the summerhouse, Laura not only relives the events that caused her trauma, but also voices them for the first time: 'I haven't told anyone. I have never spoken these words.'[51] This reclamation allows her to reassert her agency in an act of ultimate destruction which is also a purge: she burns the place that kept her secret. Joy also realizes the imperative to act: 'The trick is not to think. Just act dammit. Act.'[52] Confronted with renewed harassments by Tony, Joy asserts her voice and willpower by countering his advances with a decisive 'NO.'[53]

For all three women, these acts of resistance challenge their subaltern positioning, and so function as a prerequisite to forgiveness. After urging Dominic to fight against his own dispossession, Laura notes: 'You see, we need to know how to forgive as well as to be forgiven.'[54] Laura conceives an important maxim here: the need for equitable power relations. As Backus notes, 'we cannot forgive those we are still allowing to dominate us'.[55] In the end of *The Trick*, imagining herself as a swimmer, Joy is able to forgive not only herself but also her mother and lover who both left her by drowning. The idea of swimming allows Joy to reappropriate her own abject body, as it also expresses her refusal to submit to the traumatic paradigm by which she felt entrapped: defying death or drowning, she notices that the trick is simply 'to keep breathing'.[56]

Reading these novels as subaltern trauma narratives suggests that their ethical and, indeed, political significance consists in giving a voice to women's unremembered experiences. As the indelible symptoms of a disavowed, seemingly 'impossible' history, Laura, Paula and Joy's herstories 'bring to light the deeds of violence' that must, according to Renan, remain forgotten for the success narrative of national progress and recovery to be proclaimed. The common concerns of all three novels establish affiliations that cut across national formations, attesting to Caruth's proposal that 'trauma itself may provide the very link between cultures: not as a simple understanding of the pasts of others but rather, within the traumas of contemporary history, as our ability to listen through the departures we have all taken from ourselves'.[57] The importance of listening to the traumas of others, like the subaltern other, is emphasized by

Caruth's claim that trauma 'addresses us in the attempt to tell us of a reality or truth that is not otherwise available'.[58] This address triggers, from us as readers, a response, which becomes the appeal for responsibility – a quasi Lévinasian demand to take on responsibility for the Other in order to remember the possibility of a more equitable and ethical history.

REFERENCES

Backus, M.G., *The Gothic Family Romance: Heterosexuality, Child Sacrifice and the Anglo-Irish Colonial Order* (Durham, NC: Duke University Press, 1999).

Caruth, C., 'Trauma and Experience: Introduction', in C. Caruth (ed.), *Trauma: Explorations in Memory* (Baltimore, MD: Johns Hopkins University Press, 1995), pp.3–12.

Caruth, C., *Unclaimed Experience: Trauma, Narrative and History* (Baltimore, MD: Johns Hopkins University Press, 1996).

Craig, C., *The Modern Scottish Novel: Narrative and the National Imagination* (Edinburgh: Edinburgh University Press, 1999).

Doyle, R., *The Woman Who Walked into Doors* (London: Minerva, 1996).

Fogarty, A., 'Uncanny Families: Neo-Gothic Motifs and the Theme of Social Change in Contemporary Irish Women's Fiction', *Irish University Review*, 30, 1 (2000), pp.59–81.

Galloway, J., 'Introduction', in Janice Galloway (ed.), *Meantime: Looking Forward to the Millennium* (Edinburgh: Polygon, 1991), pp.1–8.

Galloway, J., *The Trick Is to Keep Breathing* (London: Vintage, 1999).

Gandhi, L., *Postcolonial Theory: A Critical Introduction* (Edinburgh: Edinburgh University Press, 1998).

Gifford, D., 'Janice Galloway', in Douglas Gifford and Dorothy McMillan (eds), *A History of Scottish Women's Writing* (Edinburgh: Edinburgh University Press, 1997), pp.607–12.

Graham, C., *Deconstructing Ireland* (Edinburgh: Edinburgh University Press, 2001).

Guha, R. (ed.), *Subaltern Studies I: Writings on South Asian History and Society* (Oxford: Oxford University Press, 1982).

Herman, J.L., *Trauma and Recovery: From Domestic Abuse to Political Terror* (London: Pandora, 2001).

Johnston, J., *The Invisible Worm* (Harmondsworth: Penguin, 1991).

Kennedy, A.L., 'The Role of Notable Silences in Scottish History', in A.L. Kennedy, *Night Geometry and the Garscadden Trains* (London: Phoenix, 1990), pp.62–72.

Leerssen, J., '1798: The Recurrence of Violence and Two Conceptualizations of History', *Irish Review*, 22 (1998), pp.37–45.

Lloyd, D., *Ireland After History* (Cork: Cork University Press, 1999).

Massé, M.A., 'Gothic Repetition: Husbands, Horrors, and Things That Go Bump in the Night', *Signs*, 15, 4 (Summer 1990), pp.679–709.

McMullen, K., 'Decolonizing Rosaleen: Some Feminist, Nationalist and Postcolonialist Discourses in Irish Studies', *Journal of the Midwest Modern Language Association*, 29, 1 (Spring 1996), pp.32–45.

O'Brien, E., *Down By the River* (London: Phoenix, 2000).

Peach, L., *The Contemporary Irish Novel: Critical Readings* (Basingstoke: Palgrave Macmillan, 2004).

Reizbaum, M., 'Canonical Double Cross: Scottish and Irish Women's Writing', in K. Lawrence (ed.), *Decolonizing Tradition: New Views of Twentieth-Century 'British' Literary Canons* (Chicago, IL: University of Illinois Press, 1992), pp.165–90.

Renan, E., 'What is a Nation?', in G. Eley and R.G. Suny (eds), *Becoming National: A Reader* (New York and Oxford: Oxford University Press, 1996), pp.41–55.

Said, E., *Culture and Imperialism* (London: Chatto & Windus, 1993).

Smyth, A., 'The Floozie in the Jacuzzi', *Feminist Studies*, 17, 1 (1991), pp.6–28. First published in *The Irish Review*, 6 (Spring 1989), pp.7–24.

St Peter, C., 'Petrifying Time: Incest Narratives from Contemporary Ireland', in L. Harte and

M. Parker (eds), *Contemporary Irish Fiction* (Basingstoke: Macmillan, 2000), pp.125–44.

Žižek, S., 'Symptom', in E. Wright (ed.), *Feminism and Psychoanalysis: A Critical Dictionary* (Oxford: Blackwell, 1992), pp.423–7.

Žižek, S., *The Sublime Object of Ideology* (London: Verso, 1989).

NOTES

1 In allusion to D. Lloyd, 'Colonial Trauma/Postcolonial Recovery?', *Interventions*, 2.2. (2000), pp.212–28

2. M. Reizbaum, 'Canonical Double Cross: Scottish and Irish Women's Writing', in K. Lawrence (ed.), *Decolonizing Tradition: New Views of Twentieth-Century 'British' Literary Canons* (Chicago, IL: University of Illinois Press, 1992), p.169.

3. E. Renan, 'What is a Nation?', in G. Eley and R.G. Suny (eds), *Becoming National: A Reader* (New York and Oxford: Oxford University Press 1996), p.45.

4. L. Gandhi, *Postcolonial Theory: A Critical Introduction* (Edinburgh: Edinburgh University Press, 1998), p.4.

5. See, for example, the work of A. Memmi and F. Fanon.

6. For the Irish postcolonial context, see specifically C. Graham's important work on this in relation to the Subaltern Studies critic: C. Graham, *Deconstructing Ireland* (Edinburgh: Edinburgh University Press, 2001), pp.81ff.

7. See R. Guha (ed.), *Subaltern Studies I: Writings on South Asian History and Society* (Oxford: Oxford University Press, 1982).

8. J. Galloway, 'Introduction', in Janice Galloway (ed.), *Meantime: Looking Forward to the Millennium* (Edinburgh: Polygon, 1991), pp.9–10.

9. A. Smyth, 'The Floozie in the Jacuzzi', *Feminist Studies*, 17, 1 (1991), pp.6–28, pp.910. First published in *The Irish Review*, 6 (Spring 1989), 7–24. Article 41 of the Irish constitution demonstrates the painful material effects of transferring the symbolism of the Mother Ireland trope to the legislative domain. See K. McMullen, 'Decolonizing Rosaleen: Some Feminist, Nationalist and Postcolonialist Discourses in Irish Studies', *Journal of the Midwest Modern Language Association*, 29, 1 (Spring 1996), p.37.

10. Smyth, 'Floozie', pp.25–6.

11. Ibid.

12. A.L. Kennedy, 'The Role of Notable Silences in Scottish History', in A.L. Kennedy, *Night Geometry and the Garscadden Trains* (London: Phoenix, 1990), p.64.

13. D. Lloyd, *Ireland After History* (Cork: Cork University Press, 1999), pp.77–8.

14. See J. Leerssen, '1798: The Recurrence of Violence and Two Conceptualisations of History', *Irish Review*, 22 (1998), pp.37–45.

15. A. Fogarty, 'Uncanny Families: Neo-Gothic Motifs and the Theme of Social Change in Contemporary Irish Women's Fiction', *Irish University Review*, 30, 1 (2000), p.61.

16. J. Galloway, *The Trick Is to Keep Breathing* (London: Vintage, 1999); J. Johnston, *The Invisible Worm* (London: Penguin, 1991); R. Doyle, *The Woman Who Walked into Doors* (London: Minerva, 1996).

17. E. O'Brien, *Down By the River* (London: Phoenix, 2000), p.4. See also C. St Peter, 'Petrifying Time: Incest Narratives from Contemporary Ireland', in L. Harte and M. Parker (eds), *Contemporary Irish Fiction* (Basingstoke: Macmillan, 2000), p.127.

18. J.L. Herman, *Trauma and Recovery: From Domestic Abuse to Political Terror* (London: Pandora, 2001), p.37.

19. C. Caruth, 'Trauma and Experience: Introduction', in C. Caruth (ed.), *Trauma: Explorations in Memory* (Baltimore, MD: Johns Hopkins University Press, 1995), p.5.

20. M.A. Massé, 'Gothic Repetition: Husbands, Horrors and Things That Go Bump in the Night', *Signs*, 15, 4 (Summer 1990), p.682.

21. M.G. Backus, *The Gothic Family Romance: Heterosexuality, Child Sacrifice and the Anglo-Irish Colonial Order* (Durham, NC: Duke University Press, 1999), p.226.

22. Ibid., p.228.

23. Johnston, *Invisible Worm*, p.1.

24. Doyle, *Woman Who Walked*, p.163.

25. Ibid., p.181.

26. Ibid., p.177.

27. Ibid., p.184.
28. Ibid., p.186–7.
29. Galloway, *Trick*, p.7.
30. Ibid., p.10.
31. Ibid., p.38.
32. Ibid., p.176.
33. Ibid., p.79.
34. Ibid., p.146.
35. C. Craig, *The Modern Scottish Novel: Narrative and the National Imagination* (Edinburgh: Edinburgh University Press, 1999), p.199.
36. S. Žižek, 'Symptom', in E. Wright (ed.), *Feminism and Psychoanalysis: A Critical Dictionary* (Oxford: Blackwell, 1992), p.426.
37. Lacan's coinage implies that 'woman', foreclosed from the symbolic domain, becomes the symptom of man – that is, 'woman' functions to safeguard the consistency of the (male) subject while simultaneously pointing to its inconsistency. See S. Žižek, *The Sublime Object of Ideology* (London: Verso, 1989), pp.73–5.
38. Johnston, *Invisible Worm*, p.163.
39. D. Gifford, 'Janice Galloway', in D. Gifford and D. McMillan (eds), *A History of Scottish Women's Writing* (Edinburgh: Edinburgh University Press, 1997), p.608.
40. L. Peach, *The Contemporary Irish Novel: Critical Readings* (Basingstoke: Palgrave Macmillan, 2004), p.176.
41. E. Said, *Culture and Imperialism* (London: Chatto & Windus, 1993), p.19.
42. Galloway, *Trick*, p.49.
43. Galloway, 'Introduction', p.7.
44. Žižek, 'Symptom', p.426.
45. Johnston, *Invisible Worm*, p.52.
46. C. Caruth, *Unclaimed Experience: Trauma, Narrative and History* (Baltimore, MD: Johns Hopkins University Press, 1996), p.92.
47. Johnston, *Invisible Worm*, p.66.
48. Doyle, *Woman Who Walked*, p.200.
49. Galloway, *Trick*, p.198.
50. Ibid., p.104.
51. Johnston, *Invisible Worm*, p.161.
52. Galloway, *Trick*, p.205.
53. Ibid., p.209.
54. Johnston, *Invisible Worm*, p.86.
55. Backus, *Gothic Family Romance*, p.232.
56. Galloway, *Trick*, p.235.
57. Caruth, 'Trauma and Experience: Introduction', p.11.
58. Caruth, *Unclaimed Experience*, p.4.

PART 4
REBELLIOUS FEMININITY

14

'What Kate Did': Subversive Dissent in Kate O'Brien's *The Ante-Room*

Sharon Tighe-Mooney

Early reviews of Kate O'Brien's (1897–1974) work suggest that she was largely perceived as a popular writer of romantic fiction much concerned with Catholicism.[1] Indeed, many of her critics also thought the same, an impression that is challenged by recent scholarship such as Eibhear Walshe's standard-setting biography on O'Brien, *Kate O'Brien: A Writing Life*. Terence Brown, in his highly influential study, *Ireland: A Social and Cultural History*, shows that the Irish writers who chose to remain in Ireland in the early decades of Independence had two options available to them: either to perpetuate or to oppose the new state ideology through their art. The author, he writes, 'could furnish the new order with an art, which whether in its self-conscious nativism or idyllic celebration of the rural folk tradition, would nourish the dominant essentialist ideology of the state or, disgusted with the unreality of such programmatic artistic endeavours, he might seek to define his artistic identity in terms of opposition and dissent'.[2] According to this, we may consider O'Brien as a dissenter, as her work, at many important levels, opposed the new state ideology, despite on occasions appearing to be conservatively implicated in it. Indeed, this conferred on her a certain heroism for, as Brown continues, 'the writer prepared to employ literature and the profession of letters as weapons of dissent' became involved 'in a certain heroism'.[3] This heroism involved risking not just their respectability, but also their livelihood, as writers who fell foul of the Censorship Board suffered in terms of their reputation, as well as a loss of income.[4] As one of those who suffered under the Censorship of Publications Act, it is productive to read O'Brien's seemingly bourgeois oeuvre as more politically inflected, and this essay will explore some of the ways in which O'Brien engaged with literary, religious, social and cultural conventions in *The Ante-Room*, in literary acts of dissent from the politically determined contemporary mores of her day. O'Brien's use of the romance genre, and the respective characterizations of Agnes Mulqueen and her mother, Teresa, as well as Caroline Lanigan in *Without My Cloak*, will be examined in the context of the contribution of the Catholic Church to constructions of women's sexuality and gender roles.

Determining the genre into which we might easily fit O'Brien's work is problematic, as Eibhear Walshe points out in his introduction to *Ordinary People Dancing: Essays on Kate O'Brien*. O'Brien, he writes, 'falls into no ready category, judged as appearing to vacillate between popular fiction and "literature", Catholic conscience and Wildean dissidence, English letters and Irish writing, bourgeois history and feminist fable'.[5] O'Brien's novels include a family saga, *Without My Cloak*; two novels with strong political themes, *Pray for the Wanderer* and *The Last of Summer*; as well as novels dealing with family dynamics and dysfunction, education for women and Irish culture, such as *The Land of Spices* and *The Flower of May*. Also included is a historical novel set in sixteenth-century Spain, and a novel about the lives of two Irish girls who train as opera singers in Europe – O'Brien's final novel, *As Music and Splendour*. The sexual agenda of many of her novels affirms not the inevitable closure of the hetero-normative ending, but instead implies the greater desirability of same-sex relationships, whether consummated or not, and interrogates the happy-ever-after expectations of romantic fiction. It appears erroneous, therefore, to categorize O'Brien as a writer of romantic fiction.

In O'Brien's second novel, *The Ante-Room*, set in 1880 and published in 1934, historical and religious realism provides a frame-work that complicates its simple definition as a love story. O'Brien's manipulation of the genre of romantic fiction here proves fruitful for challenging the perception of O'Brien as a 'safe' writer of popular, romantic fiction. The historical framework works as a distancing device to allow O'Brien to question and comment on her contempo-rary Ireland and ask whether the hopes and dreams of Independence were realized. The opposing political opinions expressed by Dr William Curran and Vincent de Courcy O'Regan in the novel prefigure the bitter Civil War that broke out as soon as the reins of power had been transferred to Irish hands in 1922. Equally, to suggest as simply romantic the struggles of the individual conscience in situations of emotional crisis, as instanced by Agnes's abnegation of self-fulfilment worked through the medium of personal desire, moral edicts and sisterly love, is to seriously under-read the psychological complexity of the characters struggling with a changing relationship to a controlling and dominant Catholic Church in Ireland. There is a profound seriousness in O'Brien's engagement with issues of morality, respectability and individual determinism of her time.

The fact that O'Brien's books were seen as popular and romantic was critically detrimental to her reputation, as popularity is often associated with being 'trashy'. As Walshe writes, 'her popularity with a wide reading audience worked against her, leading to the dismissive categorization of her work as that of a "lady novelist"'.[6] Brian Moore's comment on O'Brien's literary reputation, cited in Julia Carlson's *Banned in Ireland: Censorship and the Irish Writer*, appears to bear this out: 'There was something wrong with you if you were a "darling" writer. In my childhood I knew that the most popular sort of Irish writers, like Maurice Walsh[7] and Kate O'Brien, were all trashmongers – third rate. I knew that people liked them because they were safe, so I wanted to do something different.'[8] Moore's perhaps rather hasty judgement may echo that of those who have only ever judged her books by their covers. O'Brien's book covers, which feature designs that suggest light romantic reads, misrepresent her work. Although marketed as romantic fiction, the books do not necessarily deliver what the covers promise. For instance, the cover of the 2001 edition of *Without My Cloak* depicts a woman posed in a supine position, dressed in clothes of luxurious material, her hair spread out around her.[9] Yet in this novel the principal characters are men; the novel follows the lives of three generations of Considine men, Honest John, Anthony and Denis. The cover of the 1959 edition of the same novel is even more misleading, and even quite shocking, given the contents.[10] It displays a naked woman holding a length of material which is draped about her. Such covers suggest titillation, sensationalism and the promise of forbidden sexual encounter, and although O'Brien's work at one level partakes of the romance genre, to read it as only romantic fiction is to miss the many subtleties and interventions her work makes outside the formulaic tale of the obstructed journey to everlasting love.

The impact of the book cover on the reading public's expectation of its content is discussed in Janice Radway's *Reading the Romance: Women, Patriarchy and Popular Literature*. Indeed, Radway notes that the disjunction between content and cover is one of the major irritations for readers of romantic fiction.[11] Radway's key study of women readers and romantic fiction in the United States recounts that when choosing a book, readers are deliberate in their selection and do not appreciate misleading advertising or unrepresentative book covers. In Radway's investigation into the attractions of reading romantic fiction, she considers the actual act of reading, as well as the reasons given by readers for choosing romance fiction. In this way, Radway's study takes into account the huge number of readers who derive pleasure and satisfaction from reading romantic fiction and asks what this pleasure can tell us. Radway's research found that one of the main reasons for reading romance novels is to 'escape' temporarily from real-life demands and responsibilities and to gain 'emotional gratification'.[12] She then theorizes that the act of reading allows women to rebel because they are focusing on a private, indulgent experience that blocks out any demands on their attention from others. The typical romantic ending of the heroine's marriage to the perfect man provides room for the fantasy whereby women can temporarily shelve their roles as nurturers and carers of others, with 'happy endings'. In addition, a 'happy ending' provides women with reassurance about the value of marriage and their role in the institution of marriage as they know it within a patriarchal system. On the other hand, critics of romance see the heroine's passive surrender to the strong male as an approval of patriarchy. Tania Modleski, in *Loving with a Vengeance: Produced Fantasies for Women*, suggests that this is because 'many critics tend to take at face value the novelists' endorsement of the domestic ideal and ignore the actual, not very flattering portraits of domesticity which emerge from their works'.[13] This posits the argument that the genre derives from the false-advertising of patriarchy itself, for, as Radway argues, 'all popular romantic fiction originates in the failure of patriarchal culture to satisfy its female members'.[14] Modleski shares a similar view, arguing that romances act as wish-fulfilments that 'inoculate' women against the problems and dangers they experience in patriarchal societies.[15] In situations where women play the roles of nurturer and carer, women themselves are often under-nurtured and supported. In the Irish context, woman's role as nurturer is enshrined in the 1937 Irish Constitution. Article 41.2.1 of *Bunreacht na hÉireann* states: 'In particular, the State recognizes that by her life within the home, woman gives to the State a support without which the common good cannot be achieved.'[16] The import of the words 'by her life within the home' is particularly striking. It demands a selfless dedication on the part of women to the service of others in a private domestic space, the home – a view also promulgated by the Catholic Church, whose Social Teaching principles were incorporated into this section of the Constitution.[17] This self-sacrificing role is evident in the depictions of both Agnes and Teresa Mulqueen in *The Ante-Room*. Agnes denies herself the future that she desires in order to avoid causing pain to her sister, while Teresa fights against relinquishing her hold on life, despite severe bodily pain, until a substitute carer is found for her ailing son.

Romantic fiction requires a romantic heroine and while O'Brien's novels appear to have romantic heroines, they are often far from typical, both in narratorial and in psychological terms. Lorna Reynolds, in a journal article about O'Brien, wrote: 'In her second novel, Kate O'Brien created her first *typical* heroine, a girl caught in the conflict between the attractions of love and the restraints of religious prohibitions.'[18] Agnes Mulqueen may be the main protagonist of the novel, but she is not the typical heroine of romantic fiction: her physical attractions are not immediate; the male protagonist with whom Agnes is in love, Vincent de Courcy O'Regan, having met the Mulqueen sisters at the same time (as recounted in *Without My Cloak*), marries the shallow, vivacious Marie-Rose.[19] Moreover, *The Ante-Room* suggests that Marie-Rose is more typical of a romantic heroine. In a scene where the family doctor, Dr Curran, first encounters Marie-Rose, he describes her as follows: 'The classic feminine of polite literature, William Curran thought, the sort of heroine whom lady novelists visualize as holding the hero in the hollow of her little hand.'[20] This self-referential device subtly distances O'Brien from stereotypical 'lady novelists', and her heroine from the 'typical' romantic heroine, as Marie-Rose does not have 'the hero in the hollow of her little hand'. At the same time, Nicola Beauman suggests that by 'employing the familiar strategies of popular romance, O'Brien is signalling her allegiance with the traditions of women's writing'.[21] O'Brien's subtle manipulation of the boundaries of the popular romance genre is evident when she invites her readers to think about her work through a different lens. *The Ante-Room* makes a well-placed reference to Henry James's novel, *Washington Square*,[22] making a connection to a writer whose work in many respects could have been termed 'romantic fiction' had it been written by a woman, but whose relation to the romance genre has been read as ironic, subversive and strategic. In James's novel, the heroine, Catherine Sloper, is equally untypical as she is neither brilliant nor beautiful, and the object of her affections only courts her for her money. Indeed, Agnes even compares herself to Catherine in the conversation about the novel at the dinner table. Agnes and Catherine both refuse to comply with the norms of society in terms of securing a husband, but not in the usual heroic manner, as to remain unmarried is to choose another mode of oppression. It is unlikely that Agnes will marry her admirer, Dr Curran, as she does not love him. Likewise, Catherine refuses to marry Morris Townsend because she realizes that he does not love her. Thus, as Anne Fogarty argues in 'The Business of Attachment: Romance and Desire in the Novels of Kate O'Brien', Agnes's desire 'defiantly resists the demands of the family romance which stipulates that love must end in marriage'.[23]

At the end of *The Ante-Room*, Vincent commits suicide as he cannot live without Agnes who, for her sister's sake, refuses to contemplate a future with him. Vincent's suicide frees Marie-Rose from an unhappy marriage, leaving her respectable position in society undamaged. Teresa Mulqueen's attractive, intelligent death-bed nurse, Nurse Cunningham, whose orphaned status has left her financially insecure, decides to marry Reggie, Agnes's syphilitic brother, purely for financial security. Thus, Reggie and Marie-Rose appear to fare quite well in spite of their respective moral 'weaknesses', while Agnes's future remains unresolved. From the viewpoint of romantic fiction, this is an unjust ending, as one of the points of romantic fiction is to reward sacrifice, selflessness, restraint and lack of self-interest, thereby reinvesting an ideology of selflessness among women in economic systems that ask them to perform low-paying or non-paying jobs for the greater good. The novel does not end with Agnes being united with the man she loves. It can be productively argued, therefore, that Agnes is not a typical romantic heroine, as her strength of character and selflessness go unrewarded within the terms of the genre. Accordingly, the ending of *The Ante-Room* is undecided and unhappy; consequently, the novel does not fulfil the terms of a work of romantic fiction, but instead produces an outcome that frustrates the romantic readers' expectations and therefore highlights the actual 'unromantic' outcome for many women. This juxtaposition between the inner terms of the genre and the outer reality of such ideological faith is echoed in the disparity between the public and private lives of the family in *The Ante-Room*. The failures of patriarchy and its own self-advertising are dramatically depicted, as the romantic hero – dashing, devilish and daring, masterful, menacing and magnificent – is replaced by ineffectual male characters. Strength, decisiveness and mastery are embodied by the female characters, and when these traits appear in males they are evidence of self-important posturing, as opposed to depth and strength of character. The strong female characters in the text suggest that while the outer society may be patriarchal, the inner reality can be quite different, while operating within socially patriarchal constraints. At the same time, no alternative role for woman is presented, as O'Brien does not offer a radical alternative for Agnes, although she leaves her unattached in the matrimonial sense. As Fogarty comments, the fates of characters such as Agnes 'bespeak an impossible yearning for escape rather than an outright attempt at rebellion'.[24]

Such escape may be detected in the framing of the novel which sets the events of *The Ante-Room* on three consecutive holy days in the Catholic Church calendar, All Hallows Eve, All Saints Day and All Souls Day, placing Catholicism firmly at the centre of the novel. This frame, however, suggests the possibility for internal dissent as each of these holy days, although outwardly Christian, is historically bound with a past that unsettles the claim of the Magisterium of the Church, as each assimilates pre-Christian rites, and occurs on a day that was originally a pagan feast. Each day, although an opportunity for diligent Christian observances, also provides the ludic possibility of disobedience, for not observing the conventions of the romance novel. Religious realism is markedly featured in *The Ante-Room*, as characters negotiate their own desires via religious dictates and teachings, echoing the conventions of the highly charged Gothic novel, as suggested by the references in the text to sensation fiction novelist Mary Elizabeth Braddon. Indeed, they exceed these conventions by virtue of the theological sophistication with which each main player, and especially Agnes, struggles with the dilemma of human instinct coming into conflict with religious and moral duty. Agnes is not, despite initial appearances, a typical Irish Catholic. While she does embody the internalization of Catholic feeling, the individualistic examination of conscience, as Walshe explains in his biography on O'Brien, is more characteristic of English Catholicism,[25] or indeed, of a pre-Christian way of being that did not demand such a straitened existence for a woman, such as the Brehon system of laws that accorded women marital, property and divorce rights similar to those of men.[26] What O'Brien did, therefore, as Adele Dalsimer argued in *Kate O'Brien: A Critical Study*, was to treat Irish Catholicism 'as an inner, psychological dynamic rather than an external, social force', the latter being the predominant mode of Irish

Catholic practice at the time.[27] In explaining Irish religious practice during the period in question, Tom Inglis writes, in *Moral Monopoly: The Rise and Fall of the Catholic Church in Modern Ireland*, that outward appearances of piety outweighed inner conviction, as public displays of religious behaviour were crucial for gaining respect culturally, socially and politically in a country where the Catholic Church held 'a monopoly on morality'.[28]

When Agnes's uncle, Canon Tom Considine, suggests Mass for his dying sister, Agnes is forced to go to confession, as her feelings for her brother-in-law have 'withheld her, for she was honest, from those practices of the Church which are the routine of a good Catholic'.[29] Her pagan desire is thus prayed out of her, as the sacrament gives her courage, when the priest assures her that her love for Vincent, 'with prayer, real prayer … will die'.[30] In *Kate O'Brien: A Literary Portrait*, Lorna Reynolds writes that Irish society at that time would have assumed that all good Catholics would have 'firmly and successfully subjugated mere human affections to the dictates of their religion'.[31] But in the text this does not happen, and Agnes's courage and confidence does not last. Indeed, one touch from Vincent is enough to shatter her resolution. Although Agnes's renunciation of love for Vincent at the end of the novel 'accords fully with her Catholic training',[32] it is, in fact, her strong sense of duty and obligation to her sister, Marie-Rose, that is the primary factor in her decision not to pursue a love affair with Vincent. For Agnes, the family bond proves too strong to break. She cannot leave aside Marie-Rose whom Vincent no longer loves, as she tells him: 'I think that now I'm the only living soul she feels safe with.'[33] This both breaks with and explicitly plays out the rules of romantic fiction. The selfless, dutiful heroine must, at the end, relinquish her selflessness in order to give in to her desire to have someone for herself, at the last minute swerving away from the real implication of self-sacrifice in the text. Here, Agnes treats the terms of self-sacrifice with utter fidelity, to the extent that she cannot in fact claim the hero for herself. The romantic heroine usually breaks a bond with another woman (who is generally shown to have deceived her) in order to identify with the hero, yet here the bond with the other woman is affirmed, while the hero is rejected. Accordingly, while Agnes works through a religious medium to negotiate her emotional dilemma, it is not the driving motivation for her decision to end the relationship with Vincent.

The denial of the heteronormative ending for Agnes explicitly subjects the family unit, dependent on marriage and motherhood, to scrutiny. Following Catholic Church Social Teaching guidelines, the State safeguarded the institution of Marriage in the 1937 Constitution. Article 41.3.1 of *Bunreacht na hÉireann* states: 'The State pledges itself to guard with special care the institution of Marriage, on which the Family is founded, and to protect it against attack', while Article 41.3.2 stated: 'No law shall be enacted providing for the grant of a dissolution of marriage.'[34] In a country where divorce was sanctioned by neither Church nor State, the wives depicted in O'Brien's texts negotiate positions for themselves within these twin pillars of patriarchal mandates. The pagan possibility of divorce haunts *The Ante-Room* through the repressed aspects of the structuring holy days, and the unhappy wife in *Without My Cloak*, Caroline Lanigan, attempts an escape from her less than ideal circumstances. In Catholic teaching, the sacrament of marriage is imbued with solemn promises, as Pope Pius XI's 1930 encyclical on Christian marriage, *Casti Connubii*, indicates:

> By the very fact, therefore, that the faithful with sincere mind give such consent, [that is, to marriage] they open up for themselves a treasure of sacramental grace from which they draw supernatural power for the fulfilling of their rights and duties faithfully, holily, perseveringly even unto death. Hence this sacrament ... adds particular gifts, dispositions, seeds of grace, by elevating and perfecting the natural powers.[35]

In *Without My Cloak*, Agnes's aunt, the unhappily married Caroline Lanigan (nee Considine), having fled her marital home to seek refuge with her brother in London, explains her expectations of marriage to her potential lover, Richard Froud. She tells him that before her marriage, a priest explained that 'the sacrament of matrimony would give me grace to be a good and happy wife. I didn't know what he meant. But often afterwards I wondered what I had done wrong that I hadn't been given that grace. Oh, Richard, I prayed so much!'[36] In this context, Caroline has not, in her terms, received this grace, and in her own eyes has been deemed unworthy by God for the receipt of the 'particular gifts' to fulfil her 'duties'. From the believer's perspective, therefore, a failed marriage was a source of personal failure and divine disregard. Moreover, Caroline has no recourse to changing her situation, as divorce in Ireland was not socially acceptable and, after Independence, not legally available. Karen Armstrong's view, in *The Gospel According to Woman*, is that in circumstances where marriage is imbued with such high expectations, 'marriage has been transformed into an earthly paradise; expectations are raised for both men and women that cannot possibly be fulfilled. For woman particularly, as marriage is her only world, this is catastrophic.'[37] The text indicates that Caroline's marriage had been a social triumph, but personally empty: 'Her marriage had been staggeringly correct and had come to pass without the least manoeuvring ... [James Lanigan was] a fine fellow, of distinguished appearance, and coming of dignified middle-class stock.'[38] The word 'staggeringly' is striking, implying that Caroline's marriage is so suitable with regard to James's status, looks and prospects as to be almost exaggerated in terms of its perfection as a union. In this way, the contrast between outer appearances of exemplariness and Caroline's inner unhappiness is established. Moreover, 'staggeringly' conveys unsteadiness, which suggests the instability of Caroline and James's marriage. In a similar vein to Agnes, Caroline is unable to extract herself from familial bonds and returns home, as is expected of her. The impact of Caroline's unhappy situation is depicted in *Without My Cloak* in terms of her decline from vivaciousness to bitterness, while in *The Ante-Room*, Caroline's sister, Teresa Mulqueen, in reaction to an inadequate husband, lavishes all her love on one of her children.

Teresa Mulqueen is first introduced in *Without My Cloak*, and in that novel the narrator writes: 'The only great love that Teresa had known was the maternal. Passion for a man, though she could have felt it, had never come her way.'[39] Consequently, Teresa deals with her unsatisfactory union with Danny Mulqueen by investing all her emotions in her son, Reggie. In the text, Teresa's husband, Danny, is described as having 'no appearance to speak of ... He was stupid and without viciousness, very much the sort of "in-law" that turns up in most families at one point or another.'[40] As Reynolds argues, Teresa 'is one of the many Irish women who have tried to compensate themselves for an inadequate husband by lavishing all their tenderness on a son'.[41] Danny, is aware of where Teresa's heart lies and is 'jealous of the lifted look that Reggie could bring to the tortured woman's face'.[42] Hence, in the initial portrayal of Teresa, that well-known cliché, the 'Irish Mother', is dramatized. Aine McCarthy, in ' "Oh Mother Where Art Thou?" Irish Mothers and Irish Fiction in the Twentieth Century', writes:

> The most cursory examination of the representation of mothers in Irish fiction reveals three widely, almost obsessively, reproduced stereotypes: Good Mammy, an idealized mother figure (dutiful, self-sacrificing paragon, devoted to God and family,

provider of selfless love and good dinners); Moaning Mammy, her negative counterpart (whining or silent martyr, drained by her feckless/alcoholic husband and enormous brood of children); and [the type that Irish-American novelist J.T. Farrell (1929) dubbed] the 'Smother Mother', a dominant matriarch who insists on her children's adherence to her principles.[43]

Although O'Brien depicts various mothers who include elements of all of the above – as well as absent or dying mothers – in her fiction, there is generally a satirical gap in the portrayals that allows for a break with character stereotyping. Teresa 'had built for her wasted son a life that was safe from life'.[44] Her single-minded mothering of Reggie has allowed him to avoid confronting his syphilitic condition. He shuffles through the novel in a sort of limbo and also avoids dealing with the implications of Teresa's cancer. In exercising her power over him, Teresa denies Reggie his own power. Anthony Roche elaborates on this further in 'The Ante-Room as Drama' when he writes:

> It is in the wasting away of Teresa's body that her symbolic power is greatest and that she is able to induce guilt for the denial of that body for so long. The classic compensation in Irish Catholic terms for the woman's withdrawal from the husband after marriage and the transfer to the son, the male body over whom she may (as mother) exercise power.[45]

Accordingly, as Armstrong writes, 'Guilt makes a woman feel she is important and that her actions count and have a significance which, in reality – where women are so often thrust on to the sidelines of life – they simply do not have.'[46] Teresa's power has been misplaced, and as she lies dying, she recognizes her mistake in sheltering Reggie: 'For she saw that her method of making his spoilt life liveable had been a mistake.'[47] By revealing Teresa's realization of her mistake, the self-sacrificing mother who needed to fulfil the aspirations of the Irish Constitution for the family departs from her blind convictions, thus undoing the fidelity and faith needed to protect the State that requires support from the very women it fails to support. Agnes's excessive faith contrasts with Teresa's loss of faith, but both undermine the romance architecture that supports an ideology that discriminates against women's own self-determination.

At the end of The Ante-Room, Agnes Mulqueen's future is as uncertain as it was when the novel opened. Conventional romantic love is denied to her and if Radway's readers' definition of romantic fiction is considered, which is 'that an unhappy ending excludes a novel that is otherwise a romantic love story from the romance category',[48] then clearly *The Ante-Room* cannot be described as romantic fiction. Neither is there any 'escapism' involved for the reader, as Agnes, at the end of the novel, is left to live with the heart-break caused by Vincent's death. This will be done in private, as her love for him cannot be acknowledged publicly. Denying the usual 'happy ending' to Agnes is, therefore, a radical move to make in a patriarchal society. Moreover, the questioning of expectations of marriage in dramatized personal, religious and legal terms, in the representation of Caroline Lanigan, further augments the interroga-tion of the family. Teresa Mulqueen's dying epiphany introduces a different sort of radical departure. Dalsimer writes: 'As mothers, Kate O'Brien's characters, denied education, careers, even political opinions, frequently lost themselves in the lives of their children.'[49] Armstrong has argued that limited roles for women have had a negative impact on their lives and on the lives of their children. She writes: 'The life of self-sacrifice which defines the way a woman functions in the male world can be not only infantile but damaging to other people. It can be a ferocious form of blackmail and a destructive assertion of the rights and claims of the ego.'[50]

In O'Brien's work, mothers are represented as regressive or negative forces in their children's lives, as freedom is only possible for O'Brien's heroines away from the control of or in the absence of their mothers. At the same time, O'Brien, in her explorations of women's roles in the cultural context, recognized that Irish women were inculcated to such mothering practices by their own restrictive roles in society, as dictated by Church and State. Although religion is central to *The Ante-Room*, there are no romantic notions of divine support for Agnes. Her Christian and social duty, combined with sisterly love, proves to be stronger than romantic love. It is Agnes's human strength of character rather than the strength provided by a divine source that informs her decision not to pursue a relationship with Vincent. Dalsimer wrote that O'Brien, 'although painfully sensitive to the negative effects of Irish Catholicism upon her as a woman and a writer ... treats it with the utmost credibility and respect',[51] even though, as Eamon Maher points out in *Crosscurrents and Confluences*, 'she made no secret of her agnosticism'.[52] In *Pray for the Wanderer* and *The Land of Spices* especially, O'Brien, as Walshe argues, contrasted 'the cultural insularity of the Irish Free State with the enlightened, European Catholicism of her imagined bourgeoisie. She began to differentiate between the "Eternal" Roman Catholic

Church and the narrow-mindedness of the new Irish Catholic state.'[53] Thus, while O'Brien respected the rights of others to have the buttress of faith in their lives, she called for a religion that appealed to the intellect as well as to the heart. In that regard, O'Brien's interest in Irish Catholicism was a subversive one, testing faith and fidelity not only in her characters, but also in narrative structures and the expectations attaching to genre. We could speculate that the European religious perspective provided by her schooling shaped her intellectual engagement with Catholicism in that she questioned the tenets of the faith, which is also manifested as a testing of form. Indeed, many of her characters, as Maher writes, went on to 'break free of their Catholic upbringing to do things that could imperil their eternal salvation'.[54] He continues: 'the raising of these issues was a bold step at a time when a Jansenistic distrust of the flesh was prevalent in Ireland and when the Censorship Board was particularly active'.[55]

In the *Ante-Room*, there is an implied criticism of the Ireland of 1934 in that O'Brien did not provide an imaginative alternative outside that of wife and mother for her heroine. Echoing the respectable or desirable choices available to women at the time (outside of being a nun), there was no alternative to life within the family in the text. However, while there appeared to be no future for Agnes in this text, in having her reject the role of wife and mother, O'Brien set the tone for her future work, as she began to engage with and challenge the prevailing culture by imagining and creating the possibilities of alternative roles for her untypical heroines outside those prescribed by Church and State. The banning of two of O'Brien's books confirms the radical engagement with patriarchal ideals perceived by the contemporary body politic. Walshe explains her subversive approach: '[O'Brien's] strategies of attack were much more sophisticated, locating her novels within the culture that sought to marginalize her, intellectualizing her religious and moral dissent, respecting and at the same time opposing the true nature of the Catholic paternalism that attempted to outlaw her.'[56]

O'Brien's talent lay in probing images of female stereotypes that questioned the perception of human beings as homogenous, just as 'lady writers' do not all write in the same manner or about the same subjects. Appearances can be deceptive and the fact that Kate O'Brien engaged with stories of love, or what may appear to be traditional or conservative issues, certainly does not mean that she cannot be considered a heroic, subversive dissenting voice.

REFERENCES

Armstrong, K., *The Gospel According to Woman: Christianity's Creation of the Sex War in the West* (London: Elm Tree Books, 1986).

Beauman, N., *A Very Great Profession: The Woman's Novel 1914–39* (London: Virago, 1963).

Boland, E., 'Preface', in K. O'Brien, *The Ante-Room* (Dublin: Arlen House, 1984).

Brown, T., *Ireland: A Social and Cultural History 1922–1985* (London: Fontana, 1985).

Bunreacht na hÉireann, Second Amendment edn (Dublin: Government Publication Office, 1942).

Carlen, C., *The Papal Encyclicals 1903–1939*, Vol. 3 (Ann Arbor, MI: Pierian, 1990).

Carlson, J. (ed.), *Banned in Ireland: Censorship and the Irish Writer* (London: Routledge, 1990).

Dalsimer, A.M., *Kate O'Brien: A Critical Study* (Dublin: Gill & Macmillan, 1990).

Fogarty, A., 'The Business of Attachment: Romance and Desire in the Novels of Kate O'Brien', in E. Walshe (ed.), *Ordinary People Dancing: Essays on Kate O'Brien* (Cork: Cork University Press, 1993), pp.101–19.

Fuller, L., *Irish Catholicism Since 1950: The Undoing of a Culture* (Dublin: Gill & Macmillan, 2004).

Inglis, T., *Moral Monopoly: The Rise and Fall of the Catholic Church in Modern Ireland*, 2nd edn (Dublin: University College Dublin Press, 1998).

James, H., *Washington Square*, in *The Bodley Head Henry James*, Vol. 1 (London: Bodley Head, 1967), pp.195–392.

Kenny, M., *Goodbye to Catholic Ireland* (Dublin: New Island, 2000).

Keogh, D. and McCarthy, A.J., *The Making of the Irish Constitution 1937* (Cork: Mercier, 2007).

Maher, E., *Crosscurrents and Confluences* (Dublin: Veritas, 2000).

McCarthy, A., ' "Oh Mother Where Art Thou?" Irish Mothers and Irish Fiction in the Twentieth Century', in P. Kennedy (ed.), *Motherhood in Ireland* (Cork: Mercier, 2004), pp.95–108.

Modleski, T., *Loving with a Vengeance: Mass Produced Fantasies for Women* (Hamden, CT: Archon, 1982).

O'Brien, K., *Pray for the Wanderer* (London: Penguin with Heinemann, 1951).First published in 1938.

O'Brien, K., *Without My Cloak* (London: Panther, 1959). First published in 1931.

O'Brien, K., *The Land of Spices* (London: Virago, 1986). First published in 1941.

O'Brien, K., *The Ante-Room* (London: Virago, 1988). First published in 1934.

O'Brien, K., *Without My Cloak*, 3rd edn (London: Virago, 2001).

Ó Corráin, D., 'Women in Early Irish Society', in M. MacCurtain and D. Ó Corráin (eds), *Women in Irish Society: The Historical Dimension* (Dublin: Arlen, 1978).

Radway, J., *Reading the Romance: Women, Patriarchy and Popular Literature* (Chapel Hill, NC: University of North Carolina Press, 1984).

Reynolds, L., *Kate O'Brien: A Literary Portrait* (Gerrards Cross: Colin Smythe, 1987).

Reynolds, L., 'Kate O'Brien and her "Dear Native Place"', *Ireland of the Welcomes* (September/October 1990), pp.33–5.

Roche, A., 'The Ante-Room as Drama', in E. Walshe (ed.), *Ordinary People Dancing: Essays on Kate O'Brien* (Cork: Cork University Press, 1993), pp.85–100.

Walshe, E. (ed.), *Ordinary People Dancing: Essays on Kate O'Brien* (Cork: Cork University Press, 1993).

Walshe, E., *Kate O'Brien: A Writing Life* (Dublin: Irish Academic Press, 2006).

Waugh, E., *Brideshead Revisited* (London: Penguin, 1981). First published in 1945.

NOTES

1. For example, a review of *Mary Lavelle*, a novel banned on grounds of obscenity by the Irish Censorship Board in December 1936, cited it as a 'superior type of romantic novel' (P. Craig, Review of *Mary Lavelle*, *Times Literary Supplement*, 1 June 1984). The reviewer of the reissued 1985 copy of *That Lady* wrote that the novel was 'written in Kate O'Brien's usual romantic manner' (*Times Literary Supplement*, 5 July 1985). In the 1984 Arlen House preface to *The Ante-Room*, Eavan Boland reads O'Brien's interest in the bourgeois as representing her acquiescence to the religious and cultural codes of her class, thereby deeming O'Brien as essentially conservative. See E. Boland, 'Preface', in K. O'Brien, *The Ante-Room* (Dublin: Arlen House, 1984).

2. T. Brown, *Ireland: A Social and Cultural History 1922–1985* (London: Fontana, 1985), pp.312–13.

3. Ibid., p.313.
4. In the 1929 Censorship of Publications Act, books and magazines were banned on two basic grounds, that they were either 'indecent or obscene' or that they advocated contraception and abortion. The Act, an extract of which is quoted in Samuel Beckett's article, 'Censorship in the Saorstat', reproduced in J. Carlson (ed.), *Banned in Ireland: Censorship and the Irish Writer*, stated that 'the word "indecent" shall be construed as including suggestive of, or inciting to sexual immorality or unnatural vice or likely in any other similar way to corrupt or deprave'. See J. Carlson (ed.), *Banned in Ireland: Censorship and the Irish Writer* (London: Routledge, 1990), p.142.
5. E. Walshe, 'Introduction', in E. Walshe (ed.), *Ordinary People Dancing: Essays on Kate O'Brien* (Cork: Cork University Press, 1993), p.1.
6. E. Walshe, *Kate O'Brien: A Writing Life* (Dublin: Irish Academic Press, 2006), p.110.
7. Maurice Walsh (1879–1964) was a writer of fiction and a native of Co. Kerry. His novels and stories are mostly romantic adventures, sometimes with a historical setting, that engage with country life, its tensions, disputes and genialities.
8. Quoted in Carlson (ed.), *Banned in Ireland*, pp.117–18.
9. K. O'Brien, *Without My Cloak*, 3rd edn (London: Virago, 2001). This will be the edition referred to hereafter, unless stated otherwise.
10. K. O'Brien, *Without My Cloak* (London: Panther, 1959).
11. J. Radway, *Reading the Romance: Women, Patriarchy and Popular Literature* (Chapel Hill, NC: University of North Carolina, 1984).
12. Ibid., p.96.
13. T. Modleski, *Loving with a Vengeance: Mass Produced Fantasies for Women* (Hamden, CT: Archon, 1982), p.22.
14. Radway, *Reading the Romance*, p.151.
15. Modleski, *Loving with a Vengeance*, p.43.
16. *Bunreacht na hÉireann*, Second Amendment edn (Dublin: Government Publication Office, 1942).
17. The close relationship between papal encyclicals and Articles 41 of the 1937 Irish Constitution on The Family can be seen in the 1931 encyclical, *Quadragesimo Anno* (On the Restoration of the Social Order). The purpose of *Quadragesimo Anno* was to adapt and develop the doctrine outlined in an earlier encyclical, *Rerum Novarum* (Of New Things or Of the Conditions of the Working Classes). The political context was the Great Depression, the threat of communism and mounting totalitarian movements. Pope Pius XI (1922–39) wrote: 'Mothers, concentrating on household duties, should work primarily in the home or in its immediate vicinity. It is an intolerable abuse, and to be abolished at all cost, for mothers on account of father's low wage to be forced to engage in gainful occupations outside the home to the neglect of their proper cares and duties, especially the training of children.' *Quadragesimo Anno* (15 May 1931), Section 71a, in C. Carlen, *The Papal Encyclicals 1903–1939*, Vol. 3 (Ann Arbor, MI: Pierian, 1990), p.426. Likewise, in *Bunreacht na hÉireann*, Article 41.2.2 states: 'The State shall, therefore, endeavour to ensure that mothers shall not be obliged by economic necessity to engage in labour to the neglect of their duties in the home' (*Bunreacht na hÉireann*, Article 41.2.2). For an account of the construction and composition of the Irish Constitution, see D. Keogh and A.J. McCarthy, *The Making of the Irish Constitution 1937* (Cork: Mercier, 2007).
18. L. Reynolds, 'Kate O'Brien and her "Dear Native Place"', *Ireland of the Welcomes* (September/October 1990), p.34.
19. O'Brien, *Without My Cloak*, pp.423–4.
20. K. O'Brien, *The Ante-Room*, 2nd edn (London: Virago, 1988), p.93.
21. Cited in A. Fogarty, 'The Business of Attachment: Romance and Desire in the Novels of Kate O'Brien', in Walshe (ed.), *Ordinary People Dancing*, p.105. See N. Beauman, *A Very Great Profession: The Woman's Novel 1914–39* (London: Virago, 1963).
22. H. James, *Washington Square*, in *The Bodley Head Henry James*, Vol. 1 (London: Bodley Head, 1967), pp.195–392.
23. Fogarty, 'Business of Attachment', p.110.
24. Ibid., p.116.
25. Walshe, *Kate O'Brien*, p.50. Walshe understands this in the sense of the individual examination of conscience as typified in the novel, *Brideshead Revisited*, by Evelyn Waugh. I am grateful to Catherine Smith, University College Cork, who provided me with Walshe's interpretation of this term. See E. Waugh, *Brideshead Revisited* (London: Penguin, 1981).

26. D. Ó Corráin, 'Women in Early Irish Society', in M. MacCurtain and D. Ó Corráin (eds), *Women in Irish Society: The Historical Dimension* (Dublin: Arlen, 1978), pp.1–13.
27. A.M. Dalsimer, *Kate O'Brien: A Critical Study* (Dublin: Gill & Macmillan, 1990), p.21.
28. T. Inglis, *Moral Monopoly: The Rise and Fall of the Catholic Church in Modern Ireland*, 2nd edn (Dublin: University College Dublin Press, 1998), p.67. For an example of questions printed in the pages of the *Irish Messenger of the Sacred Heart* that reflect the concern with rules, see M. Kenny, *Goodbye to Catholic Ireland* (Dublin: New Island, 2000), pp.183ff. See also L. Fuller, *Irish Catholicism Since 1950: The Undoing of a Culture* (Dublin: Gill & Macmillan, 2004), pp.30–2.
29. O'Brien, *Ante-Room*, p.34.
30. Ibid., p.89.
31. L. Reynolds, *Kate O'Brien: A Literary Portrait* (Gerrards Cross: Colin Smythe, 1987), p.118.
32. Dalsimer, *Kate O'Brien*, p.21.
33. O'Brien, *Ante-Room*, p.264.
34. *Bunreacht na hÉireann*, Articles 41.3.1, 41.3.2.
35. *Casti Connubi*, Section 40, in Carlen, *Papal Encyclicals*, p.397.
36. O'Brien, *Without My Cloak*, pp.191–2.
37. K. Armstrong, *The Gospel According to Woman: Christianity's Creation of the Sex War in the West* (London: Elm Tree Books, 1986), p.290.
38. O'Brien, *Without My Cloak*, p.41.
39. Ibid., p.372.
40. Ibid., pp.38–9.
41. Reynolds, *Kate O'Brien*, p.45.
42. O'Brien, *Ante-Room*, p.8.
43. A. McCarthy, ' "Oh Mother Where Art Thou?" Irish Mothers and Irish Fiction in the Twentieth Century', in P. Kennedy (ed.), *Motherhood in Ireland* (Cork: Mercier, 2004), p.97.
44. O'Brien, *Ante-Room*, p.19.
45. A. Roche, '*The Ante-Room* as Drama', in Walshe (ed.), *Ordinary People Dancing*, p.96.
46. Armstrong, *Gospel According to Woman*, p.218.
47. O'Brien, *Ante-Room*, p.25.
48. Radway, *Reading the Romance*, p.99.
49. Dalsimer, *Kate O'Brien*, p.xv.
50. Armstrong, *Gospel According to Woman*, p.207.
51. Dalsimer, *Kate O'Brien*, p.25.
52. E. Maher, *Crosscurrents and Confluences* (Dublin: Veritas, 2000), p.93.
53. Walshe, *Kate O'Brien*, p.77.
54. Maher, *Crosscurrents*, p.104.
55. Ibid., p.104.
56. Walshe, 'Introduction', in Walshe (ed.), *Ordinary People Dancing*, p.8.

15

'Mastered yet controlling what they were mastered by': John McGahern's *Amongst Women* and the Female Dandy

Graham Price

The critic Rodney Shewan observed in his book, *Oscar Wilde: Art and Egotism*, that 'dandyism exists in an ambivalent relationship with convention, playing with the rules while apparently respecting them'.[1] It is this definition of the dandy that will be examined in relation to the female characters in John McGahern's *Amongst Women*. Firstly, this article is going to explore the relevance of Shewan's theory of dandyism to the Wildean character that is the most perfect incarnation of the liberated female dandy in the plays of Oscar Wilde, Lady Bracknell, and, by so doing, a Wildean element in *Amongst Women* will be established. Lady Bracknell has been perceived by many critics as the personification of a repressive and dictatorial Victorian society. Neil Sammells's assessment of Lady Bracknell in his book, *Wilde Style*, epitomizes the majority view with regard to her character: 'Her [Lady Bracknell's] remarks on education and democracy, her prophetic warnings about acts of violence in Grosvenor Square, all betoken a deep-seated conservatism, an institutionally enforced style of normativity.'[2] It is certainly the case that Lady Bracknell does present herself as the champion of the normative standards of her age in lines such as: 'Never speak disrespectfully of society ... Only people who can't get into it do that.'[3] However, because she is a woman and therefore considered to be a second-class citizen in that world, her championing of its social codes is itself an act of transgression. In essence, Lady Bracknell is presenting herself 'as the protector of society but fashions it after her own image'.[4] That Lady Bracknell is performing the dandy's trick of subverting the societal norms to which she seems to be conforming is explicitly stated when she tells Jack that she could easily alter both the fashion and the side of the street that he was living on, if such a course of action were necessary.

The way in which the marriage between Lady and Lord Bracknell came about, while not actually depicted in the play, is hinted at by Lady Bracknell as having been the result of her machinations and her subversion of social norms. Despite insisting that she is not in favour of mercenary marriages, Lady Bracknell goes on to say: 'When I married Lord Bracknell I had no fortune of any kind but I never dreamed for a moment of allowing that to stand in my way.'[5] This statement indicates that Lady Bracknell did the extremely unladylike thing of pursuing her intended husband instead of demurely allowing herself to be pursued. Thus we see that Lady Bracknell, far from being purely a conservative defender of a restrictive society, is in fact a dandy subversive par excellence, who expertly controls and manipulates societal codes from a secure position inside that society. It is the transgressive quality of the dandy, as personified by Lady Bracknell, which will be analysed in relation to Rose Moran and her stepdaughters in McGahern's *Amongst Women*. While it is certainly not the case that Rose is a virtual replica of the far more exaggerated figure of Lady Bracknell, who is memorably described as 'a monster without being a myth',[6] subtle similarities do exist between the two characters. That McGahern was familiar with Wilde's play is certainly true, since McGahern quoted *The Importance of Being Earnest* in a book review: 'While [Ackerley] might acknowledge with Wilde that truth is rarely pure and never simple, he could hardly do so with his heart. This obsessiveness alarmed and saddened his friends. When you go down a mineshaft, Forster counselled, enjoy the lumps of coal, don't look for gold. Late in life Ackerley took up Rights of Animals with the same obsessiveness.'[7] This direct usage of Wilde by McGahern demonstrates that Wilde did exert an artistic influence over McGahern's writing. The full quotation that McGahern made partial usage of in the above passage is spoken by Algy in *The Importance of Being Earnest*: 'The truth is rarely pure and never simple. Modern life would be very tedious if it were either, and modern literature a complete impossibility.'[8] By referencing this Wildean line, McGahern is, I would argue, giving a very good summation of the philosophy that he applied to his literary craft. McGahern's works very often deconstruct ideas and concepts that are supposedly simple and true, such as notions of gender binaries, essentialist conceptions of nationhood and right and wrong, as this essay will endeavour to demonstrate.

In the very first sentence of *Amongst Women* many of the central preoccupations of the novel are implicitly present: 'As he weakened,

Moran became afraid of his daughters.'[9] This opening sentence of the novel contains the themes of masculinity in crisis and the rise of a feminine form of power. These are ideas that permeate the rest of the text and will be examined in this article with reference to how a female version of power is constructed through apparent adherence to societal dictates, while at the same time covertly subverting them in a manner very similar to many of Wilde's female dandies.

The character of Rose Moran is established very early on in *Amongst Women* as being a modern day incarnation of the Wildean dandy in the following summation of her attitude to life and human interaction: 'Her true instinct was always to work behind the usual social frameworks: family, connections, position, conventions, those established forms that can be used like weapons when they are mastered. Behind them she could work with a charm and singleness of attention that became so smooth as to be almost chilling.'[10]

While the character of Michael Moran may be the domineering individual of this novel, it is Rose who manipulates and orchestrates many of the events and characters that exist in the world of Great Meadow (the Moran household). On the surface, Rose might appear to be Moran's slave and drudge, and certainly that is the impression that one would get of her character in the RTÉ dramatization of *Amongst Women*. The reality is, however, that she is the person who wields the balance of power in the house into which she marries. As Lori Rogers has written, 'Rose desires access to law which is the household in Ireland; more importantly, she desires to wield that law, rather than just receive it ... [By] taking part in patriarchy as a woman, Rose cannot help subverting [its structures].'[11] The relationship between Moran and Rose is very similar to the one that existed between John McGahern's father and his second wife, who is described by McGahern in his *Memoir* as being both his father's 'slave and master'.[12]

From the beginning of their courtship together, Rose is the one who manipulates Moran into pursuing her, while still refusing to go outside the codes of convention that govern her society by being too obviously desirous of him. When Moran refuses to make any overt advances towards her, Rose withdraws from him. This withdrawal forces Moran to pursue her, something that the conventions of mid-twentieth-century Ireland dictated that a man should do in a courtship. As Antoinette Quinn has stated, '[Rose] mounts a shrewd tactical campaign designed to flush his [Moran's] interest out into the open.'[13] In the matter of setting a date for the wedding, it is Rose who skilfully gets Moran to agree a time and place for the nuptials despite his reluctance to do so. In reality, Moran 'exercises very little control in the manner of his marriage'.[14] By coaxing him and using all the social charm that is at her disposal, Rose manages finally to have the wedding that she desired. As the novel makes clear: '[Rose] set the time and was too happy to notice that he [Moran] was more like a man listening to a door close than one going towards his joy.'[15] Rose and Lady Bracknell are thus united by the fact that they both play proactive roles in securing themselves a husband, contrary to the mores of their respective eras. Marriage for them is something that they have made happen as opposed to something that happened to them.

Once they are married, Rose plays the role of the typical, subservient wife to perfection. She looks after her husband's children and keeps his house in pristine condition. In short, she does everything that society and convention require of a wife. Lori Rogers has defined the place of women in Irish society of that period as follows:

> The woman's only valid role in a traditional Roman Catholic society was Mother, and Ireland was … to be a Roman Catholic nation. Irish leaders clung to Ireland's Catholic heritage as proof of Ireland's status as the first civilized western people … and therefore they departed from the usual policy of post-colonial nations which affirmed and harkened back to ancient, pre-colonial matriarchy or equality for women.[16]

Rose's position as mistress of the house is consolidated when she begins to 'clean and paint the house room by room'.[17] This need to create for herself a beautiful house is evidence of how Rose is a very Wildean figure, because Wilde had championed very emphatically the importance of the decorative arts in his essay 'The House Beautiful'.[18] Whether consciously or otherwise, Rose is complying with the concluding paragraph of that essay:

> And so let it be for you to create an art that is made with the hands of the people, for the joy of the people too, an art that will be a democratic art, entering into the houses of the people, making beautiful the simplest vessels they contain, for there is nothing in common life too mean, in common things too trivial, to be ennobled by your touch, nothing in life that art cannot raise and sanctify.[19]

Furthermore, when Moran supplicates himself before Rose by

telling her that the house was never as well run before she came to be mistress, he is inadvertently agreeing with the opening passage of 'The House Beautiful': 'The decorative arts have flourished most when the position of women was highly honoured, when women occupied that place on the social scale which she ever ought to do. One of the most striking facts of history is that art was never so fine, never so delicate, as where women were highly honoured, while there has been no good decorative work done in any age or country where women have not occupied a high social position.'[20]

Although the Moran household had been kept in order by Moran's daughters since he became a widower, they did not have the same elevated status in the household that Rose occupied. With Rose's attainment of a position of authority in the household, the home became a more aesthetically pleasing place and also a less oppressive environment. Liberation and artistic beauty are thus linked together in this work.

At certain moments, however, Rose is required to use her knowledge of the nuances of human contact for her own self-preservation. When Moran verbally abuses her for tidying the house by telling her that 'There's no need for you to go turning the whole place upside down. We managed well enough before you ever came into the place',[21] Rose withdraws to her room in an extremely theatrical manner that is comparable to the dandy's love of performance and play-acting. She tells Moran that she will 'have to go away from here'.[22] While this statement appears to be a passive submission to her husband's wishes, since he seems unhappy with her presence in the house, the truth is that it is a shrewd, tactical move that is designed to offer an ultimatum to Moran, in the guise of a dutiful wife submitting to the will of her husband. That Rose is playing a game of tactics is emphasized in this description of her announcement of her intended departure: 'she spoke with the quietness and desperate authority of someone who discovered they could give up no more ground and live'.[23] This description makes clear the fact that, for Rose, social interaction is a battleground.

Moran's response to Rose's threats to leave indicates her power to reduce him to the position of supplication: 'I never meant anything like that. The whole world knows that the house was never run right until you came. A blind man can tell that the children think the world of you.'[24] While there is no formal reconciliation between the two, Moran has been out-manoeuvred by his socially more experienced wife, who has used the pose of the passive wife to gain the upper hand in their gender battle. As Robert F. Garratt has contended, Rose is 'a character who can work around the role given to mid-century Irish women'.[25] After this altercation 'Rose's place in the house could never be attacked or threatened again.'[26] It is worth noting that Rose's tactic of passive resistance is a perfect example of the Wildean observation that 'the tyranny of the weak over the strong ... is the only tyranny that lasts'.[27]

Rose's entrance into this familial world also has an extremely liberating effect on Moran's three daughters, Maggie, Mona and Sheila. As James Whyte has written, 'In *Amongst Women*, Rose uses her perfect mastery of social niceties to convey a sense of their own individuality to each of the Moran children.'[28] That Rose has achieved something of a 'dandification' of Moran's children is implicitly stated in the following passage: 'Rose and the girls smiled as the tea and the plates circled around him [Moran]. They were already conspirators. They were mastered and yet they were controlling together what they were mastered by.'[29]

This description of the Moran females being both mastered and mastering bears a striking resemblance to Jules Barbey d'Aurevilly's observation concerning one of the traits of the dandy: '[The Dandy] ... while still respecting the conventionalities, plays with them ... dominates and is dominated by them in turn.'[30] The Moran girls will now use the rules of society as a mask to disguise their rebellious natures and attempt to find what freedoms they can within the strictures that are placed on them. Denis Sampson, while never actually bringing up the subject of the dandy, offers a similar evaluation of Rose's influence on the Moran girls: '[Rose] teaches [the Moran girls] that diplomacy and tact is another source of power.'[31]

The daughter who most successfully embodies the dandy's spirit of 'conformist rebellion' is the youngest, Sheila. The earliest description of this daughter demonstrates this fact: '[she was] too self-centred and bright ever to challenge authority on poor ground'.[32] These character traits of cunning and respecting authority make Sheila the ideal dandy figure. The incident in which Sheila first shows her perfect mastery of social codes occurs when she is offered a scholarship to go to university and possibly study medicine. This offer is met with vehement resistance from Moran, who was a veteran of the Irish War of Independence: 'It was the priest and the doctor and not the guerrilla fighters who had emerged as the bigwigs in the country that Moran had fought for. For his own daughter to lay claim to such a position was an intolerable affront.'[33] In the face of this opposition,

Sheila turns down the scholarship and takes the more secure path of a job in the civil service. 'When he is certain that Sheila is securely set towards the civil service',[34] Moran then begins to offer some financial support in respect of Sheila going to university. Sheila, true to form as a social gameswoman, refuses these offers: 'She knew the offers would disappear again the very moment she tried to take them up.'[35] By giving ground to her father, Sheila has ensured that her place in the family will be secure and that she can return home for sustenance whenever she wishes. Having her home available to her as a place of asylum is more important to Sheila than academic achievement, so she cedes ground in order that her position in Great Meadow may be assured.

As she grows older and becomes a wife, Sheila dutifully returns home frequently, but begins to act out her rebellion in this familial environment in a more overt fashion. The haymaking scene near the novel's close is where Sheila's subversion of the social sphere in which she has immersed herself is evident. Instead of remaining with her family out in the fields, Sheila goes back into the house halfway through the day with her husband Seán. Thus, she remains within the family circle, while at the same time subverting the rituals and customs that Moran has made inviolate over the years. During this section of the novel, McGahern gives his readers an insight into Sheila's psyche that provides another of the book's descriptions of the dandy's mindset: '[Sheila] would belong to the family but not on any terms. She knew instinctively that she could not live without it: she would need it, she would use it, but she would not be used *by* [my italics] it except in the way she wanted.'[36]

In this passage, McGahern has solidified Sheila's status as a dandy: an individual who is such a skilful performer of the codes of society that he/she can bend those rules to suit his/her own purpose. That their country home in Great Meadow is considered almost a utopian space by the Moran girls is evidenced by the fact that they return to it with such eager regularity. As we are told in one of the earliest passages in the work: 'On the tides of Dublin or London they [the Moran girls] were hardly more than specks of froth but together they were the aristocratic Morans of Great Meadow, a completed world, Moran's daughters.'[37]

While the life of Moran's daughters seems to be a repressive one, the girls have found in it a means of creating freedom and individuality for themselves. This obsessive returning to the country has many similarities with the character of Algy in *The Importance of Being*

Earnest. He regularly travels down to the country in order that he might gain a sense of his individuality by playing the part of his alter ego, Bunbury.

The fact that his wife and daughters have this subversive potential is keenly felt by Moran, and his intimidation by their feminine wiles is made clear in the first sentence of the book which was quoted earlier: 'As he weakened, Moran became afraid of his daughters.'[38] By the end of his life, Moran is completely in the power of the women in his life, in much the same manner as Lord Bracknell is dominated by his wife, Lady Bracknell, in Wilde's *The Importance of Being Earnest*. Rose and the daughters believe that their feminine power will be enough to restore Moran back to health. They are completely convinced that 'since they had the power of birth there was no reason why they couldn't will this life free of death'.[39] Faced with this firm insistence that he get well again, 'for the first time in his life Moran began to fear [his daughters]'.[40] The fear that Moran feels for the women in his life is a recognition that he 'may have been ostensibly in control as far as the life of his family was concerned, but surreptitiously he has, for the greater part, been manipulated by his wife and his children'.[41]

As Moran is lying on his deathbed and his daughters are saying the Rosary over him, Moran realizes that the women in his life have finally usurped him, since it is their female voices that are intoning the Rosary over his dying body – a ritual in which his masculine voice had led his family for the majority of his life. This scene indicates the women's mastery of the important conventions of the religion-dominated society of which they are a part. As Moran is dying, his last words are an attempt to silence this now dominant female voice: 'Shut up.'[42]

With Moran's death, the androgyny that is one of the hallmarks of the dandy and has been a character trait of the Moran women throughout *Amongst Women* is explicitly attributed to them: 'It was as if each of them in their different ways had become Daddy.'[43] What this line suggests is that Rose, Maggie, Sheila and Mona will use their mastery of masculine dogma and turn it into what Lori Rogers has called a 'partially feminized authority'.[44] As a result, they will create a less essentialist and more androgynous psyche. The movement of the Moran family away from sole identification with masculine dominance is suggested near the novel's conclusion: 'Not only had they never broken that pledge [to Moran and the family] but they were renewing it for a second time with this other woman who had come in among them.'[45] What the reader has been told is that the family now centres around the female that is Rose. Moran's spectral presence may continue to be a part of the essence of the family but it now shares pride of place with Rose, who is very deliberately referred to by her gender so as to reinforce a partial power-shift from masculine to feminine. This shift has been made possible as a result of the female dandies who have surrounded Moran for the later part of his life and whose presence, we have been told, Moran had begun to fear. As Gerardine Meaney has written, 'At least since the 1890s dandyism has been a strategy of refusal of ... fixed masculinity'[46] – and it was his masculinity that had been Moran's defining characteristic.

That such a fusion of gender characteristics is already emerging in the world of this book is explicitly stated by Sheila in the novel's concluding paragraph: ' "Will you look at the men. They're more like a crowd of women" Sheila said, remarking on the slow frivolity of their pace. "The way Michael, the skit, is getting Sean and Mark to laugh you'd think they were coming home from a dance."'[47]

Thus, *Amongst Women* ends with an affirmation of the erosion of fixed masculinity and an emergence of a new androgyny to replace all the old certainties. In *The Importance of Being Earnest*, Algy laments what he perceives as the incapability of men and women to embrace the 'other' in their natures: 'All women become like their mothers. That is their tragedy. No man does. That's his.'[48] At the conclusion of *Amongst Women*, the Moran daughters have successfully avoided this tragic fate by becoming (at least in part) their *father* as opposed to their mother. This embracing of androgyny is what enables them to attain a certain degree of mastery over a world that has always attempted to master them. It is an entirely fortuitous coincidence that the year in which *Amongst Women* was first published was 1990. This was the year in which Mary Robinson became the first female president of Ireland, signifying a shift away from an essentially male-dominated country and a move towards a more female-influenced society of the kind that is prophesied at the conclusion of John McGahern's *Amongst Women*.

REFERENCES

Garrat, R., 'John McGahern's *Amongst Women*: Representation, Memory and Trauma', *Irish University Review*, 35, 1 (Spring/Summer 2005), special issue on McGahern, pp.121–35.
Imhof, R., *The Modern Irish Novel: Irish Writers Since 1945* (Dublin: Wolfhound, 2002).
Killeen, J., *The Faiths of Oscar Wilde* (Basingstoke: Palgrave Macmillan, 2005).
Lane, C., 'The Drama of the Imposter: Dandyism and Its Double', *Cultural Critique*, 28 (Autumn 1994), pp.29–52.
McGahern, J., *Amongst Women* (London: Faber & Faber, 1990).

McGahern, J., 'The Man Who Fell In Love With His Dog', review of *Ackerley: A Life of J.R. Ackerley* by P. Parker, *The Irish Times*, 23 September 1989.

McGahern, J., *Memoir* (London: Faber & Faber, 2005).

Meaney, G., *Nora*, Ireland into Film Series (Cork: Cork University Press, 2002).

Quinn, A., 'A Prayer for My Daughter: Patriarchy in *Amongst Women*', *Canadian Journal of Irish Studies* 17, 1 (July 1991), special issue on McGahern, pp.79–90.

Rogers, L., *Feminine Nation: Performance, Gender and Resistance in the Works of John McGahern and Neil Jordan* (New York: University Press of America, 1998).

Sammells, N., 'Oscar Wilde and the Politics of Style', in S. Richards (ed.), *The Cambridge Companion to Twentieth Century Irish Drama* (Cambridge: Cambridge University Press, 2004), pp.109–21.

Sampson, D., *Outstaring Nature's Eye: The Fiction of John McGahern* (Dublin: Lilliput, 1993).

Shewan, R., *Oscar Wilde: Art and Egotism* (London: Macmillan, 1977).

Whyte, J., *History, Myth and Ritual in the Fiction of John McGahern: Strategies of Transcendence* (Lewiston, NY: Edwin Mellen Press, 2002).

Wilde, O., 'The House Beautiful', in O. Wilde, *Collins Complete Works of Oscar Wilde* (Glasgow: Harper Collins, 2003), pp.913–25.

Wilde, O., *The Importance of Being Earnest*, in O. Wilde, *Collins Complete Works of Oscar Wilde* (Glasgow: Harper Collins, 2003), pp.357–419.

Wilde, O. *A Woman of No Importance*, in O. Wilde, *Collins Complete Works of Oscar Wilde* (Glasgow: Harper Collins, 2003), pp.465–514.

NOTES

1. R. Shewan, *Oscar Wilde: Art and Egotism* (London: Macmillan, 1977), p.150.
2. N. Sammells, 'Oscar Wilde and the Politics of Style', in S. Richards (ed.), *The Cambridge Companion to Twentieth Century Irish Drama* (Cambridge: Cambridge University Press, 2004), p.110.
3. O. Wilde, *The Importance of Being Earnest*, in O. Wilde, *Collins Complete Works of Oscar Wilde*, 5th edn (Glasgow: Harper Collins, 2003), p.409.
4. J. Killeen, *The Faiths of Oscar Wilde* (Basingstoke: Palgrave Macmillan, 2005), p.150.
5. Wilde, *Importance of Being Earnest*, p.409.
6. Ibid., p.370.
7. J. McGahern, 'The Man Who Fell In Love With His Dog', review of *Ackerley: A Life of J.R. Ackerley* by Peter Parker, *The Irish Times*, 23 September 1989.
8. Wilde, *Importance of Being Earnest*, p.362.
9. J. McGahern, *Amongst Women* (London: Faber & Faber, 1990), p.1.
10. Ibid., p.24.
11. L. Rogers, *Feminine Nation: Performance, Gender and Resistance in the Works of John McGahern and Neil Jordan* (New York: University Press of America, 1998), pp.80–1.
12. J. McGahern, *Memoir* (London: Faber & Faber, 2005), p.5.
13. A. Quinn, 'A Prayer for My Daughter: Patriarchy in *Amongst Women*', *Canadian Journal of Irish Studies*, 17, 1 (July 1991), special issue on McGahern, p.84.
14. R. Imhof, *The Modern Irish Novel: Irish Writers Since 1945* (Dublin: Wolfhound, 2002), p.232.
15. McGahern, *Amongst Women*, p.37.
16. Rogers, *Feminine Nation*, p.21.
17. McGahern, *Amongst Women*, p.48–9.
18. O. Wilde, 'The House Beautiful', in Wilde, *Collins Complete Works of Oscar Wilde*, pp.913–25.
19. Ibid., p.925.
20. Ibid., p.913.
21. McGahern, *Amongst Women*, p.69.
22. Ibid., p.71.
23. Ibid.
24. Ibid.
25. R.F. Garrat, 'John McGahern's *Amongst Women*: Representation, Memory and Trauma', *Irish University Review*, 35, 1 (Spring/Summer 2005), special issue on McGahern, pp.121–35.
26. McGahern, *Amongst Women*, p.73.
27. O. Wilde, *A Woman of No Importance*, in Wilde, *Collins Complete Works of Oscar Wilde*, p.494.

28. J. Whyte, *History, Myth and Ritual in the Fiction of John McGahern: Strategies of Transcendence* (Lewiston, NY: Edwin Mellen Press, 2002), p.181.
29. McGahern, *Amongst Women*, p.46.
30. Quoted in C. Lane, 'The Drama of the Imposter: Dandyism and Its Double', *Cultural Critique*, 28 (Autumn 1994), p.29.
31. D. Sampson, *Outstaring Nature's Eye: The Fiction of John McGahern* (Dublin: Lilliput, 1993), p.233.
32. McGahern, *Amongst Women*, p.8.
33. Ibid., p.88.
34. Ibid., p.89.
35. Ibid., p.89.
36. Ibid., p.167.
37. Ibid., p.2.
38. Ibid., p.1.
39. Ibid., p.178.
40. Ibid., p.178.
41. Imhof, *Modern Irish Novel*, p.232.
42. McGahern, *Amongst Women*, p.180.
43. Ibid., p.183.
44. Rogers, *Feminine Nation*, p.87.
45. McGahern, *Amongst Women*, p.183.
46. G. Meaney, *Nora*, Ireland into Film Series (Cork: Cork University Press, 2002), p.56.
47. McGahern, *Amongst Women*, p.184.
48. Wilde, *Importance of Being Earnest*, p.371.

16

'Anything neurotic, exotic, experimental or new':
Trauma and Representation in Women's Writing
on the Troubles

Anthea E. Cordner

Women's writing from and about Northern Ireland frequently challenges, through form and style, traditional concepts of gender, class, race and other identity precepts. Anna Burns, in particular, exemplifies the growing changes in women's writing; her exploratory work of fiction moves beyond the boundaries of realist representation to explore ways of narrating the traumatic events of the recent northern Troubles. Her 2001 novel, *No Bones*, stands out from other novels about the Troubles because Burns's narrative style and form refuses generic classification as it moves from childlike narration towards the grotesque, black humour, Gothic horror, magic realism and the absurd.[1] What Burns ultimately achieves is a meshing together of the personal and the public as she depicts the individual within a given society and delineates the processing of traumatic memory. Political analyst Jenny Edkins argues that trauma can rupture the individual's sense of identity within the state politics as they become aware of the power structure between the state and its citizens.[2] During trauma it is possible to refuse official stories by encircling the trauma in a non-linear narrative to produce new ideas, concepts and ways of seeing. This is particularly important when considering a society that has a history of sectarianism based on strict oppositional binaries in religion, politics and gender categories. By exploring Burns's use of the grotesque alongside Jenny Edkin's theories on the role of memory, language and witnessing in periods of trauma, it is possible to uncover how experimental writing has been used to express the trauma of the Troubles without taking recourse to the accepted language and images of the media or political authority.

No Bones draws on the dark humour of the grotesque in twenty-three chapters, progressing chronologically from the years 1969 to 1994, to tell the story of Amelia Lovett and her family and neighbours in the Ardoyne area of Belfast. Amelia Lovett's name suggests several interpretations that are relevant to the storyline. Amelia Street in Belfast was once a red-light area frequently reported in the press for violent incidents, and which is represented in a Frank Ormsby poem entitled 'Amelia Street' as 'the sum of lasting miseries'.[3] The verb 'ameliorate' means to improve something or make it better – an ironic reference, as the events of Amelia's life work to destroy her. The Lovett surname is similarly ironic. Ann Lovett is a familiar name in Ireland, linked to female trauma: she was a 15-year-old girl who gave birth and died by herself near the grotto to the Virgin Mary outside Granard.[4] The majority of the plot is narrated through Amelia's eyes so we hear first hand how her childhood was scarred by the strangely erratic and frequently violent behaviour of her elders. Interspersed with this is a third-person view of events and the psychotic narrative view of other characters such as Vincent, whose unusual voice brings us into his distorted world view. On first reading, this text appears as a strange novel about a group of dysfunctional characters living in horrific circumstances, expounded through a variety of different stylistic techniques. However, after a closer reading of the plot along historic lines, it becomes apparent that it is an exploration of and commentary on the traumatic three decades of the Troubles. This is evidenced most strongly in Burns's final chapter where the peace talks are referenced through the characters' participation in various slapstick comedic scenes, with the key characters falling out and making up (like the key players in the peace talks) during a day trip to Rathlin Island. Other examples can be found in her inclusion of the hunger strikes (mainly through the eating patterns of the anorexic Amelia and her friends), the introduction of internment, the first meeting of the Northern Ireland Assembly in 1973 and the events surrounding the IRA truce of 1975. Thus, throughout the novel a variety of scenes and characters suggest other ways of seeing, contrary to the accepted authoritative voice. The events are transformed by the bizarre actions and reactions of the frequently dysfunctional characters who act to defamiliarize the well-known media portrayal of key moments during the Troubles. In this way, Burns comments on both the events themselves and the traditional interpretation of the events.

Burns principally achieves an eschewment of traditional portraiture through her use of psychotic episodes as experienced and narrated from the viewpoint of her unusual characters. In addition to Amelia, who slowly unravels her growing traumatization, Burns introduces us to Amelia's sadistic family, her violently psychotic boyfriend Janto, her friendship group, and in particularly to the character of Vincent, who joins Amelia in narrating the middle section of the novel. In the chapter titled 'Mr Hunch in the Ascendant, 1980', Vincent is placed in a psychiatric ward where he plays off various characters in a war of words against the voice of his doctor. We are never able to distinguish who has the 'true' story in this chapter, which references an important year in the politics of the Troubles. Burns highlights this talks-about-talks period using Vincent's psychotic character voices, Mr Hunch and the Inner Circle, who include characters such as Mary Dolan, who, although we have met them elsewhere in the book, are now changed through Vincent's vision.

Another key tool that Burns utilizes in her displacement of traditional views, thus opening up the narrative of the Troubles, is her use of the grotesque. There is a tradition in Irish literature of exploring sociopolitical issues through form – as, for example, in the works of James Joyce, Flann O'Brien and Patrick McCabe. These writers follow the traditions in Irish literature of the comic grotesque, a custom noted by Vivian Mercier as dating from the ninth century in Ireland, where it was believed to be as powerful a tool as magic. Mercier defines the varying forms of comedy that are present in Irish culture and art by placing them into the two main strands of fantasy and the grotesque. He notes that although most comedy has some elements of the absurd within it, which emphasize the irrationality of character, action and plot, the grotesque has a peculiar psychological aspect within its form: 'It is true that life is cruel and ugly, but the macabre and grotesque do not become humorous until they have portrayed life as even more cruel and ugly than it is.'[5] This, he suggests, is an indicator of hidden fears and can be read using Freud's theories of dreams and the unconscious. Mercier points to the mixing of death with the merrymaking or life-giving fertility rites as presented together in figures such as the Sheela-na-gig and in rituals such as Irish wakes. He highlights the original meaning of the word grotesque as an Italian term *grottesco*, coming from the word grotto, which refers to emblems, statues and paintings found in Italian excavations. As these emblems were frequently exaggerated forms of human bodies, either in whole or in part, and more often than not of the genitalia, Mercier concludes that the grotesque is 'inseparable from awe and serves as a defence mechanism against the holy dread with which we face the mysteries of repro-duction'.[6] There are many comparisons that can be drawn between Mercier's theories of the grotesque and Burns's writing of the Troubles, not least in her exaggeration of character and plot, but also in her interweaving of death, sexuality and fertility.

There are various examples in the novel where Burns introduces the grotesque into her dark humour in a way similar to that suggested by Mercier. One striking example is in her chapter 'Troubles, 1979', when Burns focuses on Amelia's relationship with her dysfunctional family. In a grotesque version of a family meal, Burns depicts Amelia's brother Mick and his wife Mena using food and violence as part of a sex-game. They tie each other up and eat curry with their hands from a pot and when they tire of this game they turn on Amelia, who, we are told is – according to Mena – 'outrageously, sexually thin'.[7] Their attempt to rape Amelia is watched by their daughter and other members of the family and is only stopped when food hits one of the other sisters as they come to join in the family violence. The ensuing fight that breaks out turns the violence into a sickening version of slapstick comedy. The ending of the chapter, however, hints at the dark undertones for the future generation as the young Orla, Mick and Mena's daughter, acts out the scene before her with her dolls. In this section Burns uses the phrase 'hunger-striker' to describe Amelia, thus guiding the reader to see the trauma incurred during the political battles of that period, its effect upon those who lived through it, and the ongoing nature of such traumas.

Burns's novel appears to be attempting to combine two clear issues in its use of the grotesque: a commentary on the socio-history of that period in Belfast and an exploration of an individual's responses to trauma. Mary Russo in *The Female Grotesque* notes that there are two distinct categories embracing the grotesque: the comic and playful form, and the darker Gothic form of the grotesque. Russo acknowledges that while these two apparently opposing forms would suggest a division between the comic exploration of society and the darker world of the hidden psyche, it also shows an overlap in the way that both forms of the grotesque express the repressed or suppressed political unconscious. She explores how the latter are discussed by Bakhtin in his work on Rabelais which suggests that such forms are a social phenomenon found in a specific time and space. The tragic or strangely criminal form associated with Gothic horror (which is linked to Freud's concepts on the uncanny) can be explored in Wolfgang Kayser's work. Kayser suggests that nineteenth-century forms of Gothic grotesque were expressions of alienation of the self from the world-made-strange. Russo sums this up by saying that 'the grotesque, particularly as a bodily category, emerges as a deviation from the norm'.[8] The body is an important element in Burns's use of the grotesque, as the above example from her novel illustrates. She uses both the comic and the uncanny aspects of the grotesque to explore the social and the personal. By creating abnormal characters and perverse situations, Burns is using the grotesque as a way of refusing to normalize her narrative and any attempts to cement a singular identity or history.

A particular poignant early example of Burns's use of the grotesque is in the chapter 'Babies, 1974', where Amelia's uncertain narration leaves us not knowing whether her friend Mary Dolan is pushing a dead baby or a bomb around in her doll's pram. Amelia's opening narration to this chapter highlights the horrors behind the life that Mary Dolan had led to this point, with hints of incest and an emphasis on the broken youth of both characters. However, even as the reader is shocked at the offhanded narration of abuse, Amelia's descriptions also suggest that Mary's toy pram may contain a bomb: 'It wasn't a baby. It was a strange-looking parcel, grey and plumped up with bits of dark wire and putty at the top.' At this point we are made aware of the danger that the young girls are in. Amelia's fear focuses on the soldiers who are mocking Mary while training their guns on both girls. Amelia is frightened that they will discover what is in Mary's pram and she will be 'dragged to the Saracen, in the court, in the jail, forever'.[9] The sound of the ice-cream van, which was used by local paramilitary to transport guns, increases Amelia's fear. As the tension heightens, Amelia wheels the pram to safety away from other people. Amelia and Mary disagree as to whether the pram contains a bomb or a baby and Amelia goes for a closer look:

> I pulled off the cover and lifted all the cloths. The cabbage smell was thick. It was sickening. I peered at the grey package. There were definitely strings or thin wires, you know, just under the surface. Was it a bomb? What did a bomb look like? Not like a soldier anyway. I touched it. It felt leathery and dry and a bit soft. I pulled at the thick putty at the top to open it. And that's when I realized the material was see-through. Most of the putty was on the inside only it wasn't putty. It was a bit of a baby's head.[10]

In this upside-down world, Amelia's gruesome discovery of a dead baby, born from a child who has been abused by her father, is less shocking and frightening for Amelia than if it had been a bomb. This unsettling description serve two purposes: firstly, its use of grotesque imagery narrated through Amelia's eyes brings the reader into close proximity with the trauma, and secondly, Burns uses the image as a metaphor to explore the public expressions of specific events in Belfast.

Mary Dolan appears several times in the novel and her baby is symbolic of the political crises of 1974, and later of 1980, which, instead of bringing the peace process together, brought further violence to Ireland. In 1974, the official opening of the power-sharing Northern Ireland Executive on 1 January turned what was supposed to be a year of reconciliation into a year of political chaos, violence and general strikes. It is officially recorded as the year with the largest death toll in a single day, when four loyalist car bombs exploded in Dublin and Monaghan, killing thirty-three people and injuring a further 258 individuals. (In addition to these statistics was the news that one of the dead was a pregnant woman.) The bombs were part of the backlash against the Sunningdale Agreement and the power-sharing Executive. Burns appears to have transformed these facts in her chapter into a dead baby, which also looks like a bomb, in both cases signifying death and trauma. In the official recordings of the bombings, the account exists as a catalogue of death, injury and collateral damage. These bare recorded facts, separated from the trauma, have lost the power to do more than reference the emotive details. Mary and Amelia's story, however, seeks to recreate the horror of that day for those involved and the responses felt by those watching the images on the television. Thus at the heart of Burns's chapter is the message of the trauma: shocking, unknowable and indescribable.

Trauma produces metaphoric and flawed narratives that seek to acknowledge the inarticulate nature of certain experiences. The key characteristic of psychological trauma is its unknowability for, as Cathy Caruth states in *Unclaimed Experiences*, 'Trauma is not located in the simple violent or original event in an individual's past, but rather in the way that its very unassimilated nature – the way it was precisely *not known* in the first instance – returns to haunt the survivor later on.'[11] There simply is no language available to describe what is beyond the normal human understanding of life. The experience of trauma is thus a gap in the sequence of events available to the conscious mind as the story of a particular event or series of events making up an individual's understanding of the past and thus making it impossible for the self or others to fully know a trauma. This subsequently creates problems of knowing, telling, hearing and representing, for as Caruth suggests, 'what returns to haunt the victim, these stories tell us, is not only the reality of the violent event but also the reality of the way that its violence has not yet been fully known'.[12] After the trauma, the event is continually experienced in a fragmented and fluid form that tries to build up an interpretation of the experience in a way that helps it become assimilated into the previous understandings. In addition, during trauma, the sight of the event happens long before the knowledge catches up with the experience of the event. The senses take priority so that there is a movement toward the mind and understanding from an awareness of the position of the body. This can be reflected in a variety of literary devices, such as using a narrator who expresses the story in a pre-human, animalistic, or childlike form, in sensual and unfamiliar images. For example, in Burns's chapter 'War Spasms, 1988', Amelia's visit to her friend Bronagh culminates in rape. The emphasis is clearly on the effects of trauma on the body, as Bronagh describes her need for sex as an 'urgency' to remove the stress she feels when preparing her bomb, and Amelia's body is once again shown as the unwelcome recipient of sexual violence. Amelia's body is described as 'missing' during this scene, which is partly depicted through the eyes of Bronagh's children and partly by the traumatized Amelia:

> She kept looking and a chunk of meat began to crawl its way across. It was raw, bright red, glistening and crawling over the teddybears. After that, it crawled over the jelly [baby] heads, coming closer and closer to her thigh. When it touched her thigh, she kicked ... As she reached for the [gin] bottle, stretching her hand out to take it, a shadow passed through her forearm and disappeared into the wall ... She grabbed her jacket, rushed out the back way, running from that house and all the unholy things it stood for. [13]

In this description Burns creates Amelia's initial response to the trauma through the use of a metaphor for a raw wound. In addition, she acknowledges that the trauma remains as a ghosting or 'shadow' that will continue to follow Amelia. Both images are physically attached onto Amelia's body. Burns's text is here and elsewhere exemplifying the problems of 'not knowing' in trauma by instead creating a fluid narrative that acknowledges the gaps in personal and social understanding, while simultaneously challenging (as described above) the standardized public representations of events. One theorist who is particularly important in elucidating the social aspects of trauma is Jenny Edkins, who expands the social element in trauma by examining the interaction between individual, family, social groups and the nation state. Edkins suggests that the root of trauma is found in the shock felt by an individual when the state responds to them or to others in such a way as to expose the breaking of the illusion of safety within the power relationship between themselves and the state. She suggests that the true basis of trauma is not helplessness but a 'betrayal of trust' by the individuals or author-ities that are perceived to be protectorates: 'What we call trauma takes place when the very powers that we are convinced will protect us and give us security become our tormentors: when the community of which we considered ourselves members turns against us or when our family is no longer a source of refuge but a site of danger.'[14] It is undeniable that many of the people living in Northern Ireland have experienced this sense of betrayal and danger. The events of Bloody Sunday are one example of instances when the representatives of a state behaved in a violent and suppressive fashion. Although there are a variety of opinions surrounding this event and a distinction on how it is portrayed in nationalist and loyalist areas, it has undoubtedly held an important position in the public psyche. The decades of questions, calls for justice and enquiries concerning this incident are evidence of the traumatic nature of this event in the lives of the nationalist Derry community. This is summed up in the poem 'I Wasn't Even Born', quoted in Patrick Hayes and Jim Campbell's *Bloody Sunday: Trauma, Pain and Politics*.[15] This poem is a long list of things that the poet suggests she 'remembers' about that day, including a list of the dead, which ends by acknowledging 'And I wasn't even born.' What this suggests is the way in which traumatic events are absorbed by those who are asked to bear witness to the dead and of the continued suffering of their communities. The repeated relaying of the events by family and community means that it remains part of the social memory and part of how the Troubles are represented after the event. The trauma is caught in the iconic images of the media footage and in the well-rehearsed language of a repeated story. What novels such as Burns's do is to break down the repetitious and commonly accepted symbols of the past, to explore the heart of the trauma and the various exposed power relationships.

The social traumas are represented throughout Burns's novel through Amelia's responses to the Troubles. She is both an individual female character and a representative. The social responses can be best illustrated by looking at 'In the Crossfire, 1971', which is an early chapter describing the day when the teachers at Amelia's school force the children to write a peace poem following the correct guidelines set out by the state authority. Amelia does not want to write the poem as she has been commanded; she wants instead to read her story about Ethelred, but she is violently forced to write the poem:

> Miss Hanratty was now explaining the ground rules for peace poems, for apparently there were some, made up by somebody, somewhere. Clutching her long cane, she slapped the desk between each major point ... Miss Hanratty would multiple-slap anybody who didn't get it right. She wouldn't stand for unreadable writing, anything neurotic, exotic, experimental or new ... and, concluded Miss Hanratty, 'I want nice little borders drawn all the way round.'[16]

The teachers are portrayed by Burns as representatives of the state authority in this Catholic community and, as such, are shown as determined to enforce their wishes upon the powerless children. They will do this through whatever force is necessary and will not tolerate equivocations by the children. This once again echoes events of this period as seen through the eyes of the nationalist communities in the Ardoyne who were forced to accept army patrols, house searches, questioning and so on during the 1970s. Amelia is reminded of a previous occasion when the powerful authority of the police forced the whole school to be fingerprinted. This chapter is symbolic of the events surrounding Internment, which was introduced in August 1971 and saw the detainment of almost 2,000 people, most of whom were Catholics with no paramilitary associations. By using a child's viewpoint and symbolic figureheads, Burns once again attempts to re-create the moment of trauma and its effects upon a shaken community.

In an interview, Burns suggested of the violent world she depicts that 'you have to become disconnected and/or delusional in order to survive'.[17] Her characters certainly play out this description, particularly during moments of trauma. As the above episodes show, the most interesting aspect of Burns's novel is her style of writing: the way she moves from straightforward realist sections of dialogue to bizarre surreal worlds. Burns said of her novel: 'The book reflects the feeling reality rather than necessarily what happened.'[18] This 'feeling reality' is in essence the emotive responses of the community and the individual to the ongoing trauma, and thus requires a very different style of writing. Burns creates caricatures, psychotic episodes, the grotesque, the Gothic, allegorical dark humour and fantastical situations. The bizarre unreality of sections of her story work to highlight the bizarre madness of the reality they underpin. The inclusion of these narrative viewpoints and techniques allows for an exploration of the traumatic by highlighting the influence that such events would have on young children growing up to expect, as part of their 'normal' everyday occurrences, bombings, night-time raids, soldiers with guns, death and various forms of violence. In this way this novel becomes an examination of a specific kind of trauma: a war in which all binaries break down to create a space where the barriers of the public and private are completely eroded, where a child could be both a target and a threat, and a neighbour, or relative, either an ally or an enemy. In such circumstances as Caruth and Edkins suggest, the truth is unknowable and not to be found in official records. In many respects, it is the subject matter that appears to dictate the need to move beyond realism to grasp the emotional and traumatic elements at the heart of these stories.

REFERENCES

Burns, A., *No Bones* (London: Flamingo-HarperCollins, 2002).
Caruth, C., *Unclaimed Experiences: Trauma, Narrative, and History* (Baltimore, MD, and London: Johns Hopkins University Press, 1996).
Edkins, J., *Trauma and the Memory of Politics* (Cambridge: Cambridge University Press, 2003).
Gee, L., 'Interview with Anna Burns', in 'Orange Shortlist Online 2002', http://www.orangeprize.co.uk/2002prize/shortlist/burnsi.html.
Hayes, P. and Campbell, J., *Bloody Sunday: Trauma, Pain and Politics* (London: Pluto Press, 2005).
Mercier, V., *The Irish Comic Tradition* (Oxford: Clarendon Press, 1962).
Ormsby,. F., 'Amelia Street', in F. Ormsby *Business as Usual* (Belfast: Honest Ulsterman Publications, 1974).
Russo, M., *The Female Grotesque: Risk, Excess and Modernity* (New York and London: Routledge, 1995).

NOTES

1. A. Burns, *No Bones* (London: Flamingo-HarperCollins, 2002).
2. J. Edkins, *Trauma and the Memory of Politics* (Cambridge: Cambridge University Press, 2003), p.6.
3. F. Ormsby, 'Amelia Street', in F. Ormsby, *Business as Usual* (Belfast: Honest Ulsterman Publications, 1974).
4. Emily O'Reilly's subsequent report on the death of Anne Lovett in *The Sunday Tribune* (6

February 1984, p.1) shocked the public and gave rise to a national campaign which led to profound changes in attitudes towards unmarried pregnant teenagers in Ireland.
5. V. Mercier, *The Irish Comic Tradition* (Oxford: Clarendon Press, 1962), p.1.
6. Ibid., p.49.
7. Burns, *No Bones*, p.123.
8. M. Russo, *The Female Grotesque: Risk, Excess and Modernity* (New York and London: Routledge, 1995), p.11.
9. Burns, *No Bones*, p.67.
10. Ibid., p.69.
11. C. Caruth, *Unclaimed Experiences: Trauma, Narrative, and History* (Baltimore, MD, and London: Johns Hopkins University Press, 1996), p.4.
12. Ibid., p.6.
13. Burns, *No Bones*, pp.229–30.
14. Edkins, *Trauma and the Memory of Politics*, p.4.
15. P. Hayes and J. Campbell, *Bloody Sunday: Trauma, Pain and Politics* (London: Pluto Press, 2005), p.xv.
16. Burns, *No Bones*, p.35.
17. L. Gee, 'Interview with Anna Burns', in 'Orange Shortlist Online 2002', http://www.orangeprize.co.uk/2002prize/shortlist/burnsi.html, accessed 6 July 2004.
18. Ibid.

17

The Other Side of the Story: Femininity, Sexuality and Patriarchal Ireland in the Short Stories of Mary Lavin, Clare Boylan and Emma Donoghue

Lori Bennett

In her introduction to *Re-reading the Short Story*, Clare Hanson observes that 'In one way or another each [short story] questions or resists the story we were all told from earliest day – the story which told us how to feel and what we want and who we are.'[1] For no 'submerged population group', to use Frank O'Connor's phrase, is such questioning and resistance more important or necessary than for women, whose needs and ambitions have been defined by a male-constructed story.[2] Particularly in Ireland, where until late in the twentieth century Irish women were defined as second-class citizens by their government, their society and the Catholic Church, Irish women writers used the short story to redefine the feminine identity. By giving dimension to the complexity of a woman's feelings, the breadth of her desires and the multifariousness of her character, authors like Mary Lavin, Clare Boylan and Emma Donoghue gave voice to a silenced community.

The most glaring omission in the Irish 'story that we were all told from earliest day' is that of the body and its sexuality. As Cheryl Herr explains in 'The Erotics of Irishness', 'the Irish body is or was construed as worthless, endangering, and constantly threatened'.[3] Physically weaker, sexually more vulnerable and ideologically most 'endangering', the female body has been particularly censored (and censured) in the Irish story from its written beginnings in medieval Catholic monasteries through the modern publications of the late twentieth century.[4] Herr regards this mentality in Irish culture as a result of 'the cult of the virgin' in which society worships the Virgin Mary and condemns the fallen woman.[5] This latter category, of course, encompasses all women. The result is a 'virgin–whore dichotomy' that burdens women with the ideal of the Virgin's maternal purity and the impossibility of ever attaining it.[6] Consequently, the female body is a source of shame, and female sexuality a sin. This is not an Irish construction; the idea permeates cultures, religions and histories of all varieties. However, Catholic ideology is especially conscribed by the virgin–whore through its embodiment of the two as opposites – Mary, the virgin mother of Christ, and Mary Magdalene, the prostitute. In twentieth-century Ireland, the newly-formed Irish government embraced the influence of the Catholic Church over its legal and domestic policies. The result was a governmental structure that required women to be pious wives and mothers and condemned the existence, and certainly the enjoyment, of female sexuality as morally criminal.[7]

Clare Boylan provides a good introduction to this issue in her 1990 story, 'A Little Girl, Never Out Before'.[8] This tale is about Frankie, a young girl who comes to work as a maid for Mrs Deveney in her boarding house. Mrs Deveney hires Frankie because 'she liked the idea of a little girl, never out before. She pictured something as new and unprinted as the Holy Communion wafer, unspoilt, unknowing, modest, and cheap.'[9] Her specific desire for 'a little girl' privileges childhood innocence. Furthermore, by describing her future servant in religious terms, she circumscribes Frankie within the virginal dogma of Ireland's Catholic Church. This holy image is contrasted with the purpose of the advertisement – to solicit a 'cheap' maid. 'Cheapness' in its double meaning, of economy and of character, undermines Frankie's unprinted nature, returning us again to the suggestion of the fallen woman.[10] Indeed, upon returning to Mrs Deveney's cold and barren house after a visit with her family, Frankie is driven to seek the physical touch of one of the male boarders because she is now otherwise isolated from warmth and affection. Boylan uses this moment to expose the delusion of the virginal and feminine ideal. Frankie's 'unspoilt' surface gives way to her 'cheap' nature (despite the language of innocence and purity ascribed to her) because she was denied all other forms of physical and emotional affection. Thus Boylan's Frankie embodies Herr's 'virgin–whore dichotomy'.

'Sunday Brings Sunday',[11] Mary Lavin's 1944 story, also examines the loss of childhood innocence. 16-year-old Mona, though full of adolescent curiosity, is as pious and obedient a girl as any parent or priest could wish. In Mona's case, however, piety breeds ignorance. The suppression of sexuality in her Catholic community does not cause Mona to rebel, but the end result is the same; she commits the most damning sin for an unmarried Irish woman – fornication resulting in pregnancy. The Church's moratorium on sexuality, including sexual education, leaves Mona unaware of what the sins of lust entail: 'When she shook [Jimmy] and asked him if it was any harm what they did, he said how did he know ... She didn't know herself, but you'd expect a fellow would know. It was his fault. If it was any harm it was his fault.'[12] Though Mona desperately blames Jimmy here for 'any harm' they caused themselves, the consequences of 'what they did' will fall exclusively on her. Her virtue, her reputation and her social status will plummet once her pregnancy reveals itself. Ignorance is not an acceptable defence, even if the arbiter is responsible for that ignorance.

Mona's future looked grim, as did the lives of all girls facing such a dilemma in 1940s Ireland. In her study of female sexuality in Ireland, historian Dympna McLoughlin acknowledges that 'If the man refused to marry them and if their fathers were unable or unwilling to provide them with a dowry then they remained unmarriageable and a humiliation upon the family as well as an economic burden.'[13] Lavin allows her reader to foresee the humiliation that Mona will face because the taboos of her community remained obscure until it was too late for her to adhere to them.

In her 2002 collection entitled *The Woman Who Gave Birth To Rabbits*, Emma Donoghue writes about stolen rather than lost innocence in 'Cured'.[14] Though the story takes place in nineteenth-century England, Donoghue uses the character of Miss F. to highlight the very Irish theme of savagely exploited and violated femininity. As Stacia Bensyl argues, Donoghue's work is always 'intrinsically Irish and deeply rooted in her sense of both sexuality and nationality'.[15] In 'Cured', Miss F.'s ignorance of her own sexuality, fear of social repercussion and subsequent failure to publicize her victimization align her with a majority of Irish female protagonists.

Miss F. suffers from a chronic backache and seeks treatment from a Mr Baker Brown. This 'doctor' is a cruel caricature of the mad scientist who declares that the source of feminine sexual pleasure is the cause of woman's physical, mental and emotional affliction. He promises to alleviate Miss F.'s problem with a special procedure that is eventually revealed to be a clitoridectomy. He tells her: 'I have seen women who were morally degraded, monsters of sensuality – until my operation transformed them. Women have come to this clinic ... in rage, talking of divorces, and afterwards I sent them home restored, to take up their rightful places by their husbands' sides.'[16] In Mr Baker Brown's estimation, female sensuality and sexual pleasure is something to be 'cured' as the cause of moral degradation. He claims these women are 'restored' to a proper state through the desecration of their genitalia. Furthermore, he considers marital disloyalty to be an indication of illness because a woman's 'rightful' place is beside her husband, and to think otherwise constitutes a 'rage'.

Miss F. is thereafter subjected to mental as well as physical manipulation and abuse. While locked and chained in her clinical room after the operation, she is psychologically diminished by Mr Baker Brown. He threatens: 'For a woman of your pretensions to modesty and respectability, Miss F., to attempt to convey such intimate information to a young man – her own brother … who would cover his ears at such shamelessness in a sister … what words would you use to make your complaint, may I ask?'[17] His sardonic tone taunts her ignorance by challenging her to express what she has lost. As a result, she is forced to accept the crime committed against her without retribution. She says and does what is expected of her and quietly retreats into a shamed 'ghost' of her former self.[18]

Both Miss F. and Mona embody the emerging (perceived) associations between femininity, sexuality and mental illness throughout nineteenth- and twentieth-century Ireland. One consequence of disobeying social or religious law for women in Ireland during this period was to be labelled 'mad' and ostracized or sent to an asylum. Áine McCarthy notes: 'The [traditional] lunatic was replaced by the youthful, victimized and sexualized madwoman … [because of a supposed] link between femininity and madness … One of the first questions put to a woman on committal was the pattern of her menstrual cycle … several distinctive forms of female insanity were "diagnosed" at this time.'[19]

The exploitation of mental illness gave a male-dominated society scientific validation for submerging and repressing women. This effectively removed any threat to the social framework of patriarchal authority. True to this form, Miss F. is questioned extensively about her menstruation upon arrival at Mr Baker Brown's clinic. Though as a member of the working class there are several logical explanations for her aching back, Mr Baker Brown blames female sexuality for causing everything from back pain to divorce. Miss F. is only released from confinement and allowed to re-enter society once her sexuality has been neutralized and her voice of accusation – it is too late to protest – is silenced.

Mona embodies an alternative manifestation of madness in 'Sunday Brings Sunday'. Before she fully understands the physical and social consequences of her act of sexuality, she can sense the guilt of religious iniquity. Fear of sin becomes hysteria as she listens to her priest's sermon. McCarthy explains that many women in Ireland were 'troubled by thoughts of their sexual "misconduct" ... real or imagined,' which could escalate into mental illness.[20] The weight of Mona's guilt causes her dementia.

Her story ends aptly in a state of narrative delirium marked by nonsensical repetitions and confused memories. Mona's 'crime' took place on a haystack, so when she is mentally transported during Mass to a place that is 'dirty and yellow and warm like hay', Lavin confirms for her reader that sexuality is the source of Mona's insanity.[21] Lavin also weaves the character of 'Mad Mary' through the story, a mentally ill woman stationed outside the church who constantly repeats the title of the story. In this way, Lavin parallels Mona and Mad Mary, suggesting that just as 'Sunday Brings Sunday', Mona might replace Mad Mary as the local madwoman after becoming an unwed mother. In this case, the overwhelming zeal for female purity, driven by patriarchal fear of feminine sexuality, obscures the act of sex so completely that those trying to obtain the purified ideal do not know enough about the sin to avoid it. Thus, Mona's fate is that of the fallen woman despite her best efforts and intentions to be the opposite.

As a consequence of the systematic suppression of feminine sexuality, females were girls until their wedding nights, at which point they entered – alone and afraid – into the ranks of fallen women. This new role as wife and sexual being defined and separated girls from women, leaving no room for an independent adult identity. Boylan takes a look at one such experience in 'You Don't Know You're Alive', published in 1990.[22] Annie, who is caught in what the narrator calls 'the claustrophobic act of marriage', is a girl acting as a wife during the Second World War.[23] Boylan illustrates this nicely by calling attention to Annie's marital costume, dressing her 'in women's clothes, making herself presentable for the neighbours. [Annie] was unconvinced by her married woman's uniform and it bothered her that others seemed to take it seriously.'[24] Annie is disconcerted by the fact that such a simple, superficial gesture as this 'uniform' is enough to convince her society that she belongs to the institution called marriage. Perhaps this is why Annie wishes for an extenuating circumstance to release her from the need to wear such a costume.

However, Annie is trapped as much by her own devotion to social and religious norms as by the norms themselves. Boylan introduces Annie 'in the kitchen with … the Sacred Heart'.[25] She is framed by images of the ideal female as wife and devout Catholic. Annie even synchronizes her food shopping to the 'virginal clamour' of the 'Angelus bells'.[26] She yearns to be free without making herself so, because any proactive behavior in this direction would not be socially or religiously acceptable and therefore would be impossible for Annie.

Annie feels that life might be better for her if she had children, but during three years of marriage she has never conceived. In truth, when Annie goes to the doctor to learn why she cannot get pregnant, the reader learns that she does not understand how sex and reproduction work. By calling menstruation 'the curse' and only knowing that when it stops you are pregnant, Boylan exposes Annie's ignorance of and disrespect for the female body and its mechanism of reproduction.[27] Such ignorance, attributed to single girls in 'Sunday Brings Sunday' and 'Cured', was not uncommon even among married women. In an article entitled 'Health and Sexuality', Alan Hayes and Diane Urquhart argue that for Irish women, 'the dominant Catholic ideology of the newly established Irish Free State … in a sense desexualized women to such an extent that even sex within marriage was considered too risqué for public and often even for private discussion'.[28] This is certainly true for Annie, whose doctor must explain to her that she is still a virgin, protected from penetration by vaginal spasms. She is duly 'desexualized', first by religion and society, then by her own body.

Annie has seemingly achieved the impossible: she has taken on the role of wife without sacrificing her virginity, thus confounding the virgin–whore dichotomy. Inexplicably, however, Annie attributes her previous despondency in marriage to what she now knows was a lack of sexual intercourse. The reader infers that a 'simple procedure' will be done and Annie will join the ranks of fallen women.[29] Though she believes that this will remedy her claustrophobia and her costumed charade, Boylan undermines her 'second chance' by refusing to reconcile women to the domestic sphere.[30] Boylan ends the story with Annie 'behind two women with prams', highlighting their 'dull domestic chatter'.[31] These women have had sex with their husbands and produced children, but still their lives are 'dull'. Boylan encourages the conclusion that domesticity is the key to Annie's problem, a key that she will not accept or use to open the door of other possibilities.

Like Annie, Flora in Lavin's 'The Becker Wives' (1946) fails to conceive a child, but there is no procedure that will remedy her infertility.[32] Her failure to fulfil the procreative role ascribed to Irish women destroys her already fragile mental stability. Lavin introduces the female characters in this story by opposing Flora, an 'extraordinarily exciting young woman', with the other four Becker wives who exude 'an air of ordinariness and mediocrity'.[33] Lavin establishes a preference for the 'extraordinarily exciting' by suggesting that her reader dismiss the other Becker wives as traditionally ensconced in the domestic sphere.

When Flora does not get pregnant, which the other robust and fecund Becker women believe is a result of her waiflike body, the problem overwhelms her. She begins to mimic her sister-in-law's mannerisms and pregnant body with increasing frequency. Only when Flora is entirely consumed by her charade do the Beckers understand and accept her madness. In this way, Lavin comments on the improbability of a woman being exceptional and exciting while still being able to meet society's requirements for her as wife and mother. Until this moment, the Beckers are entertained by Flora's performative nature because it was contained within the social code of acceptable behaviour. As Flora steps beyond these borders, the Beckers are immediately compelled to 'make arrangements to have her taken away somewhere'.[34] It does not matter where or with whom, as long as she is removed from their respectable sphere of normality.

Donoghue focuses on an extreme version of Flora in 'The Tale of the Kiss', the final story from her 1997 collection *Kissing The Witch*.[35] The narrator of the story is barren, and she acknowledges that such women are 'hated' in her community because they 'never earned a bite of bread', as though bearing children is a woman's job and the payment demanded of her by society for allowing her to survive within it.[36] McLoughlin substantiates the narrator's claim: 'There was the same degree of contempt for women who sold sex in transient contact as there was for spinsters who remained on as an unwelcome burden ... [such women] were hardly recognized at all, as was the case with other women who were failing to conform to the dominant stereotype of an appropriate feminine destiny.'[37] Such parallel mentalities connect the generic setting of the tale to Irish social standards. Only by existing beyond the borders of society can the narrator in 'The Tale of the Kiss' evade this strict gender ideology. Nevertheless, this character's ability to abandon social responsibility and establish her own 'feminine destiny' gives us a new narrative to contemplate and a hint of the freedom some women in short stories will gain.

These short stories vary widely in narrative and style, but their common themes unite them in the expression of a problem suffered silently by Irish women in the twentieth century. Femininity, sexuality and the right to embrace them were denied to Irish women as they are in these stories. Art reflects life during what was truly, as Ann Owen Weeks says, 'an era of female discriminization and marginalization'.[38] Only through fiction, specifically the short story, could Irish women writers enlighten the public domain about the issues and concerns of femininity. By giving us insight into this sidelined reality, Lavin, Boylan and Donoghue have worked to establish themselves, their sex, their culture and their genre as important inclusions in the literary tradition.

REFERENCES

Bensyl, S., 'Emma Donoghue', in M. Molino (ed.), *Dictionary of Literary Biography, Volume 267: Twenty-First-Century British and Irish Novelists* (Chicago, IL: Bruccoli Clark Layman, 2002), pp.68–74.

Bitel, L., *Land of Women: Tales of Sex and Gender from Early Ireland* (London: Cornell University Press, 1996).

Boylan, C., *Concerning Virgins* (London: Penguin, 1990).

Donoghue, E., *Kissing the Witch: Old Tales in New Skins* (New York: Joanna Cotler, 1997).

Donoghue, E., *The Woman Who Gave Birth To Rabbits* (London: Virago, 2002).

Hanson, C., 'Introduction', in C. Hanson (ed.), *Re-reading the Short Story* (London: Macmillan, 1989), pp.1–9.

Hayes, A. and Urquhart, D., 'Health and Sexuality', in A. Hayes and D. Urquhart (eds), *The Irish Women's History Reader* (London: Routledge, 2001), pp.79–80.

Herr, C., 'The Erotics of Irishness', *Critical Inquiry*, 17, 1 (Autumn 1990), pp.1–34.

Lavin, M., *The Stories of Mary Lavin: Volume Two* (London: Constable, 1974).

McCarthy, Á., 'Hearths, Bodies and Minds: Gender Ideology and Women's Committal to Enniscorthy Lunatic Asylum, 1916–25', in A. Hayes and D. Urquhart (eds), *The Irish Women's History Reader* (London: Routledge, 2001), pp.102–9.

McLoughlin, D., 'Women and Sexuality in Nineteenth-Century Ireland', in A. Hayes and D. Urquhart (eds), *The Irish Women's History Reader* (London: Routledge, 2001), pp.81–6.

O'Connor, F., *The Lonely Voice: A Study of the Short Story* (London: Macmillan, 1965).

Smith, J., 'The Politics of Sexual Knowledge: The Origins of Ireland's Containment Culture and "The Carrigan Report" (1931)', *Journal of the History of Sexuality*, 13, 2 (2004), pp.208–33.

Weeks, A.O., 'Figuring the Mother in Contemporary Irish Fiction', in L. Harte and M. Parker (eds), *Contemporary Irish Fiction: Themes, Tropes, Theories* (London: Macmillan, 2000), pp.100–24.

NOTES

1. C. Hanson, 'Introduction', in C. Hanson (ed.), *Re-reading the Short Story* (London: Macmillan, 1989), p.9.
2. F. O'Connor, *The Lonely Voice: A Study of the Short Story* (London: Macmillan, 1965), p.133.
3. C. Herr, 'The Erotics of Irishness', *Critical Inquiry*, 17, 1 (Autumn 1990), p.22.
4. L. Bitel examines the early Christian representations and retellings of Irish stories, and

specifically of the female characters in those stories, in the first chapter of her book *Land of Women: Tales of Sex and Gender from Early Ireland* (London: Cornell University Press, 1996).

5. Herr, 'Erotics of Irishness', p.11.
6. Ibid.
7. For further discussion on Irish governmental policies regarding female sexuality in the early twentieth century and its lasting effects on Irish social morality, see J. Smith, 'The Politics of Sexual Knowledge: The Origins of Ireland's Containment Culture and "The Carrigan Report" (1931)', *Journal of the History of Sexuality*, 13, 2 (2004), pp.208–33.
8. C. Boylan, *Concerning Virgins* (London: Penguin, 1990).
9. Ibid., p.3.
10. Ibid., p.1.
11. M. Lavin, *The Stories of Mary Lavin: Volume Two* (London: Constable, 1974).
12. Ibid., pp.109–10.
13. D. McLoughlin, 'Women and Sexuality in Nineteenth-Century Ireland', in A. Hayes and D. Urquhart (eds), *The Irish Women's History Reader* (London: Routledge, 2001), p.85.
14. E. Donoghue, *The Woman Who Gave Birth To Rabbits* (London: Virago, 2002).
15. S. Bensyl, 'Emma Donoghue', in M. Molino (ed.), *Dictionary of Literary Biography, Volume 267: Twenty-First-Century British and Irish Novelists* (Chicago, IL: Bruccoli Clark Layman, 2002), p.70.
16. Donoghue, *Woman Who Gave Birth To Rabbits*, p.122.
17. Ibid., p.121.
18. Ibid., p.118.
19. Á. McCarthy, 'Hearths, Bodies and Minds: Gender Ideology and Women's Committal to Enniscorthy Lunatic Asylum, 1916–25', in Hayes and Urquhart (eds), *Irish Women's History Reader*, pp.102–3.
20. Ibid., p.104.
21. Lavin, *Stories of Mary Lavin: Volume Two*, p.116.
22. Boylan, *Concerning Virgins*.
23. Ibid., p.52.
24. Ibid., p.50.
25. Ibid., p.41.
26. Ibid.
27. Ibid., p.51.
28. A. Hayes and D. Urquhart, 'Health and Sexuality', in Hayes and Urquhart (eds), *Irish Women's History Reader*, p.79.
29. Boylan, *Concerning Virgins*, p.56.
30. Ibid.
31. Ibid.
32. Lavin, *Stories of Mary Lavin: Volume Two*.
33. Ibid., pp.333, 304.
34. Ibid., p.363.
35. E. Donoghue, *Kissing the Witch: Old Tales in New Skins* (New York: Joanna Cotler, 1997).
36. Ibid., p.208.
37. McLoughlin, 'Women and Sexuality in Nineteenth-Century Ireland', p.84.
38. A.O. Weeks, 'Figuring the Mother in Contemporary Irish Fiction', in L. Harte and M. Parker (eds), *Contemporary Irish Fiction: Themes, Tropes, Theories* (London: Macmillan, 2000), p.101.

18

Intertextuality, Parody and *Jouissance* in Emma Donoghue's Dissenting Fairy Tales

Libe García Zarranz

She stood there, by that beech trunk – a hag like one of those who appeared to Macbeth on the heath of Forres.

Charlotte Brontë, *Jane Eyre* (1847)

Devising groundbreaking paths in the tradition of postmodern fantasy, contemporary women writers like Anne Sexton, Angela Carter and Margaret Atwood systematically employ intertextuality, self-reflexivity and parody as powerful devices to denounce the moral purpose and patriarchal ideology of traditional tales.[1] Moving within this literary framework, the dissenting voice of Irish-Canadian author Emma Donoghue starts to be heard in the late 1990s with the publication of thirteen revisionist fairy tales. This article examines the workings of sexual politics in Donoghue's collection *Kissing the Witch: Old Tales in New Skins* by discussing some of the postmodern techniques she deploys in her transgressive stories.[2] By using intertextuality and parody as political strategies, Donoghue subverts the often heterosexist ideology of canonical fairy tales and novels, where wickedness and immorality is mostly incarnated in powerful female figures that must ultimately be destroyed. Drawing on Kristevan theory, this essay also explores the kind of poetic language that Donoghue develops to inscribe lesbian desire in the stories, radically clashing with the discourse of compulsory heterosexuality promoted in traditional tales.

Mikhail Bakhtin's celebration of heteroglossia, together with his defense of a dialogic view of language, helped critics Roland Barthes and Julia Kristeva launch the controversial term 'intertextuality' into the roaring 1960s. Defending the idea of the intertext, Barthes argues that 'the text is a tissue of quotations' while Kristeva claims that 'every text is an absorption and transformation of another text'.[3]

Significantly, Kristeva's concept of intertextuality not only refers to texts, but also to human subjects as points of intersection of multiple voices and plural entities. With the advent of postmodernism, the use of intertextuality has frequently become the kernel of the literary work. In this respect, Foucault states that 'the frontiers of a book are never clear-cut ... it is caught up in a system of references to other books, other texts, other sentences: it is a node within a network'.[4] In order to discuss intertextuality in *Kissing the Witch*, I will start by hinting at the several intertexts working below the surface of 'The Tale of the Needle'. The story, itself a revision of Perrault's version of 'Sleeping Beauty', echoes Charlotte Brontë's *Jane Eyre* in the relationship between space and female curiosity. In the well-known nineteenth-century novel, the orphan Jane moves from a harsh boarding school to Thornfield Hall to work as a governess at Mr Rochester's command. Being a paradigmatic example of a Bildungsroman narrative, Jane undergoes a process of emotional and psychological transformation through her progressive care for self, in Foucauldian terms, and her love for the Byronic Mr Rochester. Throughout the story, Brontë's heroine wanders about the mansion, moving through endless chambers and passages: 'I ... found the outlet from the attic, and proceeded to descend the narrow garret staircase. I lingered in the long passage to which this led, separating the front and back rooms of the third story: narrow, low, and dim ... like a corridor in some Bluebeard's castle.'[5] Containing itself an intertext, Jane's description of the old manor resonates in Donoghue's story: 'I took my mother's keys from where they hung, slipped away to the west wing and waited in the shadows ... I took the stairs one by one, oddly frightened of what they might lead to. Round and round they spiralled; this had to be the tower.'[6] Echoing the scene in which Jane gets to the frightening attic, attracted by the piercing screams of the evil siren, Bertha, the young woman in 'The Tale of the Needle' reaches the tower in her mansion to find an old spinster who unveils new truths. The wise woman in Donoghue's story, far from being mad, tells the young protagonist what she needs to hear to transform herself into a fulfilled woman: 'What's there to hurt you in a bit of work? ... What do you know of dirt, little precious, swaddled up in gold since the day you were born? ...Wake up, princess.'[7] And indeed the princess is transformed, not thanks to the kiss of a Prince Charming figure but with the help of an old spinster. Following Umberto Eco's term,[8] the intertextual dialogue in 'The Tale of the Needle' is used by Donoghue to debunk the patriarchal ideology behind the monstrous figure of the mad woman as an agent of fear by transforming it into a liberating force.

Yet another shared motif between *Jane Eyre* and 'The Tale of the Needle' is the unreal quality of the experiences lived by the young female heroines, emphasized through the dreams they all have and the eerie descriptions of the landscapes surrounding the mysterious mansions they inhabit. In this respect, Daphne du Maurier's *Rebecca* (1938) also works as an intertext in Donoghue's tales.[9] In fact, Hitchcock's masterful adaptation of the novel helps to visualize the illusory quality of the narrative by translating the dream-like atmosphere into images. In Donoghue's story, the young princess inhabits a palace where the boundaries of reality blur: 'It felt more like sleep than joy. The manor had a drowsy air to it. Even the fire seemed lazy as it ate away at the logs.'[10] This unreal atmosphere contributes to interpreting the life that this young woman leads as monotonous, decadent and static. The protagonist is trapped within a metaphorical sleep that does not allow her to achieve agency in the narrative. Significantly, the childish woman in 'The Tale of the Needle' initially describes herself as 'innocent of all effort' and 'blank as a page'.[11]The image of women as tabula rasa recurs in many folk tales and traditional stories where young heroines must undergo a rite of initiation into womanhood, a destiny usually written out by men. As Gubar argues, 'while male writers like Mallarmé and Melville also explored their creative dilemmas through the trope of the blank page, female authors exploit it to expose how woman has been defined symbolically in the patriarchy as a *tabula rasa*, a lack, a negation, an absence'.[12] Jane Eyre and the nameless protagonist in *Rebecca* stand for symbols of innocence, inexperience and vulnerability in the tradition of female Gothic fiction. In contrast, the story of 'The Blank Page' (1957) by Karen Blixen (Isak Dinesen) provides uncharted possibilities of interpretation in terms of female creative force and power. A veiled woman tells the story of an ancient tradition held in a Portuguese convent devoted to the production of flax. Princesses from different regions have always maintained the ritual consisting in giving their wedding sheet to the nuns in the Carmelite order to attest to their virginity. The nuns then proudly hang all the blood-stained sheets on their walls to be admired as symbols of woman's purity. Yet, among all the hung pieces, there is one snow-white sheet which is mysteriously framed and suspended on the same walls of the convent. As Gubar claims, 'Dinesen's blank page becomes radically subversive, the result of one woman's defiance … a mysterious but potent act of resistance ... a dangerous and risky refusal to certify purity.'[13] The enigma of the story is left unsolved; instead, the female narrator urges the reader to value the story of the blank page as tribute to all storytelling women. The tale, however, can also be approached from a lesbian perspective if we consider the blank page as the refusal of the woman to engage in compulsory heterosexuality. Indeed, some lesbian fiction has subverted the motif of woman's 'unwritten story' to transform it into a powerful strategy for developing woman's possibilities. Unfulfilled by heterosexuality, their complete subjects are not entirely developed yet. In Donoghue's 'The Tale of the Rose', a lesbian revision of Mme de Beaumont's classic '*La Belle et la Bête*', the young beauty sees her own image in the mirror to find out 'a face with nothing written on it'.[14] The heroine's identity, however, is transformed in the story in her journey towards life with another woman. Donoghue therefore inscribes lesbian love in the tale as a way of writing a different story for these female characters.

Working as a clear intertext for Brontë and du Maurier, Bluebeard's disturbing tale also haunts many of the stories in Donoghue's collection. In search of adventure, the young beauty in 'The Tale of the Rose' wanders through the beast's palace: 'I had keys to every room in the castle except the one where the beast slept. The first book I opened said in gold letters: You are the mistress: ask for whatever you wish.'[15] The motif of the key and the book are well-known symbols of the danger of female curiosity in Bluebeard's story. On the contrary, in Grimms' 'The Golden Key', it is a boy who finds a key and a box containing not death but 'wonderful things'.[16] Well-known narratives such as Carter's short story 'The Bloody Chamber',[17] or Sexton's poem 'The Gold Key',[18] subvert traditional warnings against female curiosity sustained by mythical figures like Eve or Pandora and, instead, provide alternative possibilities for women. Donoghue moves a step further in 'The Tale of the Rose', where she parodies the patriarchal ideology of traditional stories like Bluebeard by furnishing her tale with a lesbian happy ending.

In *A Poetics of Postmodernism*, Linda Hutcheon proposes the concept of postmodern parody as a valuable subversive strategy, since it features an author who actively encodes a text as an imitation with critical distance.[19] Following this argument, Donoghue exploits parody as a weapon to expose part of the ideology of traditional fairy tales, which is mainly based on the promotion of compulsory heterosexuality. Heroines thus elude stereotyped gender roles through the use of parody, as in 'The Tale of the Shoe', where

Donoghue self-consciously parodies the romance scene, which is one of the key moments in the classical stories: 'Out of the steps he led me, under the half-full moon, all very fairy-tale.'[20] In her theory on gender as performance, queer theorist Judith Butler argues that 'gender is an "act", as it were, that is open to splittings, self-parody, self-criticism, and those hyperbolic exhibitions of "the natural" that, in their very exaggeration, reveal its fundamentally phantasmatic status'.[21] Through the parody strategy, Donoghue portrays gender as a fabrication historically maintained for patriarchal and heterosexist purposes. A hilarious and highly significant moment occurs when Donoghue's alternative 'Cinderella' starts vomiting over the balcony while she awaits the prince: 'I had barely time to wipe my mouth before the prince came to propose.'[22] The woman's subversive bodily act symbolizes her refusal to engage heterosexual norms. In this respect, Kristeva's theories on abjection are useful to examine the reaction of the female protagonist. As Kristeva claims, 'food loathing is perhaps the most elementary and most archaic form of abjection', arguing that the spasms, the nausea, symbolically mean the non-assimilation of a subject in a society and culture structured around patriarchal norms.[23] The subject thus needs to expel that which is resisted in order to become a renewed self. In Donoghue's story, the heroine's body seems to be in an ambiguous borderline situation, since it expels the food that represents the royalty of the castle ruled by a patriarchal heterosexist norm. Consequently, the woman undergoes an allegorical rebirth of her sexuality and identity through the act of resisting society's rules on female appropriateness.

Donoghue also deploys intertextuality and parody in 'The Tale of the Apple' as strategies of dissent, disrupting the heterosexist ideology of Grimms' 'Snow White' and Andersen's tale 'The Red Shoes'. Near the end of Donoghue's story, the not-so-wicked stepmother confesses to the young heroine that she really misses her, and she explains her suffering in this way: 'I haven't had a night's sleep since you left … it feels like dancing in shoes of red hot iron.'[24] Notice the parody in this sentence when compared to the ending of 'Snow White' where the wicked queen is finally punished: 'Iron slippers had already been put upon the fire … and sent before her. Then she was forced to put on the red-hot shoes, and danced until she dropped down dead.'[25] Donoghue reverses the traditional meaning of the red shoes as a cautionary symbol for rebellious women by providing it with alternative possibilities, like lesbian desire.

It should be borne in mind that since the publication of

Andersen's story of 'The Red Shoes' in 1845, the image of the coloured shoes has been recurrently employed with different purposes. In Andersen's story the orphan, Karen, is fascinated by a pair of bright red shoes. Unaware of the associations of the colour red with sin, sexuality and death for the Christian community, Karen decides to wear them everywhere, including church. In Gothic manner, the shoes start dancing compulsively and the little girl is left at their will. The consequences for Karen are terrible, since she is severely punished by an angry angel to dance to exhaustion. Becoming a grotesque figure, Karen dances till she begs an executioner to cut off her feet to get rid of the red shoes. Condemned to wear wooden feet, the little girl is forgiven by God and dies. In contrast, as Linda Rohrer argues in her article on *The Wizard of Oz*, the image of the red shoes has also been interpreted as a symbol of woman's power and imagination. Gilbert and Gubar insist on the association between the red shoes and female creativity, as they call them 'the shoes of art', so the dancing shoes might also represent transgression and freedom.[26] Through the strategy of postmodern parody, Donoghue lets her heroines enjoy the pleasures of wearing dancing shoes in several stories. The motif is mentioned in 'The Tale of the Shoe' when the new Cinderella experiences transformation through her encounter with another woman: 'I was dancing on points of clear glass.'[27] The dancing metaphor becomes a celebration of the woman's new lesbian identity and sexuality. In 'The Tale of the Brother', a resewn version of Andersen's classic, 'The Snow Queen', Donoghue reintroduces the motif of the red shoes in a self-reflexive way. The young heroine's brother mysteriously disappears and so she tries to discover what has happened to him. The villagers give the girl a pair of crimson shoes, so she decides to use them in her search: 'I put on my new scarlet shoes that my brother had never seen and set off to find him.'[28] The pair of shoes gives the protagonist the strength to embark on her adventure. Along her journey, a strange woman tries to steal them but the girl fights her. The frustrated thief, however, laughs heartily, arguing that she can manage to get a pair of red shoes whenever she wants. Once again, the symbolic charge of the pair of shoes is linked to woman's agency and power.

Shifting our attention to a different postmodern device, Donoghue develops a new poetic language in which hidden meanings and double purposes pervade, inviting the reader to participate in an active task of decoding. According to Kristeva, poetic language is a type of discourse that subverts mainstream conventions. It can be found 'wherever language challenges and reorders the principles of everyday communication and the structures of grammar and syntax, and whenever an artist chooses to experiment ... with sounds and images in a fashion reminiscent of oneiric representation'.[29] In this respect, I will first discuss the poetic language employed in some of the tales from a psychoanalytic angle. Providing a different perspective to Freud and Lacan's theories, Kristeva distinguishes between the *symbolic* and the *semiotic* dimension of language. As Vincent Leitch clarifies: 'The *symbolic* is that aspect of language that allows it to *refer*. It is systematic, propositional, rule-bound, tied to the social order ... The *semiotic* ... is that aspect that bears the trace of the language user's own body ... the babbling of the infant who tries out the vocal repertoire before he or she learns to speak.'[30]

    The female character of Little Sister, who appears in a couple of stories in the collection, articulates language in a striking manner that could be considered in terms of the Kristevan semiotic. This peculiar woman is first introduced in 'The Tale of the Spinster' as assistant to the female protagonist, who explains that 'sentences seemed too much for [Little Sister]'.[31] The mystery surrounding her origins could at first associate her with the world of fairies, a female Rumpelstiltskin. Nevertheless, Little Sister is given a narrative voice in 'The Tale of the Cottage', where she tells her own story in her own language: 'I once had brother that mother say we were pair of hands one fast one slow. I once had father he got lost in woods. I once had mother.'[32] The broken language of this woman does not fit established grammar or syntax, yet still she contrives to be understood and so gains a voice. As Rosemary Jackson aptly argues, 'to break the symbolic by dissolution or deformation of its language (or "syntax") is taken by Kristeva to be a radical, subversive activity'.[33] Following this argumentation, 'The Tale of the Cottage' challenges the symbolic order by introducing the character of Little Sister as a dissenting subject. Further on in the story, this subversive woman describes the movement of the leaves by referring to the sound 'scrish scrish' and to the violence of the huntsman towards her mother with the words 'whap whap'.[34] The use of onomatopoeia reinforces the interpretation of Little Sister as subject in a semiotic realm of language.

    Donoghue also deploys poetic language in suggestive ways to incorporate a lesbian discourse into the narrative. Teresa de Lauretis maintains that the writer interested in offering a new representation of the lesbian must reinscribe language 'to dislodge the erotic from the [phallocentric] discourse of gender, with its indissoluble knot of sexuality and reproduction'.[35] In Donoghue's tales, lesbian sexuality is often described indirectly and represented in terms of a disseminate *jouissance*. According to French feminism, the term *jouissance* expresses 'a sense of pleasure, abandonment, orgasmic overflowing' and is linked with the female body and also with the experience of writing.[36] Within a psychoanalytic context, the word means 'the simultaneously organic and symbolic sexual pleasure of the speaking (human) subject'.[37] In 'The Tale of the Apple', Donoghue reinvents well-known characters like Snow White and her wicked stepmother by giving their female protagonists new identities and sexualities. The language employed in the dialogues is filled with metaphors for sexual activities: 'With her own hands she used to work the jeweled comb through my hair, teasing out the knots ... she used to feed me fruit from her own bowl, each slice poised between finger and thumb till I was ready to take it ... I took delight in what she gave me.'[38] Donoghue debunks the traditional image of the figure of the stepmother as a source of fear, providing her with a new positive identity as possible lesbian lover. Similarly, by employing the symbol of the spinning wheel, the young girl in 'The Tale of the Needle' describes her encounter with the woman in the tower as implying lesbian initiation: 'I put my hand to the wheel; she showed me where. I set it in motion. There was a moment of glorious whirling, and then I felt the needle drive itself into my finger. I screamed like a baby.'[39] As Palmer claims, the strategy of indirection 'in its avoidance of the phallocentric and scopic, represents a tactic available to writers to solve the contradictions of depicting lesbian love in a culture which denies its authenticity'.[40] In this respect, it is interesting to look at how the protagonist in 'The Tale of the Shoe' celebrates the sudden arrival of a mysterious woman in her life. Parodying the magical powers commonly attributed to the figure of the fairy godmother in Perrault's 'Cinderella', the young woman explains: 'She claimed her little finger was a magic wand, it could do spectacular things. She could always make me laugh.'[41] The lesbian sexual innuendo of this statement clashes with the ideology in the traditional tale, in which the figure of the godmother and her magic powers are used as a mere bridge for the neglected girl to gain access to a higher social stratum and thus sustain the status quo.

In order to conclude, I propose taking up again Roland Barthes's ideas, since his textual theories, which greatly influenced postmodern criticism and French feminism, are tightly related to the concept of pleasure and *jouissance*. Barthes argues that 'the goal of the literary work is to make the reader no longer a consumer, but a producer of the text'.[42] If this is achieved, a feeling of bliss and *jouissance* will overwhelm readers breaking out of their subject positions. In Donoghue's stories, comments such as those included in the last pages of 'The Tale of the Kiss' incorporate all the figures involved in the narrative act, making narrator, author and reader participate in the story: 'And what happened next, you ask? Never you mind. There are some tales not for telling, whether because they are too long, too precious, too laughable, too painful, to easy to need telling or too hard to explain ... This is the story you asked for. I leave it in your mouth.'[43] By contributing to the act of storytelling, the reader incorporates his or her own interpretation, momentarily enjoying the *jouissance* of being transformed into an allegorical Scheherazade.[44]

REFERENCES

Andersen, H.C., *Fairy Tales* (London: Penguin, 2004).
Barthes, R., *Image, Music, Text* (London: Fontana, 1977).
Blixen, K., *Last Tales* (New York: Vintage, 1991).
Brontë, C., *Jane Eyre* (London: Penguin, 2002).
Butler, J., *Gender Trouble: Feminism and the Subversion of Identity* (New York and London: Routledge Classics, 2006).
Carter, A., *The Bloody Chamber* (New York: Harper & Row, 1979).
Cavallaro, D., *French Feminist Theory: An Introduction* (London: Continuum, 2003).
de Beaumont, Mme, *La Belle et la Bête* [Beauty and the Beast], adapt. Denis Bon (Paris: Magnard, 1990).
de Lauretis, T., 'Sexual Indifference and Lesbian Representation', in P. White (ed.), *Figures of Resistance: Essays in Feminist Theory* (Chicago, IL: University of Illinois Press, 2007), pp.48–71.
Donoghue, E., *Kissing the Witch: Old Tales in New Skins* (New York: HarperCollins, 1997).
du Maurier, D., *Rebecca* (London: Arrow Books, 1992).
Eagleton, M., *Feminist Literary Criticism* (London: Longman, 1991).
Eco, U., 'Innovation and Repetition: Between Modern and Post-Modern Aesthetics', in R. Capozzi (ed.), *Reading Umberto Eco: An Anthology* (Bloomington, IN: Indiana University Press, 1997), pp.14–33.
Foucault, M., *The Archaeology of Knowledge* (London: Tavistock, 1974).
Gilbert, S.M. and Gubar. S., *The Madwoman in the Attic: The Woman Writer and the Nineteenth-Century Literary Imagination* (New Haven, CT, and London: Yale University Press, 1979).
Grimm, J. and Grimm, W., *Complete Fairy Tales* (London: Routledge, 2002).
Gubar, S., ',"The Blank Page" and the Issues of Female Creativity', in E. Showalter (ed.), *The New Feminist Criticism* (London: Virago Press, 1985), pp.292–313.
Hutcheon, L.A., *Poetics of Postmodernism: History, Theory, Fiction* (London: Routledge, 1988).
Jackson, R., *Fantasy: The Literature of Subversion* (London: Routledge, 1981).
Kristeva, J., *Powers of Horror: An Essay on Abjection* (New York: Columbia University Press, 1982).
Kristeva, J., 'Word, Dialogue and Novel', in T. Moi (ed.), *The Kristeva Reader* (New York: Columbia University Press, 1986), pp.34–61.
Kristeva, J., 'About Chinese Women', reprinted in M. Eagleton (ed.), *Feminist Literary Criticism* (London: Longman, 1991), pp.70–83.

Leitch, V.B. (ed.), *The Norton Anthology of Theory and Criticism* (New York and London: Norton & Co., 2001).

Ostriker, Alicia, 'The Thieves of Language: Women Poets and Revisionist Mythmaking', in E. Showalter (ed.), *The New Feminist Criticism: Essays on Women, Literature and Theory* (New York: Pantheon Books, 1985), pp.314–38.

Palmer, P., *Lesbian Gothic: Transgressive Fictions* (London: Cassell, 1999).

Palmer, P., 'Lesbian Gothic: Genre, Transformation, Transgression', *Journal of Gothic Studies*, 6, 1 (May 2004), pp.118–30.

Perrault, C., *Perrault's Fairy Tales* (London: Wordsworth, 2004).

Rohrer, L., 'Wearing the Red Shoes: Dorothy and the Power of the Female Imagination in "The Wizard of Oz"', *Journal of Popular Film and Television*, 23, 4 (Winter 1996), pp.146–53.

Sexton, A., *Transformations* (New York: Houghton Mifflin, 1971).

NOTES

1. Sexton's revolutionary poetry collection, *Transformations* (New York: Houghton Mifflin, 1971); Carter's influential short stories in *The Bloody Chamber* (New York: Harper & Row, 1979); and Atwood's revisionist titles like *The Handmaid's Tale* (Toronto: McClelland and Stewart, 1985) stand as major examples in the tradition of 'revisionist mythmaking', in Alicia Ostriker's words, in 'The Thieves of Language: Women Poets and Revisionist Mythmaking', in E. Showalter (ed.), *The New Feminist Criticism: Essays on Women, Literature and Theory* (New York: Pantheon Books, 1985), p.314. The rewriting of traditional fairy tales also flourished in Ireland in the late 1980s and 1990s with collections such as *Sweeping Beauties* (Dublin: Attic Press, 1989), *Ride on Rapunzel: Fairytales for Feminists* (Dublin: Attic Press, 1992) and *Rapunzel's Revenge: More Feminist Fairytales* (Dublin: Attic Press, 1995), thanks to the publishing house Attic Press.
2. E. Donoghue, *Kissing the Witch: Old Tales in New Skins* (New York: Harper Collins, 1997).
3. R. Barthes, *Image, Music, Text* (London: Fontana, 1977), p.146; and J. Kristeva, 'Word, Dialogue and Novel', in T. Moi (ed.), *The Kristeva Reader* (New York: Columbia University Press, 1986), p.36.
4. M. Foucault, *The Archaeology of Knowledge* (London: Tavistock, 1974), p.23.
5. C. Brontë, *Jane Eyre* (London: Penguin, 2002), pp.117–18.
6. Donoghue, *Kissing the Witch*, pp.175–6.
7. Ibid, pp.178–180.
8. In 'Innovation and Repetition: Between Modern and Post-Modern Aesthetics', in R. Capozzi (ed.), *Reading Umberto Eco: An Anthology* (Bloomington, IN: Indiana UP, 1997), pp.14–33, Umberto Eco defines 'intertextual dialogue' as 'the phenomenon by which a given text echoes previous texts', p.21.
9. D. du Maurier, *Rebecca* (London: Arrow Books, 1992).
10. Donoghue, *Kissing the Witch*, p.170.
11. Ibid, p.167.
12. S. Gubar, ' "The Blank Page" and the Issues of Female Creativity', in Showalter (ed.), *New Feminist Criticism*, pp.305–6.
13. Ibid.
14. Donoghue, *Kissing the Witch*, p.27.
15. Ibid, p.34.
16. J. Grimm and W. Grimm, *Complete Fairy Tales* (London: Routledge, 2002).
17. A. Carter, *The Bloody Chamber* (New York: Harper & Row, 1979).
18. A. Sexton, *Transformations* (New York: Houghton Mifflin, 1971).
19. L.A. Hutcheon, *Poetics of Postmodernism: History, Theory, Fiction* (London: Routledge, 1988).
20. Ibid., p.6.
21. J. Butler, *Gender Trouble: Feminism and the Subversion of Identity* (New York and London: Routledge Classics, 2006), p.200.
22. Donoghue, *Kissing the Witch*, p.6.
23. J. Kristeva, *Powers of Horror: An Essay on Abjection* (New York: Columbia University Press, 1982), p.2.
24. Donoghue, *Kissing the Witch*, pp.55–6.
25. Grimm and Grimm, *Complete Fairy Tales*, p.222.

26. L. Rohrer, 'Wearing the Red Shoes: Dorothy and the Power of the Female imagination in "The Wizard of Oz" ', *Journal of Popular Film and Television*, 23, 4 (Winter 1996), p.146.
27. Donoghue, *Kissing the Witch*, p.3.
28. Ibid., p.108.
29. D. Cavallaro, *French Feminist Theory: An Introduction* (London: Continuum, 2003), p.81.
30. V.B. Leitch (ed.), *The Norton Anthology of Theory and Criticism* (New York and London: Norton & Co., 2001), p.2166.
31. Donoghue, *Kissing the Witch*, p.121.
32. Ibid, p.133.
33. R. Jackson, *Fantasy: The Literature of Subversion* (London: Routledge, 1981), p.90.
34. Donoghue, *Kissing the Witch*, pp.133, 134.
35. T. de Lauretis, 'Sexual Indifference and Lesbian Representation', in P. White (ed.), *Figures of Resistance: Essays in Feminist Theory* (Chicago, IL: University of Illinois Press, 2007), p.53.
36. M. Eagleton, *Feminist Literary Criticism* (London: Longman, 1991), p.227.
37. J. Kristeva, 'About Chinese Women', reprinted in Eagleton (ed.), *Feminist Literary Criticism*, p.83.
38. Donoghue, *Kissing the Witch*, p.47.
39. Ibid., p.180.
40. P. Palmer, 'Lesbian Gothic: Genre, Transformation, Transgression', *Journal of Gothic Studies*, 6, 1 (May 2004), p.122.
41. Donoghue, *Kissing the Witch*, p.6.
42. Barthes, *Image, Music, Text*, p.4.
43. Donoghue, *Kissing the Witch*, pp.227, 228.
44. I am grateful to Dr Constanza del Río Álvaro, from the University of Zaragoza (Spain), for her feedback on my earlier research on Emma Donoghue's work.

PART 5
POP CULTURE AND HEROIC MISFITS

19

Folk Devils and Moral Panic: Sedition, Subversion and Sensation in Victorian Popular Culture

Michael Flanagan

Stan Cohen, in his study of youth culture, *Folk Devils and Moral Panics*, writes, 'Societies appear to be subject, every now and then, to periods of moral panic. A condition, episode or group of persons emerges to become defined as a threat to society. The moral barricades are manned by editors, bishops, politicians and other right-thinking people.' According to Cohen, such modern youth subcultures, from beatniks to skinheads, 'have occupied a constant position as "folk devils": visible reminders of what we should not be'.[1] An early modern example of Cohen's 'folk devils' concept may be found in Victorian Britain, a period in which complex issues of class and literacy became enmeshed in a prototypical version of what we now term 'youth culture'. Rapidly developing media formats such as, for example, the so-called 'penny dreadful' genre offered newly literate young people the opportunity to reach outside conventional value-teaching institutions (such as the family and school) for stimulation and entertainment. The ensuing 'moral panic' around such issues as anti-Establishment political pamphlets, the anti-rich sentiment of much popular literature or the glorification of criminality in the 'Bloods'[2] offer us a fascinating insight into how the middle class responded, controlling and absorbing possible dissent and eventually redirecting the latent violence and potential rebellion of the Victorian sensational literature crisis for its own ends.

In the latter half of the nineteenth century the middle class emerged as a dominant class in British society, partially replacing the rural gentry. Britain's towns and cities are full of the homes they made for themselves. The hand of the middle class was everywhere – in government and national politics, in the churches, in societies and pressure groups, on the magistrates' bench and in governing trusts, foundations, schools and colleges.[3] Giving voice to urbanization and industrialization they emphasized competition, thrift, prudence, self-reliance and personal achievement as opposed to privilege and inheritance. The moral terms of this outlook enabled the middle class to accommodate diversity. Being middle class was defined by taking responsibility for one's self, one's family and the community, but the precise terms of the place of the middle class in British society were open to individual interpretation.[4] What was certain, however, is that the concept of 'respectability' lay at the heart of middle-class life, with all that this entailed.[5] Education was a crucial agent in the drive towards a 'respectable' place in society, having as it did a critical bearing on one's position in life, marriage prospects and hopes for climbing the often precarious ladder of business or government advancement. For the Victorians, education began in the nursery.

The suppression of the folk tale and its replacement with a more acceptable representation of the popular lore of country life is an interesting aspect of the nineteenth-century British urban experience, part of what John K. Walton has termed 'the persisting tension between tradition and innovation in Victorian society'.[6] Middle-class urban dwellers were in the process of rejecting their rural roots.

The rough manners and earthy expression of previous narratives (the original 'Tom Thumb' is a good example) were considered too coarse and vulgar for the children of respectable middle-class society and thus underwent a process of sophistication. Victorian writers were presented with the opportunity to reshape the moral tale under the influence of a more refined and artificial style of 'fairy story' imported from the continent in the works of Perrault, the Brothers Grimm and Hans Christian Andersen. Parallel with this process of refinement, however, was a development which was to keep the old folk hero at the forefront of popular culture and indeed increase his popularity for British youth in a most unacceptable manner.

The Industrial Revolution had resulted in a population explosion in the manufacturing regions. The moral welfare of this underclass, if not their physical well-being, was of great concern to the respectable Establishment. The Sunday School Movement was one middle-class response to this situation. The aim of the Sunday Schools, whether run by Dissenters or Church of England patrons, was to teach the children of the poor to read the Bible. This raised a problem. Would they use the newly acquired skill of reading to study the scriptures or other improving works? Or would they read the unsuitable – old romances, tales of violence and superstition, full of the coarse jests which made the Tom Thumb chapbooks so popular?

Or, even more dangerous, would they read one of the many political pamphlets which had begun to circulate, some of which appeared to attack the roots of religion and social order?[7] Among the chapbooks and ballad sheets in the packs of the wandering pedlars, in town and village, were copies of revolutionary pamphlets like *The Rights of Man*. Far, far worse than Tom Thumb, was Tom Paine. Thomas Paine's pamphlet was a defence of the ideas of liberty, equality and fraternity, which the Establishment perceived as coming to a full and horrible expression in the French Revolution. Hawked along with copies of 'Jack the Giant Killer' and the 'Seven Champions of Christendom', it is said to have sold nearly a million copies in ten years in England. With a population of ten million, if this figure were even half true, the impact must have been enormous.

Bad harvests, industrial disruption and the economically exhausting war with Napoleon meant widespread discontent across Britain. There was a fruitful market, among former pupils of Sunday Schools or of the cheap village day schools run by a local dame, for radical pamphlets, for editions of poems by Byron and Shelley. Shelley's words, 'Shake your chains to earth like dew, Ye are many, they are few',[8] had a message that neither the hand-loom weaver nor the framework knitter made idle by new machinery could ignore. Neither the aristocracy nor the middle class could discount the potentially destabilizing impact of social disruption. The Establishment, both political and religious, was under threat.[9]

The expansion of the Victorian press and mass media paralleled in graphic form the rise of the Victorian city. The growth of printed information was faster even than the pace of Victorian urbanism and captured much of the latter's fractured, diverse and dynamic quality. New and heterogeneous populations of cities found in the press and mass media the ideal vehicle for reflecting and shaping public opinion and collective cultural identities. If few Victorians could afford prints or photographs, most could see them displayed in shop windows or through lantern-slides at school or church. By the beginning of the twentieth century, however, newspapers, magazines, photographs and printed ephemera of all kinds had proliferated to such an extent that few people could avoid encountering the printed word or image on a daily basis, even if they had wished to. The Victorian world was thus a distinctly graphic and visual production – a spectacle constructed as much from paper and glass as from bricks and iron.[10]

Improvements in printing technology had increased the ability of even the humblest publishers to greatly increase their output. These were businessmen who lost little time in supplying the urban factory workers with the escapist material that they craved. The massive expansion of the British railway system that distinguished the latter half of the nineteenth century enabled large quantities of cheap magazines and juvenile papers to be distributed rapidly from the printing press to the many channels that were created to supply the market. By the end of the century, W.H. Smith, for example, had expanded across Britain to supply an increasing demand for reading material. Railway bookstalls and an infinite number of backstreet shops were other examples of outlets which rose up to provide an increasingly literate population with the reading stimulation they desired.

A new genre of serial fiction, the 'penny dreadful', was created. This has become a familiar term for the penny-a-number serial story-parts, magazines and novelettes which purveyed cheap and sensational fiction for a mass readership in Britain from the 1830s onwards. In the last quarter of the century these serial productions came to refer more exclusively to tales for the young reader, many of whom were more literate following the 1870 Education Act.[11] These forms of popular literature were descendants both of chapbooks and broadsides and of Gothic novels such as Mrs Radcliffe's *The Mysteries of Udolpho*. Usually mass-produced by anonymous authors, they included everything that would sell, from *Varney the Vampire, or the Feast of Blood* to plagiarized Dickens stories under such titles as *Oliver Twiss*.[12]

By the 1840s there were penny dreadfuls with every sort of setting: historical, buccaneering, domestic, ghoulish. One writer, G.W.M. Reynolds, combined sensational stories of slum life and vice with schoolmasterly explanations of thieves' cant and card-sharping and passages of socialist propaganda. English and American writers pirated each other freely, relays of writers took turns at stories, and the successful tales were spun out endlessly with no regard for the shape of the plot. It is at this point that we see the reappearance of the old folk hero, a figure from the past that concerned parents had assiduously attempted to banish from the nursery. He was now to be reinvented in a more lurid and potentially corruptive incarnation.

The most notorious creation of the early penny dreadfuls was *Sweeney Todd, the Demon Barber of Fleet Street*, who first appeared in about 1840. Penny dreadfuls were not at first explicitly aimed at the juvenile market, but they were consumed by the young from the beginning, and trying them out on the office boy was a recognized editorial technique.[13] To a greater or lesser extent the legends of *Dick Turpin, Jack Shepard, Rob Roy* and *Spring-Heeled Jack* were created by early penny dreadfuls; respectable persons bewailed the glamorizing of criminals and the presentation of the rich, the aristocratic and the clergy as fair game. One Dick Turpin saga, Edward Viles's *Black Bess, or The Knight of the Road*, ran to 254 weekly parts; it was probably the longest serial by a single penny dreadful author, and was published whole in 1868. Less lasting than Turpin's was the fame of *The Wild Boys of London* (1866) whose habitat was the London sewers and whose adventures involved bodysnatching doctors, a barebreasted woman flogged by her uncle, ravishings, mutinous convict ships and countless corpses. The rerun of the serial was stopped by the police.[14]

When it became obvious that these publications actually attracted the juvenile market, some publishers, perhaps most notably E.J. Brett, realized that there was money to be made in broadening the appeal of their product. The result of this was the creation of a middle ground in juvenile popular literature and the beginning of the evolution of a new type of heroic role model which has arguably survived to this day in British popular culture. The character of Jack Harkaway (first appearing in the *Boys of England*) is one such result of this new movement away from outright blood and thunder and towards a compromise, one that would be acceptable to a people coming to terms with the intrinsic adventure of late-nineteenth-century New Imperialism. The introduction of Jack Harkaway in 1871 saw the circulation of the *Boys of England* rise from an already healthy 150,000 issues to a phenomenal 250,000. Unlike other famous Victorian schoolboys, Jack Harkaway shows no remorse for wildness. In the eyes of his creator, his role was to win the young reader from the penny dreadful and so restraint was inappropriate. But every excess in Harkaway's behaviour is shown as justified by the villainy of the villains, more often than not foreigners. Harkaway draws on the appeal of the 'rebel rogue' tradition, but unlike them he is on the right side.[15]

Reinforcements in the battle against the penny dreadful were moving up in the shape of the Amalgamated Press comics of the 1890s, owned by the Harmsworth Brothers (later to be Lords Northcliffe and Rothermere, founders of the *Daily Mail* and *Daily Mirror* and proprietors, for a while, of *The Times*). They launched their comics, not at a penny but at a halfpenny. They promised that 'these healthy tales of mystery and adventure will kill stone dead' the opposition. First *Marvel* (1893), then *Union Jack* (1894), *Boy's Herald* (1903), *Gem* (1907) and *Magnet* (1908), to name but a few, made clear where the Harmsworths drew the line on the rebel rogue of the penny dreadful. 'No tales of boys rifling their employers' cash boxes and making off to foreign lands', they promised.[16]

Where earlier publishers dealt in thousands or tens of thousands in what would, in modern publishing parlance, be termed 'units', Amalgamated Press were to deal in millions. Aided by the latest rotary press and colour printing developments, the Harmsworths did win the field from the backstreet firms. The penny dreadful was killed by substituting the 'ha'penny dreadfuller', as A.A. Milne ironically remarked. The chief aim of the publishers of this more sanitized product was to swing the spirit of violent adventure away from the anti-rich sentiment of earlier popular literature. Not surprisingly then, the closing of the nineteenth century saw the arrival of detective heroes, mostly inspired by Conan Doyle's Sherlock Holmes (1891). Sexton Blake and Nelson Lee are the best known of these fictional creations. Not short of cash themselves, these detective heroes employed boy assistants from poor circumstances. Being 'unofficial' they could use any means in fighting their chosen foes, while often ridiculing the police. They were at one and the same time outside the law and on the right side of it. Other developments on the popular literary landscape were to further the process of civilizing the penny dreadful and bring juvenile literature into the mainstream of conventional national taste, including the development of such 'externalized' fictional genres as Science Fiction, Invasion Scare narrative and Yellow Peril material.[17]

Parallel with the development of these new genres, the latter decades of the nineteenth century witnessed a reorientation of the manner in which popular literature was to be used to support contemporary priorities in such fields as imperial propaganda and the inculcation of patriotism across the social classes. This was achieved in two principal ways. Firstly, historical themes from Britain's history were taken and, as it were, 'reprocessed' in such a manner as to underpin basic tenets of Victorian and Edwardian culture. Judith Rowbotham has labelled this use of the past as a propaganda tool for the present 'History with a Purpose'.[18] Britain's history had no shortage of exciting events or heroic figures to offer the readers of the boy's papers on a weekly or monthly basis. Popular themes included the Indian Mutiny, the Napoleonic Wars (with Nelson at sea and Wellington on land), Marlborough's military campaigns and stories of the Romans, Saxons and Vikings.

The second principal way in which popular literature was to be used to communicate the moral and social agenda of the day was through using contemporary events to illustrate Britain's greatness, the natural superiority of the British race, the inevitability of their international hegemony and the invincibility of British heroic masculinity. This style of writing was to coincide with the development of a national movement within Britain towards the popularization of economic and military expansion that is termed 'New Imperialism'.[19]

The literary dilemma of 'lawless adventure' could now be legitimately solved abroad – the widespread public preoccupation with the international role of Britain that was to be such a noted feature of the late-Victorian period was to offer an unexpected solution to the problem of violence in popular literature for boys. If for both Cecil Rhodes and Salvation Army leader William Booth the Empire was the 'way out' for social problems, so it was for the writer or editor wondering what next to do with the violent but law-abiding hero. When there are no more pranks that Jack Harkaway can legitimately play on the much-abused staff of various schools, his creator sends him abroad, where his talent for fighting foul can be used without restraint.

The transition from school to Empire, written into the prospectus of Cheltenham or Wellington, is also written into the school story. As school-story writer Harold Avery put it in 1895, 'in the hard fight to save his goal we see in those grey eyes the first kindling of that light' which will shine when 'he stands face to face with danger and even death'.[20] From the 'breathless hush of the close' to the bloodstained desert sand, where 'the voice of a schoolboy rallies the ranks', in Henry Newbolt's poem, is a logical and intended step. It excites the reader without inciting him to break open the cash box.[21] Unofficial but righteous violence was the rule. In his *Fifth Form at St Dominic's* in 1887, Reed laid down that 'a pair of well-trained, athletic schoolboys with a plucky youngster to help them ... are a match any day for twice that number of half tipsy cads'.[22]

Outrageous behaviour legitimized calls for an outrageous enemy. As Isabel Quigly points out, stories both upmarket and down contain every current 'attitude compressed and therefore concentrated, not just snobbery and jingoism ... but uglier things like anti-Semitism and racism'. 'A trio of darkies', 'a nigger, a genuine nigger' – these turn-of-the-century phrases strike the modern reader in the face, but they were written with unconscious ease as the unjustifiable was justified.[23] The loyal elements in the lower class could be recruited to fight 'lesser breeds without the law' both at home and abroad.[24] Meanwhile, in the real world, in semi-military organizations like the Boys' Brigade, founded by a Nonconformist in 1883, tens of thousands of working-class youngsters were taught 'habits of obedience, reverence, discipline, self respect and all that tends towards a true Christian manliness'. By 1900 the Boys' Brigade had earned its founder a knighthood.[25]

Between the dusty pages of *Gem, Magnet, Union Jack, Chums, British Bulldog* and the dozens of other examples of boys' papers which were to evolve in response to the Victorian desire for suitable juvenile leisure reading material are to be found a unique insight into how a society uses history to reinforce its ideals and philosophy in terms of didactic fiction.

In late-Victorian fiction for boys, issues of race, class and gender were inextricably woven into the fabric of the story. Narrative structure now removed much potential subversion away from the familiar surroundings of home – except in detective fiction, and even then the enemy to the suburban status quo was frequently a foreign one. Exotic locations provided the background for the pursuit of a more subliminal rationale. The Spanish Main, Northwest Frontier, South Sea Islands, Canadian Rockies, Icy Wastelands of the Poles, Stormy China Seas or Steamy African Jungles placed the youthful reader in exciting and thrilling situations. In these locations the supporting cast of treacherous Indians, pigtailed, inscrutable Chinese or man-eating Negroes played their part as the 'Other' – the primitive, the pagan, the savage: dark contrasts with the security of the middle-class home. [26] All would be well in the end; the youthful hero would succeed, and through this process, basic and unchanging stereotypes reinforced. The often comic and occasionally threatening qualities of the foreigner were held up to ridicule, and by extension the superiority of British pluck in adversity re-emphasized. The militarization of British society was a product of the many 'little wars of empire' that distinguished the latter half of the Victorian era. Now there was endless opportunity for legitimate heroic endeavour on a global scale, a chivalric ideal that would be shattered in the harsh reality of the industrial carnage of the Western Front. By the interwar years the conventional form of the hero had evolved into a cool, detached and cynical figure, as described by Richard Usborne in *Clubland Heroes*:

They led good lives, these decent fellows. They had had good wars, and used the slang of the trenches mixed up with the slang of sport. Their money was plentiful. They were footloose and quick on the trigger. Those who operated abroad were 'scornful men who diced with death under a naked sky'. Their test of friendship with another man was whether they'd like to be with him in a scrap. They carried the insularity of the Englishman with them to the ends of the earth, even if they had a gift for foreign lingos. In bush and kraal, Hoxton or Clarges Street, Valparaiso or Singapore, they stood up for 'The King', killed the dirty dago who called them 'dirty Englishman', treated women as sacred, kept fit, shot the pip out of the ace of diamonds at twenty paces, cultivated a pleasant, lazy drawl and a good pair of riding-boots, caught the flying knife in the bar-room brawl and hurled it back to pin the dago to the wall by the fleshy part of the arm.[27]

Everything underwent great change with the coming of the industrial revolution and an automated world:

'All that is solid melts into air.' Industrial capitalism tore up the earth, 'dissolved all fixed, fast, frozen relationships'[28] and created a new, turbulent world of motion, speed and change. The perpetual movement of modernity both thrilled and terrified the new citizens of the great industrial centres. It was – and is – experienced both as an explosive kind of liberation and as an annihilating state of disintegration and disorientation.[29]

It may indeed be argued that the effects of modernity had dissolved much of the previous conservatism of the Victorian printing industry and in the process created a genre that 'both thrilled and terrified' its readers. We can trace the progress of the British hero through society's efforts to comprehend and absorb the sedition of the political pamphlet, the subversion of the penny dreadful and the sensation of the graphic revolution. In the process of this Victorian revolution in popular literature we can see the roots of many of the attributes of the British heroic archetype. The hero required certain rebellious qualities (Dick Turpin), a wildness of nature and disregard for social convention (Jack Harkaway). A cool intelligence (Sherlock Holmes) allied with a spirited resourcefulness (Richard Hannay) were other necessary traits. He may be distinguished by a superior sense of arrogance, as in the example of Sanders of the River, and engage in casual racism, as did Biggles. He required a talent for enterprise, a notable characteristic of Dan Dare. We may follow the evolution of the hero on to the quintessential figure of the modern James Bond, the latest cinema incarnation of which, it may be suggested, is more in character with Ian Fleming's original creation, owing less to previous representations which tended to be elegant, urbane and self-mocking and more to the popular culture of a previous generation – the sensational, anti-Establishment spirit and occasionally sadistic violence of the penny dreadful era.

REFERENCES

Amigoni, D. (ed.), *Life Writing and Victorian Culture: The Nineteenth Century* (Aldershot: Ashgate, 2006).

Bloom, C., *Cult Fiction: Popular Reading and Pulp Theory* (Basingstoke: Macmillan, 1996).

Carpenter, H. and Prichard, M., *The Oxford Companion to Children's Literature* (Oxford: Oxford University Press, 1999).

Carpenter, K., *Penny Dreadfuls and Comics: English Periodicals and Comics for Children from Victorian Times to the Present Day* (London: Victoria and Albert Museum, 1983).

Cohen, S., *Folk Devils and Moral Panic* (Routledge: London, 2002).

Cox, J., *Take a Cold Tub, Sir! The Story of the Boys Own Paper* (Guildford: Lutterworth Press, 1982).

Cunliffe, B. et al. (eds), *The Penguin Atlas of British and Irish History* (Penguin: London, 2002).

Davenport-Hines, R., *Gothic: Four Hundred Years of Excess, Horror, Evil and Ruin* (New York: Northpoint Press, 1998).

Disher, M.W., *Victorian Song: From Dive to Drawing Room* (London: Phoenix House, 1955).

Dixon, B., *Catching Them Young: Political Ideas in Children's Fiction* (London: Pluto Press, 1977).

Dyos, H.J. and Wollf, M. (eds), *The Victorian City: Image and Realities*, Vol. 2 (London: Routledge & Kegan Paul, 1973).

Haining, P. (ed.), *The Penny Dreadful: Or, Strange, Horrid and Sensational Tales!* (London: Gollancz, 1975).

Haining, P., *A Pictorial History of Horror Stories: Two Hundred Years of Illustrations from the Pulp Magazines* (London: Treasure Press, 1985).

Herbert, R. (ed.), *The Oxford Companion to Crime and Mystery Writing* (New York and Oxford: Oxford University Press, 1999).

Houghton, W.E., *The Victorian Frame of Mind* (New Haven, CT, and London: Yale University Press, 1972).

Howarth, P., *Play up and Play the Game: The Heroes of Popular Fiction* (London: Eyre Methuen, 1973).

Leeson, R., *Reading and Righting: The Past, Present and Future of Writing for the Young* (London: William Collins, 1985).

Loftus, D., 'The Self in Society: Middle-Class Men and Autobiography', in D. Amigoni (ed.), *Life Writing and Victorian Culture: The Nineteenth Century* (Aldershot: Ashgate, 2006).

MacKenzie, J. (ed.), *The Victorian Vision – Inventing New Britain* (London: V&A Publications, 2001).

MacKenzie, J., 'Victorian Britain', in B. Cunliffe et al. (eds), *The Penguin Atlas of British and Irish History* (London: Penguin, 2002).

Morris, J., *Heavens Command: An Imperial Progress*, Pax Britannica Triptych, Vol. 1 (Harmondsworth: Penguin, 1981).

Newsinger, J., *Dangerous Men: The SAS and Popular Culture* (London: Pluto Press, 1997).

Paris, M., *Warrior Nation: Images of War in British Popular Culture 1850–2000* (London: Reaktion Books, 2000).

Rowbotham, J., *Good Girls Make Good Wives: Guidance for Girls in Victorian Fiction* (Oxford: Basil Blackwell, 1989).

Sutherland, J., *The Longman Companion to Victorian Fiction* (Harlow: Longman, 1988).

Turner, E.S., *Boys Will Be Boys* (Harmondsworth: Penguin, 1948).

Usborne, R., *Clubland Heroes* (London: Hutchinson, 1983).

Walton, J.K., 'Home and Leisure', in J. MacKenzie (ed.), *The Victorian Vision: Inventing New Britain* (London: V&A Publications, 2001), pp.51–75.

Williams, R., *The Long Revolution* (London: Hogarth Press, 1992).

Wilson, E., *Adorned in Dreams: Fashion and Modernity* (Piscataway, NJ: Rutgers University Press, 2003).

Wollf, M. and Fox, C., 'Pictures from the Magazines', in H.J. Dyos and M. Wollf (eds), *The Victorian City: Image and Realities*, Vol. 2 (London: Routledge & Kegan Paul, 1973), pp.559–82.

NOTES

1. S. Cohen, *Folk Devils and Moral Panic* (Routledge: London, 2002), p.1.
2. So called because they were descended from the 'blood and thunder' school of Gothic literature, featuring malignantly motivated villains seeking to possess the hearts and souls of characters made vulnerable because of their youth, gender and penniless condition. See R. Herbert (ed.), *The Oxford Companion to Crime and Mystery Writing* (New York; Oxford: Oxford University Press., 1999), p.41.
3. J. Mackenzie, 'Victorian Britain', in B. Cunliffe et al. (eds), *The Penguin Atlas of British and Irish History* (London: Penguin, 2002), p.194.
4. D. Loftus, 'The Self in Society: Middle-Class Men and Autobiography', in D. Amigoni (ed.), *Life Writing and Victorian Culture: The Nineteenth Century* (Aldershot: Ashgate, 2006), pp.67–86.
5. W.E. Houghton has an interesting analysis of Victorian respectability in his *The Victorian Frame of Mind* (New Haven, CT, and London: Yale University Press, 1972), pp.184–95.
6. J.K. Walton, 'Home and Leisure', in J. MacKenzie (ed.), *The Victorian Vision: Inventing New Britain* (London: V&A Publications, 2001), p.55.
7. For an insight into the official attitude towards the political dangers of popular fiction, see R. Williams, *The Long Revolution* (London: Hogarth Press, 1992), p.165.
8. R. Leeson, *Reading and Righting: The Past, Present and Future of Writing for the Young* (London: William Collins, 1985) p.58.
9. Ibid. pp.58–61.
10. M. Wollf and C. Fox, 'Pictures from the Magazines', in H.J. Dyos and M. Wollf (eds), *The Victorian City: Image and Realities*, Vol. 2 (London: Routledge & Kegan Paul, 1973), pp.559–82.
11. J. Sutherland, *The Longman Companion to Victorian Fiction* (Harlow: Longman, 1988), pp.497–8.
12. See R. Davenport-Hines, *Gothic: Four Hundred Years of Excess, Horror, Evil and Ruin* (New York: Northpoint Press, 1998), especially pp.147–8.
13. Extracts from T.P. Prest, 'Sweeny Todd' (1846) and J.M. Rymer, 'Varney the Vampire' (1840s) can be found in P. Haining (ed.), *The Penny Dreadful: Or, Strange, Horrid and Sensational Tales!* (London: Gollanez, 1975), pp.95–133.
14. H. Carpenter and M. Prichard, *The Oxford Companion to Children's Literature* (Oxford: Oxford University Press, 1999), pp.399–400. See also P. Haining, *A Pictorial History of Horror Stories: Two Hundred Years of Illustrations from the Pulp Magazines* (London: Treasure Press, 1985), pp.6–51.
15. K. Carpenter, *Penny Dreadfuls and Comics: English Periodicals and Comics for Children from Victorian Times to the Present Day* (London: Victoria and Albert Museum, 1983), p.12.
16. For an account of the development of serial literature for boys, see E.S. Turner, *Boys Will Be Boys* (Harmondsworth: Penguin, 1948). See also J. Cox, *Take a Cold Tub, Sir! The Story of the Boys Own Paper* (Guildford: Lutterworth Press, 1982).
17. C. Bloom, *Cult Fiction: Popular Reading and Pulp Theory* (Basingstoke: Macmillan, 1996).
18. J. Rowbotham, *Good Girls Make Good Wives: Guidance for Girls in Victorian Fiction* (Oxford: Basil Blackwell, 1989), pp.141–180.
19. See J. Morris, *Heavens Command: An Imperial Progress*, Pax Britannica Triptych, Vol. 1 (Harmondsworth: Penguin, 1981).
20. Leeson, *Reading and Righting*, p.97.
21. Ibid. The full text of Newbolt's poem, *Vita Lampada*, is available in M.W. Disher, *Victorian Song: From Dive to Drawing Room* (London: Phoenix House, 1955), p.55.

22. P. Howarth, *Play up and Play the Game: The Heroes of Popular Fiction* (London: Eyre Methuen, 1973), p.56.
23. E.Quigly, *The Heirs of Tom Brown* (Chatto & Windus, 1982), cited in Leeson, *Reading and Righting*, p.97.
24. Ibid.
25. Ibid. See M. Paris, *Warrior Nation: Images of War in British Popular Culture 1850–2000* (London: Reaktion Books, 2000), for a comprehensive account of the military nature of British society. See also J. Newsinger, *Dangerous Men: The SAS and Popular Culture* (London: Pluto Press, 1997).
26. B. Dixon, 'Empire – Fiction Follows the Flag', in Bob Dixon, *Catching Them Young: Political Ideas in Children's Fiction* (London: Pluto Press, 1977), pp.74–120, presents an interesting evaluation of the manner in which children's literature supported the imperial ideal.
27. R. Usborne, *Clubland Heroes* (London: Hutchinson, 1983), p.141.
28. M. Berman, *All That is Solid Melts into Air: The Experience of Modernity* (London: Verso, 1983), cited in E. Wilson, *Adorned in Dreams: Fashion and Modernity* (Piscataway, NJ: Rutgers University Press, 2003), p.60.
29. Wilson, *Adorned in Dreams*, p.60.

20

Disobeying Gilles Deleuze: Is Quentin Tarantino the Voice of Dissent?

Jenny O'Connor

As Ian Buchanan reminds us, Gilles Deleuze has long been accused of cultural snobbery.[1] Tarantino's artistic output can be regarded in the same vein as the pop music which Buchanan discusses, as his films revel in the repetitious refrain of the familiar, luring the viewer into an encounter with new-as-old, a postmodern cobbling together of formal cinematic advances and staple narratives that passes as time-warping originality. Buchanan does not extrapolate from Deleuze's writings in order to come to this observation; rather, Deleuze himself unequivocally states his position in *Negotiations* and could easily be referring directly to Tarantino and his pop-culture style. In discussing the cerebral (not necessarily intellectual) connections that cinema creates, he tells us that 'most cinematic production, with its arbitrary violence and feeble eroticism, reflects mental deficiency rather than any invention of new cerebral circuits'. Pop videos are the worst offenders of all, because they fail to fulfil their creative potential: 'they could have become a really interesting new field of cinematic activity', he tells us, 'but were immediately taken over by organized mindlessness. Aesthetics can't be divorced from these complementary questions of cretinization and cerebralization.'[2] Thus Deleuze, the philosopher who does not deal in binaries, polarizes high and low culture, reifying one and demonizing the other. This split can be seen in terms of a modernist/postmodernist dichotomy, wherein the modernist creation of experimental and original forms of art is contrasted with a postmodernist reliance on passive modes of consumption and the representation of mass culture.

In Deleuze's rethinking of cinema, he proceeds down a structuralist path, but it is a journey into a language at once familiar and altogether new. Deleuze attempts to think a new semiotics (that is an anti-semiotics) and introduces us to a whole new lexicon of the image, but while this at first appears to reinforce the binary between high and low art, it in fact reintroduces immanence as an antidote to the suffocating laws of structuralism. Consequently, Deleuze aims to create two works that are not about understanding or interpreting film, but about *thinking* film in new ways. Enter Quentin Tarantino, a purveyor of capitalist America, a consumer and provider of mass *cult*ure. Not only does Tarantino represent the anathema to the Deleuzian directorial ideal (in his enthusiastic ingestion into capitalism and popular culture), but he also plays with time through flashbacks and flashforwards that may be regarded in Deleuzian terms as meaningless. However, rather than creating binaries of good and bad, worthy and unworthy, perhaps we should instead examine Tarantino as a dissenter, as Deleuze's 'falsifier'. This is a term that Deleuze uses in *Negotiations* when describing his relationship with Félix Guattari. For Deleuze, a 'falsifier' is a mediator, a second term in a series that tests the concepts of the first term. Yet for Deleuze, Guattari is merely an interlocutor; what happens when Deleuze is presented with a falsifier that occupies the role of 'opposite' and challenges his theories to their limits? I will aim to assess what each contributes to the other in a mode of becoming; for as Deleuze articulates, 'these capacities of falsity to produce truth, that's what mediators are about'.[3] As Deleuze's falsifier, Tarantino puts his theories to the test, by asking whether a reimagined semiotics of modernist film that claims to resist hierarchies can coexist with a postmodern cinema that shamelessly revels in the cretinization of mass culture.

While Tarantino's cinema can be 'interpreted' using Deleuze's *Cinema* books, creating an instrument of interpretation is not the objective of Deleuze's work. *The Movement-Image* and *The Time-Image* do not serve to enable the theorization of cinema, but rather the exploration of its specifically dynamic characteristics. Nonetheless, a whole new way of thinking Tarantino's cinema is elicited from examining, for example, the opsigns and sonsigns (purely optical and sound images) that Deleuze discusses in his works on cinema. I will examine a number of examples from Tarantino's films in order to discuss the mutual becomings that result when they are brought into contact with one another, and to define the point at which Deleuze and Tarantino appear to fail each other. I will also discuss whether this means that Deleuze's theories, in their denial of the postmodern, in fact fail cinema itself. Tarantino is everything Tarkovsky or Godard is not; he is a purveyor of mass culture, a director who does not appear to take cinema 'seriously', a pulp fiction-maker. However, as

Buchanan rightly points out, 'His low regard for the popular notwithstanding, Deleuze does however provide several useful critical tools for its analysis.'[4] In Buchanan's essay, the main tool for analysis is pop music as refrain, as a way to de-territorialize capitalism from within. Buchanan goes on to discuss the possibilities invoked by the modernist crisis regarding art's lack of originality and newness. He articulates that pop music's absorption into the capitalist system can be seen as an inherent characteristic of a new form of art. This absorption signals a collective alteration in the social consciousness that is as powerful as any political or cultural line of flight (or escape). Thus, Tarantino, like pop music, tests the limits of Deleuze's work by defying the 'rules' that Deleuze defines for 'good' cinema. While Deleuze promotes the rhizome in *A Thousand Plateaus*, here he is arboreal, planting the seeds of hierarchical structuralist systems off which there *must* be found offshoots and lines of flight on which to experiment. These lines of flight are as integral to cinema as they are to any other mode of expression, and while Tarantino's and Deleuze's chronosigns (or time-images) are two different entities, it is not fair to say that Tarantino does not utilize the time-image in his own way.

In *Pulp Fiction*, Tarantino manages to achieve a 'direct presentation of time',[5] a Tarantinian version of Deleuze's time-image at least. Deleuze tells us that direct images of time are based on aberrant movements, are divorced from space and are unhinged from our everyday world. In effect, they are both true and false. As Ronald Bogue articulates:

> Deleuze distinguishes two kinds of chronosigns, those that concern *the order of time* and those that concern *time as series*, and in both kinds, the true and the false are rendered undecidable or inextricable, in the one case through a coexistence or simultaneity of different times, in the other through 'a becoming of potentialization, as series of powers'.[6]

The direct time-image is a crystal-image, representing various states of virtual and actual temporality. Tarantino explores the direct time-image in *Pulp Fiction* when Butch returns to his house to pick up his father's watch (itself a literal and symbolic measure of continually passing presents). Deleuze, in discussing the peaks of the present, articulates that in the scenario of a lost key (or in Butch's case, a lost watch) chronological time is eliminated as events that occur in continuous peaks of the present are concomitant. Instants of having the key and losing the key are not discernible; rather the events cause instants to interconnect and overlap. He tells us 'at the same time someone no longer has the key (that is, used to have it), still has it (had not lost it), and finds it (that is, will have it and did not have it)'.[7] Tarantino makes this explicit to us, not only in the simultaneity of Butch having the watch, losing the watch and finding the watch, but also in the crystal image of Vincent Vega's death. When he is shot by Butch, Vince is dead (used to be alive), alive (never dead) and both dead and alive (will be dead and was not dead). Tarantino does exactly what Deleuze describes in creating a powerful time-image here. He distributes 'different presents to different characters, so that each forms a combination that is plausible and possible in itself, but where all of them together are "incompossible" and where the inexplicable is thereby maintained and created'.[8] The incompossibility exists in this event occurring in each character's world, in which the event has already and not yet taken place. It also seems incompossible for Vince to be before us, both dead and alive at the same time. When Vince emerges from the bathroom in Butch's house, he fulfils one of Deleuze's criteria for the attainment of the time-image: 'he literally emerges from time rather than coming from another place'.[9] The time that he emerges from is in the future and simultaneously in the past, and also, of course, in the present. The false continuity of the film allows Vincent to be resurrected and to walk out of the diner in the final scene, tucking his gun into his shorts. Thus, the aberrant movement of simultaneously stepping into and out of past, present and future eschews space in favour of time, upsetting not only our actual time but the virtual present peaks of time of the film. Vince is always-already dead and resurrected, always-already true and false in the Deleuzian sense. Thus, Vince's emergence falsifies the truisms of fixed perceptions of time and chronological expectations of narrative.

In *Reservoir Dogs*, we are introduced to another facet of the crystal-image, which embodies this paradox of time. Mr Orange kills Mr Blonde in a hail of bullets and Freddy Moondike, Mr Orange's 'real' identity, is subsequently introduced to the audience. This identity however, is both true and false, both virtual and actual. The virtual in this case is 'the past that has never been present',[10] that which constitutes all actualities but is distinct from them. The commode story is such a virtuality and one that Mr Orange/Freddy Moondike uses to his advantage. It is a narrative aside that Freddy learns by rote in order to convince Joe and his gang of his credentials and it creates a time-image through its ultimate coalescence with the actual. The story involves Freddy taking a trip to the men's toilets in the middle of a convoluted drug deal. He brings the drugs with him in a carrier bag and encounters four police officers and a German Shepherd in the restrooms. We move from movement-image to time-image in this sequence and from objective to subjective perception (and back again).[11] As Freddy practices his performance in his apartment, the camera remains fixed, allowing him to walk in and out of the 'obsessive framing' of the image.[12] Thus, the director and the camera create a presence, a perception-image that is both objective and subjective simultaneously. Freddy goes through his lines, creating a false past for himself, a virtual recollection-image. The scene cuts to an empty urban concrete space as he continues to practise, and finally to the interior of a club, as he carries out the 'real' performance of the virtual story in front of Nice Guy Eddie, Joe and Mr White. At this point, Freddy is no longer Freddy, but Mr Orange, his virtual identity. During the story, which Mr Orange is narrating to his cohorts in the club, the camera cuts to reveal its virtual location, the gents' toilets. There are subsequent cuts back and forth until actual and virtual coalesce in the image, via the sonsign. Opsigns and sonsigns force ruptures in the sensory-motor schema, breaks or gaps in which access to pure sensorial events can occur.[13] The intolerable image is derived directly from them, from an immersion into the optical and the sonic realms of the image. In this case, the sonsign is the bark of the German Shepherd, which causes the action around Mr Orange to freeze, while he narrates his own virtual story within the story itself. The sonsign creates an intolerable image, a situation that Mr Orange cannot physically bear. It turns Mr Orange into an observer, or observer-narrator, while he watches and simultaneously narrates a virtual act of the past that never took place. Mr Orange tells his audience about the intolerable physical state that is brought on by a connection between the sonsign and the virtual:

> Every nerve ending, all of my senses, the blood in my veins, everything I have is just screaming 'take off man, just bail, just get the fuck outta there.' Panic hits me like a bucket of water. First there's the shock of it – bam! – right in the face. I'm just standing there, drenched in panic, and all these sheriffs lookin' at me and they know man, they can smell it, as sure as that fuckin' dog can, they can smell it on me ...[14]

The camera pans 360 degrees around Mr Orange during this virtual event, taking on a specifically filmic consciousness as it moves around a point of indiscernability between the virtual of the story and the actual sensations presented through the sonsigns of the image. The moment of crisis passes unremarkably, however, forming the humour of the story so vital to its believability, and the narration of the story emanates once again from the actuality of the club. However, there is another sonsign on the horizon. Virtual Mr Orange pushes the button on the hand dryer, and the sound of an aeroplane emerges. This sonsign again marks the intolerable image that paralyses all narratives. The pure sensorial experience of the out-of-context plane noise ruptures the linear narrative of the story, creating a moment of observation, of watching, of observing, that is a pure time-image. Mr Orange's wet hands are in close-up, in slow motion under the hand dryer; the police officers stop talking and stare; the dog barks noiselessly. It is not until the sonsign disappears that the narrative can continue in the virtual context (the police officers are mid-conversation when the sonsign is over) and in the actual context (we are back in the club with Joe telling Mr Orange: 'You knew how to handle that situation: just shit in your pants and dive in and swim'). Thus, it cannot be said that Tarantino does not experiment with the various sheets of past and the coexistence of peaks of present in his films. In this sequence, the time-image displaces certainty and fixity, splits virtual and actual and creates truisms of falsities and falsities of truisms. This film explores the layers of time that Deleuze ascribes to Resnais and to Welles, yet it reserves the right to be Oedipal in its climax (Mr White holds Mr Orange in a version of the Pieta, the gangster father figure that has just been 'fucked' by his surrogate son, a cop), to make pop culture references, to create empty signifiers. It is this paradoxical refusal of Deleuze's work to engage with 'unworthy' ideas that fascinates Slavoj Žižek in his book *Organs without Bodies*.[15]

Žižek rails against Deleuze's facile classification of Lacan's reading of Oedipus and his repudiation of the structuralism to which his philosophical theories are indebted. However, Deleuze anticipates Žižek's argument almost twenty years in advance and answers these charges in *Negotiations*. Here he says that

> the concepts philosophy introduces to deal with cinema must be specific, must relate specifically to cinema. You can of course link framing to castration or close-ups to partial objects but I don't see what that tells us about cinema. It's questionable whether the notion of the 'imaginary' even has any bearing on

cinema; cinema produces reality ... It's the same with linguistics: it also provides only concepts applicable to cinema from outside ...[16]

Deleuze's response is logical and his sensible approach is evidenced in the creation of a new (anti-)semiotics of the cinema that is not based in psychoanalysis. Yet Žižek, in the Art section of the book, focuses on a microanalysis of Hitchcock's films rather than an exploration of Deleuze's contribution to cinema. He bounds from references to the movement-images and time-images to the Lacanian 'objet petit a' (the unattainable object of desire, or lack) to Hitchcock as anti-Platonic. Yet nowhere does he tackle the most obvious of paradoxes with regard to Deleuze's anti-psychoanalytic stance: the fact that Deleuze fetishizes cinema itself. If Žižek really wants to take 'Deleuze from behind', perhaps the most fertile ground is not the *'Hegelian buggery of Deleuze'* but the Deleuzian buggery of cinema.[17] While Žižek proceeds to apply a psychoanalytic reading of Hitchcock, he appears to overlook the deliciously rich psychoanalytic reading of Deleuze's work on cinema. We must return to Laura Mulvey's familiar 'Visual Pleasure and Narrative Cinema' to reveal the possibilities of such an investigation. Mulvey discusses fetishistic scopophilia, which she says, 'builds up the physical beauty of the object, transforming it into something satisfying in itself'. She underlines that fetishistic scopophilia 'can exist outside linear time as the erotic instinct is focused on the look alone'.[18] She proceeds with examples from Hitchcock to illustrate this point, just as Deleuze does when describing the transition from movement- to time-image and Žižek does in his exploration of psychoanalytic readings of art. Yet, as Mulvey discusses the magical space of the screen, which in her view is hermetically sealed, Deleuze explores the fact that 'we no longer know what is imaginary or real, physical or mental ... not because they are confused, but because we do not have to know and there is no longer even a place from which to ask'.[19] Pure opsigns and sonsigns replace motor actions to create a cinema of sensation, with the primary importance on seeing. That Deleuze places great importance on seeing and observing in order to bring the time-image into being is evidence of his own fascination with the look. An important factor here is the intolerable image, an instant within cinema in which the character (or indeed the viewer) sees something that creates an abundance of affect, creating a pure optical situation, 'a cinema of the seer and no longer of the agent'.[20] However, while 'the camera's look is disavowed' in Mulvey,[21] in

Deleuze, the camera develops a consciousness of its own, which is no longer 'defined by the movements it is able to follow or make, but by the mental connections it is able to enter into'.[22] Thus, Deleuze and Mulvey diverge, yet the resonance of scopophilic fetishization remains. Deleuze is, as Claire Perkins describes, a 'cinephile', a lover of cinema, or rather a desirer of cinema. This cinematic desire is apprehended again and again through the look, that look that defies time and creates a pure image of its own, the scopophilic-image. Even more interesting is that this is a point at which Tarantino and Deleuze really do converge.

Tarantino is a fetishist of popular culture, consuming graphic art, TV programmes and blaxploitation films,[23] and creating a postmodern homage to them in his own films. He too is a cinephile who is fascinated by the look, by watching and re-watching the same incident through different or disembodied viewpoints, by allowing the camera to gain a consciousness that is never settled or fixed. This convergence of interests can also be explored through Žižek's description of Deleuze as 'the ideologist of late capitalism',[24] a position that Deleuze would almost certainly dispute. Žižek finds Deleuze and Guattari's approach to global capitalism to be far less revolutionary than it first appears and accuses them of *'reflecting*, rather than resisting, the deterritorialized flows of global capitalism'.[25] Just as Deleuze overlooks pop music, he also misses the potential of capitalism to create affects and becomings, to achieve what postmodernism also achieves in the combination of unlikely pairings. In *Pulp Fiction*, the postmodern and the fascination with capitalism coalesce, and nowhere more than in the Jack Rabbit Slims sequence. Pulling up to the restaurant, Vincent and Mia Wallace begin to converse in a style that recalls 1950s movies. They call each other 'Daddy-o' and 'kitty cat', 'cowboy' and 'cowgirl'. The waiter also calls Mia 'Peggy Sue'. The overt desire to explore past sheets of time through moments in the present is echoed in the venue itself. Marilyn Monroe and Zorro serve tables and, as the camera rests on their side profiles, a screen behind shows black-and-white images of cars, trams and people travelling through another era. Tarantino makes good use of diner scenes in many of his films, utilizing the specifically American space of capitalist ingestion in order to explore questions of consumerist behaviour in postmodern society.[26] In this case, the preoccupation with exploring the intricacies of capitalist society is combined with Tarantino's own cinematic fetishism, where 'real' and 'virtual' characters in Jack Rabbit Slims can be told apart by someone with a 'true' knowledge of popular cinematic history. Yet a replica of a Hollywood star of the movement-image era comes free with every meal, enabling us to sample them, fresh from the past, yet also from the present, through consumption. Žižek and Tarantino both explore the possibilities of capitalism in order to challenge Deleuze. Žižek returns to Lacan to make his point, claiming that the potential of capitalism to create new types of affect is overlooked:

> ... what if what appears an obstacle is effectively a positive condition of possibility, the element that triggers and propels the explosion of affective productivity? What if, consequently, one should precisely, 'throw out the baby with the dirty bath water' and renounce the very notion of erratic affective productivity as the libidinal support of revolutionary activity?[27]

Tarantino, on the other hand, returns to the image itself. By tethering the time-image to an inherent capitalism that lives and breathes in the image itself, he creates an image that heightens our awareness of the consumerism of the present, while acknowledging our nostalgia for the movement-images of the past. The resulting postmodern image is liberating, not restrictive; exploratory and affective, not flat; full with meaning on the surface, not empty.

This is the point at which Tarantino and Deleuze must separate, for they will never be compatible enough to live together harmoniously. Yet, the question remains: does Deleuze fail Tarantino by excluding his type of cinema from his taxonomy of images? And if so, does this mean that Deleuze fails cinema itself? I do not believe so; or at least, this failure is not intentional. Deleuze wrote two books on cinema that draw on previous knowledge, yet are entirely unique in their primary aspiration. They desire to reflect a 'cinesexuality' – what Patricia McCormack describes as the altering effect of cinema, the 'unique moment of desire only available to us through that "cinema" feeling: cinema as a lover we take, a form of sexuality that is not translatable to any other circumstance'.[28] Thus, it is not film theory, it is not semiotics, it is not a manual for the interpretation of cinema. It is designed to encourage the reader to experience cinema itself, to explore movement- and time-images rather than focus on representations and readings of the image. Yet, these works make assumptions about a reader's prior knowledge of film, about a familiarity with philosophy in general, and with Deleuze's philosophies in particular, that obscure their aspirations. However, while I believe that Deleuze can be accused of being overly complicated and difficult to understand, he cannot be charged with failing cinema. His challenge to us is to persevere and to dedicate ourselves to the task of exploring our own bodily connections to cinema. Whether he fails Tarantino and other expressions of postmodernist film is another matter. By excluding postmodernism entirely from his taxonomy, he disregards it, effectively throwing it on the trash heap of 'bad' cinema. Nonetheless, Deleuze and Tarantino's cinematic works enrich each other, each challenging and testing the images the other creates. Above all, Tarantino operates as Deleuze's falsifier, interrogating his concepts and creating a dialogue about what constitutes 'worthy' cinema.

REFERENCES

Bogue, R., *Deleuze on Cinema* (New York and London: Routledge, 2003).
Botting, F. and Wilson, S., *The Tarantinian Ethics* (London and Thousand Oaks, CA: SAGE, 2001).
Buchanan, I., 'Deleuze and Pop Music', *Australian Humanities Review*, August–October 1997, http://www.australianhumanitiesreview.org/archive/Issue-August-1997/buchanan.html.
Deleuze, G., *Cinema 1: The Movement-Image* (1983), trans. H. Tomlinson and B.Habberjam (London: Continuum, 2005).
Deleuze, G., *Cinema 2: The Time-Image* (1985), trans. H. Tomlinson and R. Galeta (London: Continuum, 2005).
Deleuze, G., 'Mediators', in *Negotiations* (1985), trans. M. Joughin (New York: Columbia University Press, 1990).
MacCormack, P., 'A Cinema of Desire: Cinesexuality and Guattari's Asignifying Cinema', *Women: A Cultural Review*, 16, 3 (2005), pp.340–55.
Mulvey, L., 'Visual Pleasure and Narrative Cinema', in. S. Thornham (ed.), *Feminist Film Theory* (Edinburgh: Edinburgh University Press, 1999), pp.58–69.
Parr, A. (ed.), *The Deleuze Dictionary* (Edinburgh: Edinburgh University Press, 2005).
Reservoir Dogs, film, directed by Quentin Tarantino. USA: Dog Eat Dog Productions Inc., 1992.
Sinnerbrink, R., 'Nomadology or Ideology? Žižek's Critique of Deleuze', *Parrhesia*, 1 (2006), pp.62–87.
Žižek, S., *Organs without Bodies: On Deleuze and Consequences* (London and New York: Routledge, 2004).

NOTES

1. I. Buchanan, 'Deleuze and Pop Music', *Australian Humanities Review*, August–October 1997, http://www.australianhumanitiesreview.org/archive/Issue-August-1997/buchanan.html, p.1.
2. G. Deleuze, 'Mediators', in G. Deleuze, *Negotiations* (1985), trans. M. Joughin (New York: Columbia University Press, 1990), p.60.
3. Ibid., p.126.
4. Buchanan, 'Deleuze and Pop Music', p.2
5. G. Deleuze, *Cinema 2: The Time-Image* (1985), trans. H. Tomlinson and R. Galeta (London: Continuum, 2005) p.37.
6. R. Bogue, *Deleuze on Cinema* (New York and London: Routledge, 2003), p.135.
7. Deleuze, *Cinema 2*, p.98.
8. Ibid.
9. Ibid., p.37.

10. A. Parr (ed.), *The Deleuze Dictionary* (Edinburgh: Edinburgh University Press, 2005), p.297.
11. G. Deleuze, *Cinema 1: The Movement-Image* (1983), trans. H. Tomlinson and B. Habberjam (London: Continuum, 2005), p.74.
12. Ibid., p.71.
13. Indeed, it can also be said that the sensory-motor schema attempts to disrupt any purely sensory immersion in the image; it can be seen as 'a kind of circuit breaker for controlling image-excitations'. Ibid., p.21.
14. *Reservoir Dogs*, film, directed by Quentin Tarantino. USA: Dog Eat Dog Productions Inc., 1992.
15. S. Žižek, *Organs without Bodies: On Deleuze and Consequences* (London and New York: Routledge, 2004).
16. Deleuze, *Negotiations*, pp.58–9.
17. Žižek, *Organs without Bodies*, pp.45, 48.
18. L. Mulvey, 'Visual Pleasure and Narrative Cinema', in S. Thornham (ed.), *Feminist Film Theory* (Edinburgh: Edinburgh University Press, 1999), p.65.
19. Deleuze, *Cinema 2*, p.7.
20. Ibid. p.2.
21. Mulvey, 'Visual Pleasure and Narrative Cinema', pp.68–9.
22. Deleuze, *Cinema 2*, p.22.
23. Exploitation movies that specifically targeted urban black audiences in 1970s America.
24. Žižek, *Organs without Bodies*, p.184.
25. R. Sinnerbrink, 'Nomadology or Ideology? Žižek's Critique of Deleuze', *Parrhesia*, 1 (2006), p.63.
26. F. Botting and S. Wilson, *The Tarantinian Ethics* (London and Thousand Oaks, CA: SAGE, 2001), pp.35, 42, 44, 61, 117, 126.
27. Žižek, *Organs without Bodies*, p.185.
28. P. MacCormack, 'A Cinema of Desire: Cinesexuality and Guattari's Asignifying Cinema', *Women: A Cultural Review*, 16, 3 (2005), pp.341–2.

21

'Sinne Laochra Fáil': Heroism and Heroes in the Work of Pádraig Ó Cíobháin

Sorcha de Brún

In his seminal novel on the suppression of dissent and the totalitarian nightmare, *1984*, the writer George Orwell (1903–50) describes the nature of oligarchical rule as:

> not the father-to-son inheritance, but the persistence of a certain worldview and a certain way of life, imposed by the dead upon the living. A ruling group is a ruling group so long as it can nominate its successors. The Party is not concerned with perpetuating its blood but with perpetuating itself. Who wields power is not important, provided that the hierarchical structure remains the same.[1]

Under the watchful eye of the Thought Police and Big Brother, citizens of Oceania are under the illusion that they are at war with their neighbours, but this is, in fact, an 'imposture', one that serves the political function of preserving the 'special mental atmosphere that a hierarchical society needs'.[2] The idea of the maintenance of the fundamental structures of a particular society by one group, and the attendant efforts by another group to usurp that power, seems to me to bear a striking similarity to many of the struggles between warring factions that can be perceived within the Irish language heroic tradition. And if heroism is one of the central elements of the artistic vision of the subject of this paper, the Kerry novelist and short story writer Pádraig Ó Cíobháin, it is noteworthy that he frequently parodies the tradition, thereby upsetting the hierarchical structures 'imposed by the dead upon the living'.[3] In this paper, I will show how a particular conception of heroism in the Irish tradition is reflected in Ó Cíobháin's work, a conception that is strongly identified with the notion of hierarchies in society. I will show how Ó Cíobháin succeeds in casting his singular literary creations in such a manner that they become an embodiment of dissent within the communities which they inhabit, and that this dissent is integral to his work. I will begin by examining the conception of heroism in the Irish language heroic tradition, both literary and oral, and go on to look at how this has influenced some of Ó Cíobháin's writings.

The French scholar Marie-Louise Sjoestedt describes the etymology of the word *laochas*, the Irish word for heroism, as deriving from Latin, *laecus*, meaning 'he who bears arms'.[4] The Latin writers in Ireland in the seventh century employed the word *laicus* to describe those who plundered the countryside, and the writer Seathrún Céitinn described 'plunderers' in his comprehensive history of Ireland, *Foras Feasa ar Éirinn*. According to Céitinn's account, these were bandits who roamed Ireland, attacking and robbing villages and towns.[5] In Old Irish, the word *oc* meant hero, or *laoch*, and at this point one sees an emerging feature, which seems to mark a shift in how heroism was conceived: this word eventually became *óc-laoch*, thereby twinning the conceptions of youth and heroism. Heroes or *laochra*, then, exhibited certain characteristics, and these give us a composite picture of youth, speed and agility, love, strength and bravery. The traits of the hero and the circumstances of his life can be summarized as follows: the clandestine circumstances in which the hero is born are usually surrounded by mystery and uncertainty; his birth and the early years of his life take place in total secrecy; and he may be given a name at birth that is subsequently changed. An extraordinary youth, and usually one that is highly idealized, follows his early years. In general, the relationship of which he is conceived is forbidden in that it remains outside the parameters of what society deems to be regular conduct. His life is a brief one, and he pursues excellence in all he does, as in the case of the Homeric code.[6] And although the hero enjoys what Ó Cíobháin has described as a honeyed youth, 'Lúnasa meala',[7] he can also be *díthir*, of no fixed abode, or *écland*, having no identifiable next of kin. As a precursor to an analysis of Ó Cíobháin's novels and short stories, we may ask what the literary intention is when a writer makes indirect and direct references to heroism in his work. Declan Kiberd provides a satisfactory answer to this question with regard to the publication of Lady Gregory's *Cuchulainn of Muirthemne* in 1902. He stipulates that the use of such stories from the heroic period is 'a technique of exploring contemporary issues by means of narratives set in the past'.[8] As Sjoestedt notes, however, the heroic tradition is dualistic by nature, in that we can identify the existence of a hero within the tribe as well as a hero outside the tribe. The hero of dissent is the iconoclast who does not conform to the prevailing dominant or orthodox views and who lives with his band of warriors in the *fásach*, the desert, where this can be understood in the figurative as well as the literal sense. It is this hero who interests us most with regard to the work of Pádraig Ó Cíobháin, because he exists in a place apart from the centres of power, one with its own unique political culture and praxis.

If we take the theme of youth as being of central importance to the idea of the hero, one need look no further than the story 'Bús Allais, a Gharsúin', for an example of Ó Cíobháin's parodying of the Fiannaíocht story of Oisín and Tír na nÓg. However, Ó Cíobháin has inverted the story and a parody of elements of the original confronts us. Rather than an old man returning from Tír na nÓg and being baptized by Saint Patrick, we have a young boy overtly rejecting what that baptism represents. All the terms of the youth of the hero are fulfilled in this short story, where the child hero is in the period of his life that leads up to separation from his mother as protector.[9] Ó Cíobháin refers directly to the goddess Aphrodite, remarking that she too would live 'in this town', 'chónódh Afradaité ar an mbaile seo, leis'.[10] Aphrodite herself, then, appears to represent a succubus for the growing teenager's fantasies. The story centres around a boy called Bill who is in his early teens, and on his observations of life which Ó Cíobháin narrates through a series of internal disquisitions. Bill perceives the local culture where the clergy are regarded with uncritical reverence as one akin to serfdom and one in which the community are portrayed as vassals of the Church. The secrecy surrounding his conception and birth are mentioned only when he claims that he does not know who fathered him: 'cén chú a chac mé'.[11]

The use of the word *cú*, hound, to denote the mysterious figure of his father, could be a reference to the hero Cúchulainn, although Bill appears to have far more in common with the Irish hero Oisín. Ó Cíobháin portrays Bill as one of a trinity and does so through use of multiple narrators. He feels a kind of brotherly concern towards all humanity, and the process of maturation from boyhood to manhood is carefully drawn by Ó Cíobháin, in particular with regard to the boy's name which changes from Liamín to Bill when the protagonist has gained a new level of confidence about his identity and his own innate strengths.[12] And, as in the case of many heroes in the Irish heroic tradition, it is the emotion of anger that is one of these hidden strengths and that acts as a catalyst for this new stage in Bill's development. This is what is required, indeed, for him to break away from the abhorrent and stifling society in which he finds himself. He views life as being temporal. 'Níl sa tsaol seo ach tamall', he claims, thereby debunking the myth of Oisín's experience of life in perpetuity in Tír na nÓg.[13] The climax of the story comes when he seems to undergo a kind of renewal of energy one morning upon his feet making contact with the floor of his bedroom, an incident that brings Oisín to mind, and whose palingenesis we witness when he is initiated into old age upon touching the ground on his return from Tír na nÓg. It is only through Bill's rage towards this 'balacs de bhaile',[14] 'bollocks of a town', and towards the people within it, his own neighbours, who are impossible to kill, 'domharaithe',[15] that he succeeds in overcoming the obstacles that he perceives have been placed before him:

> Las Bill suas i bhfeirg, gan éinne aige chun iad a throid ach é féin. Fearg a chuir áthas ar a chroí. Gomh dearg. Gráin mhairbh. Shín sé amach a ucht i gcoinne na gaoithe. B'é Bill Daibhí. B'é an baile Goliath. Goliath na fuarchúise, na cúlchainte agus an achasáin.[16]

> [Bill lit up in anger, nobody to fight them but himself. An anger that delighted him, a raging anger that scoured his heart. An abiding *hatred*. He pushed his chest out against the wind. He was Bill one moment, Daibhí the next, and this town was his Goliath. The Goliath of chilly indifference, of the backbiting word, of the cool insult.]

This reference to David and Goliath suggests that, as a newly spun warrior of sorts, he will be fighting against what Ó Cíobháin calls the old warriors, all of which seems to place him in the story as a sort of *ephebe*.[17] As can be seen from the above passage, he undergoes both a regeneration of his energies as well a transformation of his identity, no longer referring to himself as Liamín, but as Bill, the English-language equivalent of the Irish Liamín (a feature which reminds us of the story of Cú Chulainn, when the boy hero Setanta becomes known as Cúchulainn after slaying the hound of Culann).[18] The emphasis that Ó Cíobháin places on duality throughout the narrative, both English/Irish, male/female, appears to underline Bill's world view of life as being temporal and transitional (even optional), similar to the changes he himself is undergoing as a young man. Moreover, it alludes to the possibility of the existence of parallel yet opposing identities within the individual and the community. By the end of the story, he comes to understand that he has the power to take matters into his own hands and, by dint of free will, can take charge of his own destiny by transforming himself through means that are intrinsic to him. It is these apparently simple acts of transformation which he initiates himself – changing his name, choosing the female over the male – that comprise dissent in the story, because he, the individual, has chosen them, as opposed to the unforgiving community in which he lives. Most importantly, perhaps, they are acts of dissent which exist only so far as he imagines them: it is the exercising of his imagination that provides the fortress that will best protect him from any external threat, and behind which he can safely take refuge with his various identities.

If anger functions as a catalyst for dissent in a story such as 'Bús Allais, a Gharsúin', music and literature are often of equally major significance in the burgeoning development of the life of the young hero in Ó Cíobháin's stories. A considerable number of his short stories are narrated around the theme of music, either in terms of the musical heroes admired by the main protagonists, or else in terms of music as symbolizing a call to maturity and greater self-awareness. However, this process of maturity is usually accompanied by growing dissent in the peer group, resulting in the destruction of relationships. In 'Conas a bheidh nuair a bheidh Morrissey 40?' the relationship between Johnny Marr and Morrissey of the pop band The Smiths is posited in a modern, English context that seems to closely mirror that of Cúchulainn and his friend, Feardia, of the Irish heroic tradition.[19] Marr and Morrissey are described by Ó Cíobháin as soldiers, 'saighdiúirí', starting out in life together as best friends and attending school together, but who intend to wage war on life very soon: 'ag dul i mbun catha'.[20] In actual fact, they end up waging war on one another. The story narrates their imagined friendship and their subsequent parting, as a relationship that begins as one of comradeship in the grey, redbrick school that they attend, but that turns to one of combat, or 'comhraic',[21] similar to the relationship of Cúchulainn and Feardia whose relationship is destroyed as they are forced by circumstances of war to fight. And although their shared passion for music brings them together as schoolboys, it is Morrissey's and Marr's growing differences once they enter the public domain as performing musicians that destroys their relationship. The community, or the public domain, therefore, is portrayed in Ó Cíobháin's story as not only the site of dissent, but as the root cause of dissent because of the emphasis the system places on competition and performance.

In the quietly complex short story 'Aosánach', Ó Cíobháin explores the power of cinema as a means of youthful escape from the control of parents who have grown up in the poor mouth milieu of 1930s Ireland, the dry, imagined world of Éamonn De Valera, 'saol tur aislingeach Éamoinn De Valera'.[22] The gently dissenting voices in this story are that of the teenagers of this Gaeltacht locality, many of whom have left school early, and who seek an escape from the hard work of the small farms where they work shoulder to shoulder, 'gualainn ar ghualainn', with their fathers.[23] The main character is a young teenager who seeks a new hero to replace that of the old one, his father, and of an older youth, Tomás, who comes to embody for him the spirit of independence and freedom of thought. His friends have chosen the heroes of stage and screen as their idols, whose films they faithfully come to watch in a community hall. As frequently happens in Ó Cíobháin's stories, however, layers of dissent are gradually uncovered and are often privately expressed, where the narrator appears to empathize with those with whom he holds the greatest differences of opinion. During a public showing of the film *The Siege of Sidney Street*, the young teenager realizes that neither the idolization of film stars by his peers, nor the hankering after the ideals of De Valera's Ireland, can be a substitute for his personal quest for love. Rejecting all his recent experiences, if even temporarily, he turns his eyes instead to his beloved in the row behind him, looking forward to new experiences in the process.

There are aspects of Ó Cíobháin's work which strongly resemble aspects of James Joyce's, in particular the novel *An Gealas i Lár na Léithe*, which Ó Cíobháin himself has claimed to be a semi-autobiographical work. Ó Cíobháin is a great admirer of Joyce, and claims that he modelled the manner in which he portrayed himself in the novel on Joyce's Stephen Hero.[24] Interestingly, the family unit in Ó Cíobháin's novel provides the security in which the young person can fully express his identity, whereas the institution of the Church is portrayed as controlling and threatening to both the private life of the individual and of the family. The Church, therefore, becomes the primary site of remove and the main focus of dissent throughout the novel, expressed by the narrator in terms such as horror, 'uafáis', remove, 'ó chian'.[25] One can especially note similarites in theme between Joyce and Ó Cíobháin in the following passages where both are depicting a 16-year-old's encounter with a priest during confessional:

Tarraingíonn sé osna fhada thraochta. Líonann an bosca de chiúnas an uafáis. Ní bhfaighead maithiúnas. Ar deireadh sroicheann a ghuth mé ó chian.
'Cén t-aos tú?'
'Sé mbliana déag, a athair'.[26]

[He takes a long, tired breath. The confessional box fills with a sickening silence.
There would be no forgiveness here. At last, his voice comes to me from some distant place.
'What age are you?'
'Sixteen, father.']

The priest was silent. Then he asked:
– How old are you, my child?
– Sixteen, father.[27]

In its treatment of relations among the Gaeltacht people on the one hand, and between those people and the local church on the other, *An Gealas i Lár Na Léithe* is a dramatic portrayal of the fundamental distinction between dissent that has positive and negative consequences. Told from the point of view of the narrator, dissent that is received positively leads to difference and diversity, thereby highlighting aspects of Gaeltacht life that are morally pluralistic.[28] For example, the elders in the novel express many world views not necessarily shared by the young narrator, but understood and accepted by him nevertheless. In one case of moral pluralism in the novel, we see one of the Blasket Islands, An Tiaracht, as a place which has connotations of heroism for the young protagonist. The elders talk to the younger members of the extended family about Tír na nÓg, but refer to it as a physical reality, one that they can see every day, an 'oileán mara' off which their grandfathers and fathers go fishing.[29] The narrator, however, refers to An Tiaracht as a place of the imagination, one that runs parallel to the life of ordinary mortals, but where there is another kind of life waiting, one that is refulgent with possibilities. In a brilliant passage, Ó Cíobháin uses the analogy of the physical landscape to describe the diversity of opinion enjoyed by the narrator in the company of his family elders, and describes the open vista of sky meeting sea and of two worlds coming together on the horizon from various points, to describe that moral pluralism and a convergence of ideas:

Saol eile ann ag rith comhthreormhar le saol an duine dhaonna

... Agus in oileán mara mar a mbuaileann an spéir leis an bhfarraige, tagann an dá shaol so le chéile ó phointí éagsúla. Thugadh na seanGhréagaigh Hades air.[30]

[It is another world that runs parallel to the one inhabited by humans...[ ] And on an island in the sea where the sky meets the ocean, these two worlds meet. The Ancient Greeks called it Hades.]

Through use of analogy, Ó Cíobháin draws comparisons between aspects of Gaeltacht life and totalitarianism by describing the region in terms of a Soviet statelet where control is sought by the Church of the private life of individuals, 'na Sóibhéide seo'. Ó Cíobháin then goes on to paradoxically describe a local man, Mic, and his clashes with the local clergy, in terms of values that directly conflict with those of totalitarianism:

Agus b'é Mic ardshampla d'áitreabhaigh óga na Sóibhéide seo. An neamhspleáchas, an spleodar, an dúil i leathar an tsaoil, an ghéarthuiscint ar fhíorthábhacht saorthoil síolchuir.[31]

[No one personified this Soviet youth more than Mic. His independence, his joy, his taste for the splendour and very sex of life, his raw understanding of the necessity of sowing the seeds of free will.]

Ó Cíobháin compares Mic's passion for freedom and free will with that of the local priest whom he describes as the guardian of selfish morality, 'garda cosanta na moráltachta leithlisí', the boatswain of the river Styx, 'fear farantóireachta na habhann Styx' and of the gate to Hades, the 'geata go Hades'.[32] In this way, we can see how Ó Cíobháin has used heroic metaphors for community, family and church life to great effect, but with very different results.

Where questions of youth and of place have been illustrated by the preceding stories, 'An Chéad Oíche' highlights one of the central themes of heroism perfectly, that of seduction, and one that evokes the escaped lovers of 'Tóraíocht Dhiarmada agus Ghráinne'. A young man and woman have met in a nightclub in Daingean Uí Chúis, and have driven to the car park of the deserted Ventry Beach, scene of the Battle of Ventry, where they sit and talk. There are many references to Fionn Mac Cumhaill throughout. A kind of heroism, a 'sórt laochais' comes over the male protagonist,[33] but the place appears to be cursed, for as soon as he mentions the history and folklore with which the area is connected, the object of his ardour loses interest. He tells her about a *leaba Dhiarmada*: 'Shín Diarmaid síos le Gráinne fé mar a táimidne sínte anseo anocht.' ['That night, Diarmaid lay down with Gráinne, just as we're lying here tonight.']³⁴ As with Gráinne in the case of Diarmuid, the young woman in question initiates the relationship, and seduces the young man with a libation. In some of the literary versions of the Irish story 'Tóraíocht Dhiarmada agus Ghráinne', a love potion is what facilitates their ultimate escape, as happens in 'An Chéad Oíche', in which the young man offers the girl a drink in order to convince her to go with him.³⁵ And, whereas Gráinne raises her skirts in the shallows in an effort to seduce Diarmaid, the young woman raises her jeans past her shins as she paddles in the water, in what seems like an act of seduction.³⁶ The young man reflects to himself, however, that what awaits him in this relationship is pain and suffering,³⁷ all too aware that, like the fate that awaits Diarmaid and Gráinne as they escape to the margins, it is only 'an chéad oíche [The First Night]'.³⁸

It has been previously noted here that a feature of Ó Cíobháin's writing is the gradual uncovering of layers of dissent within what appears initially to be unified groups, and this is nowhere more evident than in the short story 'Geniseas'. The group in question in this story is the Irish in London, 'na Gaeil',³⁹ who have a shared ethnicity, but have objective social differences based on class and region of origin.⁴⁰ The main feature of this story is the manner in which Ó Cíobháin portrays dissent and class and cultural conflict, between these various groups of young Irish people in London, a world that pitches those of low educational and economic attainment against those of a high educational and economic attainment, the 'yuppies' abroad, '*yuppies* ar imirce'.⁴¹ The story is told in the second person and centres on the narrator, a young Irish girl, and her companion, Clár, who are living in a squat in Islington with a host of other people. Ó Cíobháin uses her name, *Clár*, to refer to the region she is from, County Clare, as well as suggesting traits of intelligence and wisdom when he refers to her 'clár', her forehead. The use of *Clár* as both allusion and as metaphor seems to point to her role in the group as a leader, a hero, by underlining the link between her name and her native county in the West of Ireland. Ó Cíobháin highlights the importance of the objective social difference of region in the narrative, through the use of 'Labhras ó Leamhchán', Labhras from Lucan, for the leader of the group of high socio-economic status.⁴² In keeping with aspects of the Irish language heroic tradition, the squatters in Islington are *díthir*, of no fixed abode, and *écland*, of no identifiable kin. As immigrants they are politically marginal, living in chaos, 'mí-ord',[43] on the perimeters of English society. We can assume them to have political marginality based on the fact that they are immigrants, and because they do not speak the majority language, English, but are Irish speakers.[44] Although they are in pursuit of all things youthful, what the two groups of young people both seem to be searching for in their different ways is not an eternal Tír na nÓg, but an *alternative* Tír na nÓg. The nightclub serves as one of the few places that can allow them the space to develop their alternative vision, and they achieve this by way of the many illegal substances that they imbibe there under the liberating effects of psychedelic lights and music. When they meet up in the nightclub, however, it quickly becomes apparent that these groups are far from unified, and the forcefully expressed authoritarian views of the members of the high socio-economic group come to the fore in the form of intolerance and hostility, where authoritarianism can be understood to be a system of attitudes based on prejudice, dogmatism, low tolerance for ambiguity and obedience to authority.[45] A row breaks out, and Ó Cíobháin portrays them as warring factions. On the one hand, there are the beneficiaries of what he terms the Spartan training of the Irish education system from the eastern region, 'traenáil Spartach', a group who are under lock and key during the day as they work in their glass and concrete towers,[46] the new ruling class from the old colony, the 'seanchóilín'.[47] On the other hand, there are the narrator and Clár from the western region, the 'slaves', 'sclábhaí', who work in the local Dorchester Hotel in King's Cross, making beds from morning to night:

> Gaeil bhuirgéiseacha i mbun a gcuid suaimhnis tar éis obair an lae. Oideachas maith faighte acu ag baile. Gafa trí ollscoileanna, traenáil Spartach.[48]

> [The middle class Gaels taking it easy at the end of a working day. They had obtained their good education back home. They had passed through universities, and had undergone the Spartan training.]

Clár and her cohort do not recognize the centres of power, nor does it appear that they recognize them, and this is borne out in part by the contempt in which the rival group holds them, something that Ó Cíobháin shows through dialogue of an almost wholly political nature. This can be also seen in the way in which the young men from the rival group belittle Clár by comparing her material possessions to theirs. They mock the squat she is living in, but she berates them when she replies that she had erroneously thought them intelligent people.[49] Things then reach a crisis point with the leader of the rival group, Labhras. However, Clár wastes no time in letting the gathered assembly know that she herself has little respect for Labhras in sexual matters.[50] Despite their hatred for one another, this story – as its biblical name suggests – emphasizes rebirth as well as adventure for both groups. When Ó Cíobháin refers to them as being in pursuit, it would appear that for one group of young Irish this involves the pursuit and consolidation of money and status, while for the other it entails the pursuit of employment and of the effects of drugs in search of a life that does not really exist, 'tóraíocht shaoil ná fuil ann', undertaking yet another odyssey through the city streets, 'odaisé eile ar fuaid Londain'.[51] Ó Cíobháin's scintillating treatment in this short story of a theme as complex as political dissent arising from class and cultural conflict is an indication of the scope and range of his talent, and is as brilliantly observed as it is rare in contemporary Irish language literature. It is a further testimony to his skill as a writer that he never strays from his narrative path, and that the passion with which he writes of this subject is palpable from beginning to end. Reminiscent in tone of some of the most political works of the American writer Philip Roth, it is in itself a literary monument to dissent by virtue of the fact that the narrator never leaves us in any doubt as to whose side he is on.

A short story that also uses the signs and signifiers left on the landscape by a local female hero is that of 'Je T'Aime'. This story concerns the ability to love, revealed to us by Ó Cíobháin who draws on the oral tradition in order to support his narrative. He has acknowledged the influence that the concept of French *amour courtois*, courtly love, has had on his prose.[52] In this case, the protagonist and his *inamorata*, Laurence, are touring the peninsula of Corca Dhuibhne. Ó Cíobháin uses the word 'fásach', desert, to express the distance the lovers feel from the rest of society.[53] The tragedy of their love is intimately connected with Diarmuid and Gráinne and, espe-cially, with the hero Sibéal, she who gave her name to the famous Ceann Sibéil. Sibéal, it is said, flung herself over the cliff because of a doomed love affair. Laurence identifies strongly with her in this regard, although she notes that she herself does not have the innate ability to become a female hero:

> Cailleadh Sibéal, bás tragóideach de réir na scéalta ach
> maireann a cuimhne sa cheann tíre sin amuigh agus i

gcomhfhios mhuintir na háite seo ar nós mo ghrá anso taobh liom sa mhótar. Cónaíonn Sibéal ionam.[54]

[And so Sybil died. It was a tragic death according to the old stories, but her memory survives in that part of the country, and in the minds of those who live here. She remains on, too, in the consciousness of my lover here beside me in this car. Sybil lives on in me.]

Laurence is not up to emulating Sybil's heroic act:

Ná tóg ormsa ó Bhruz a leithéid de bhanlaoch d'alter ego a cheapadh dom féin, ach géillim go bhfuil an t-ath-tharlú ann chomh maith leis an gcomhtharlú.[55]

[Don't ask me, Laurence from Bruz, to emulate the alter ego of a female hero such as her. I admit, however, that no more than the coincidence, there is such a thing as the reoccurrence.]

All of the places described in 'Je T'Aime' are described in terms of their physical danger. Much is made of the twists and turns of the roads, the endless journeys of catabasis employed as a literary device by Ó Cíobháin with which to presage the fear of heights, of falling further and further in love. The reader is given to understand that their love is a clandestine one. In contrast, the nature in which local landmarks are realized in the story and their connections with heroes who are famous act as a tacit support for the lovers' feelings, but primarily function as harbingers of doom. (What better as a literary portent of disaster than the image of An Fear Marbh and Ceann Sibéal, the prostrate man in the sea, and the heartbroken woman about to leap from the cliff's edge?) As in the stories of Deirdre Ní Mhannanáin who falls in love with the hero, Naoise, Ó Cíobháin uses the image of the soul of the woman to express how she feels as she falls in love.[56] Even though Laurence does not want to construct an alter ego for herself, she does want to drop dead on the spot, 'bás a fháil anois díreach ar an spota so'.[57]

Ó Cíobháin's emphasis on woman taking her own life – for example, Sandra, the female protagonist of 'Sí Gaoithe'[58]– is an element in his work that closely resembles a motif in classical Greek mythology and in the lives of Greek and Roman female heroes, such as Dido, Iphigenia and Antigone. The nemesis in the Irish historic tradition with this death wish, of course, is Deirdre, who has plighted her troth to the king, Conchubhar Mac Neasa, but who loves Naoise.[59] In his novel *Desiderius A Dó*, Ó Cíobháin retells a version of the story in which the unfortunate Deirdre takes her own life.[60] The death wish of the woman, therefore, would seem to rank among the greatest assertions of independence and dissent in these stories of Ó Cíobháin's: both Deirdre and Sandra are trapped in loveless marriages and are either powerless or incapable of expressing their frustrations. Their deaths collate their dissent with their status quo and serve as their only expression of protest. And, as has been previously noted, dissent from prevailing norms in society not infrequently ends in self-destruction in Ó Cíobháin's work.

Pádraig Ó Cíobháin's reframing of heroes and heroism is remarkable in terms of the continuum of the Irish literary tradition. Words and place names which are generally held to have heroic connotations such as Tír na nÓg, the Blasket Islands and Gaels are parodied, reinvented and challenged throughout his work. He has partly achieved what Orwell describes as the search for the secondary meanings of words, where nothing can ever presume to remain uncontested. His portrayal of heroic personages and the places associated with them constitutes a world view that broadly welcomes dissent, even thrives on it. His view of the world, and of Ireland, is one where values ascribed over time to aspects of our culture constitute a palimpsest that can always be refashioned, his work carefully observant of Ireland's cultural and political landscape. And with some of the richest, most beautiful Irish being written today, Ó Cíobháin has carved dissent on the prevailing values. Ultimately, it is the act of writing itself that has made this possible.

REFERENCES

Campbell, J., *The Hero With a Thousand Faces* (Princeton, NJ: Princeton University Press, 1949).
Hadas, M. and Smith, M., *Heroes and Gods: Spiritual Biographies in Antiquity* (Liverpool and London: Charles Birchall & Sons, 1965).
Heywood, A., *Politics* (New York: Palgrave Macmillan, 2002).
Joyce, J., *A Portrait of The Artist As a Young Man* (New York: Gramercy,1992).
Kiberd, D., *Irish Classics* (London: Granta, 2000).
Newton, K. and Van Deth, J.W., *Foundations of Comparative Politics* (Cambridge: Cambridge University Press, 2005).
Ó Cíobháin, P., *Le Gealaigh* [*Of Moonlight and Madness*] (Dublin: Coiscéim, 1991).
Ó Cíobháin, P., *An Gealas i Lár na Léithe* [*The Brightness of Shadow*] (Dublin: Coiscéim, 1992).
Ó Cíobháin, P., *An Grá Faoi Cheilt* [*The Concealment of Love*] (Dublin: Coiscéim, 1992).
Ó Cíobháin, P., *Desiderius a Dó* [*Desiderius The Second*] (Dublin: Coiscéim, 1995).
Ó Cíobháin, P., 'Cathair Ghríobháin na Samhlaíochta', in M. Ó Cearúil (ed.), *Aimsir Óg: Scéalta, Aistí, Dánta* [*New Times: Stories, Essays, Poems*](Dublin: Coiscéim, 1999).
Ó Cíobháin, P., *Tá Solas ná hÉagann Choíche* [*There Is A Light That Never Dies*] (Dublin: Coiscéim, 1999).
Ó Cíobháin, P., 'An Treasruathar Turgnamhach: Féinspléachadh údair ar an Ionchur I bProslitríocht a Linne', ['Here's to the Experimental: An Author on His Contribution to Contemporary Prose Literature']in A. Ní Dhonnchadh (ed.), *Léachtaí Cholm Cille*, 36 (Kildare: An Sagart, 2006), pp.5476.

Ó Fiannachta, P., 'Litríocht Chorca Dhuibhne', ['The Literature of Corca Dhuibhne'] in *Irisleabhar Mhá Nuad* (Dingle: An Sagart, 1982).
Ó hÓgáin, D., *Fionn Mac Cumhaill: Images of the Gaelic Hero* (Dublin: Gill & Macmillan, 1987).
Ó Searcaigh, S., *Laochas* (Dublin: An Gúm, 2004).
Orwell, G., *1984* (London: Penguin, 1987).
Sjoestedt, M.L., *Gods and Heroes of the Celts*, trans. M. Dillon (London: Methuen, 1949).

NOTES

1. G. Orwell, *1984* (London: Penguin, 1987), p.218.
2. Ibid., p.207.
3. Ibid., p.218.
4. M.L. Sjoestedt, *Gods and Heroes of the Celts*, trans. M. Dillon (London: Methuen, 1949), p.57.
5. D. Ó hÓgáin, *Fionn Mac Cumhaill: Images of the Gaelic Hero* (Dublin: Gill & Macmillan, 1987), pp.34–5.
6. M. Hadas and M. Smith, *Heroes and Gods: Spiritual Biographies in Antiquity* (Liverpool and London: Charles Birchall & Sons, 1965), p.7.
7. Pádraig Ó Cíobháin discusses the notion of honeyed youth, or 'Lúnasa meala', in 'Cathair Ghríobháin na Samhlaíochta' ['In the Labyrinth of the Imagination'], in M. Ó Cearúil (ed.), *Aimsir Óg: Scéalta, Aistí, Dánta* [*New Times: Stories, Essays, Poems*] (Dublin: Coiscéim, 1999), p.105. In a similar discussion, Pádraig Ó Fiannachta examines Tomás Ó Criomhthain's portrayal of aspects of his youth in 'Litríocht Chorca Dhuibhne' ['The Literature of Corca Dhuibhne'], in *Irisleabhar Mhá Nuad* (Dingle: An Sagart, 1982), pp.21–35.
8. D. Kiberd, *Irish Classics* (London: Granta, 2000), p.401.
9. J. Campbell, *The Hero with a Thousand Faces* (Princeton, NJ: Princeton University Press, 1949), pp.49–94.
10. P. Ó Cíobháin, *An Grá Faoi Cheilt* [*The Concealment of Love*] (Dublin: Coiscéim, 1992).
11. Ibid., p.12.
12. Ibid., p.11.
13. Ibid., p.12.
14. Ibid., p.25.
15. Ibid., p.26.
16. Ibid., p.27.
17. Ibid., p.15.
18. S. Ó Searcaigh, *Laochas* [*Heroic Tales*] (Dublin: An Gúm, 2004), pp.44–9.
19. Ibid., pp.74–7.
20. P. Ó Cíobháin, *Tá Solas ná hÉagann Choíche* [*There is a Light that Never Dies*] (Dublin: Coiscéim, 1999), p.108.
21. Ibid., p.115.
22. P. Ó Cíobháin, *Le Gealaigh* [*Of Moonlight and Madness*] (Dublin: Coiscéim, 1991), p.30.
23. Ibid., p.29.
24. P. Ó Cíobháin, 'An Treasruathar Turgnamhach: Féinspléachadh údair ar an Ionchur I bProslitríocht a Linne', ['Here's to the Experimental: An Author on His Contribution to Contemporary Prose Literature'] in A. Ní Dhonnchadh (ed.), *Léachtaí Cholm Cille*, 36 (Kildare: An Sagart, 2006), p.60.
25. P. Ó Cíobháin, *An Gealas I Lár na Léithe* [*The Brightness of Shadow*] (Dublin: Coiscéim, 1992), p.239.
26. Ibid.
27. J. Joyce, *A Portrait of The Artist As a Young Man* (New York: Gramercy, 1992), p.299.
28. As Á. Heywood says, 'the idea that conflicts of values are intrinsic to human life'. *Politics* (New York: Palgrave Macmillan, 2002), p.120.
29. Ó Cíobháin, *An Gealas i Lár na Léithe* [*The Brightness of Shadow*], p.38.
30. Ibid.
31. Ibid., p.24.
32. Ibid., p.88.
33. Ó Cíobháin, *Le Gealaigh* [*Of Moonlight and Madness*], p.108.
34. Ibid., p.111.
35. Ibid., p.109.

36. Ibid., p.107.
37. Ibid., p.113.
38. Ibid., p.112.
39. Ó Cíobháin, *Tá Solas ná hÉagann Choíche* [*There is a Light that Never Dies*], p.28.
40. K. Newton and J.W. Van Deth, *Foundations of Comparative Politics* (Cambridge: Cambridge University Press, 2005), p.145. Objective social differences are described here as a condition 'based on class, ethnicity, language, religion and region'.
41. Ó Cíobháin, *Tá Solas ná hÉagann Choíche* [*There is a Light that Never Dies*], p.18.
42. Ibid., p.29.
43. Ibid., p.21.
44. Newton and Van Deth, *Foundations of Comparative Politics*, p.150: 'People categorized as "marginals" or who have political marginality include ... immigrants and those who do not speak the majority language.'
45. Ibid., p.144.
46. Ó Cíobháin, *Tá Solas ná hÉagann Choíche* [*There is a Light that Never Dies*], p.27.
47. Ibid., p.29.
48. Ibid., p.28.
49. Ibid., p.30.
50. Ibid., p.30.
51. Ibid., p.27.
52. Ó Cíobháin, 'An Treasruathar Turgnamhach: Féinspléachadh údair ar an Ionchur I bPróslitríocht a Linne' ['Here's to the Experimental: An Author on His Contribution to Contemporary Prose Literature'], p.65.
53. Ó Cíobháin, *An Grá Faoi Cheilt* [*The Concealment of Love*], p.132.
54. Ibid., p.128.
55. Ibid.
56. Ibid., p.119.
57 . Ibid., p.126.
58. Ó Cíobháin, *Tá Solas ná hÉagann Choíche* [*There is a Light that Never Dies*], pp.116–33.
59. Ó Searcaigh, *Laochas* [*Heroic Tales*], p.68.
60. P. Ó Cíobháin, *Desiderius a Dó* [*Desiderius the Second*] (Dublin: Coiscéim, 1995), p.124.

22

Captain Jack White, DSO – Anarchist and Proleptic Postructuralist

Leo Keohane

Although the politics and history of the early twentieth century in Ireland have been extensively debated, new tools of analysis can occasionally illuminate certain aspects of what initially seem to be overdone topics. Captain Jack White, DSO, has been a largely forgotten figure of that period and, if he is remembered at all, it is for his role in founding the Irish Citizen Army, a force more iconic than militarily effective.

He was, however, one of this country's few self-professed anarchists of any standing and as such provides a perspective that although up until recently was seen as largely redundant is gradually beginning to gain ground academically.[1] Studies like anarchist literary theory are being initiated in an attempt to 'offer a promising alternative to the sterility of the modes of theory dominant within the academy'.[2]

The parallels between anarchism and poststructuralist philosophy have been drawn by Todd May, among others. This is particularly so in postmodernist anarchism, nowadays often called postanarchism to distinguish it from the classical nineteenth-century anarchism, which is perceived to be redundant to some extent, although certainly not invalid.[3]

For the purposes of this essay, it is proposed to utilize the concept of the meta-narrative, since although regarded as dated by some, it admirably serves the purpose of illustrating White's anarchistic perspective on the events and people he encountered. Lyotard's dictum of incredulity being directed towards all meta-narratives matched White's critical response to almost any received wisdom and allows his introduction, albeit very prematurely, into the pantheon of poststructuralist analysts.

Anarchism, although with many unfortunate connotations of

nihilistic violence and chaos, is also a political philosophy. Up until recently the problem with anarchism, from the Greek *anarhkhos*, without rule, was its seeming impracticality. Although its analysis of the hierarchical structures of power was relevant, it was accused of idealism, utopianism and a naivety about human nature. Its critique of power and its rejection of central authoritarianism were valid, but it could be argued that without some locus of authority it would prove impossible to regulate large sophisticated structures like the economy or organize institutions like education and medicine. However, anarchists such as Pietr Kropotkin argued that it was a fallacy that humankind needed strict regulation. In his *Mutual Aid*, he maintained that an innate cooperation existed in all species and that this, more than the notion of 'survival of the fittest', was the primary dynamic of evolution.[4]

Nowadays, anarchism is perceived more as a demeanour than as a prescriptive philosophy, in the sense that a robust scepticism is brought to the arena of diagnosis rather than a list of remedies for the particular problem. Within the philosophy of postmodern anarchism itself, alternatives of organization economically and politically are not clearly drawn because, the argument goes, they are concepts that are relatively ineffable. Lewis Call draws on Foucault's concept of the *episteme* – that is, the archaeological-like strata of knowledge occupied during a particular epoch, which strongly inhibit us from postulating alternatives external to the system because of our hide-boundedness to basic premises that form part of the existing system.[5] To illustrate (and admittedly make some assumptions that might startle a sociologist), we occupy an *episteme* which could be called a capitalist system that has lasted, let us say, for more or less 500 years. To a serf occupying the previous *episteme* – that is, a feudal ethos – it would prove impossible to conceptualize phenomena like an upwardly mobile society, or the notion of modern human rights. His alternative to the existing system would be the overthrow of the ruling lords and their replacement with some kind of peasant king – an equally despotic authority. Hence today the alternatives can at best be nebulous signs of what may lie ahead. Lewis Call writes about hyper-text which can be a startlingly different way of apprehending information, illustrating a rhizomatic rather than a linear progression. More mundanely, or more understandably, there are communes such as Anonymous formed on the Internet, involved in subversive activities, which demonstrate a coherent resistance among like-minded radicals which would have been unthinkable up to very recently. These are merely glimmers, but nonetheless significantly indicative, of what may be to come.

Meanwhile, anarchism in its analysis of the current dominant hegemonies perceives the meta-narrative or Grand Narrative as the tool which buttresses the hierarchies of power. Gramsci's hegemony suggests seduction as being more effective than coercion in the exercise of power – that is, the threat of the gunboat is far more efficient than its actual deployment. But seduction, to be effective, needs a good story. Hence, the Grand Narrative is in effect power, and as such requires to be treated with a poststructuralist incredulity or to encounter anarchism's scepticism.

It is proposed to bring this theoretical method to one of the questions of Irish history of the late nineteenth and early twentieth centuries: the paucity of accounts of socialist struggles, whether Marxist, communist or anarchist, at that time. Although supporters of these ideologies certainly existed, their numbers appear to have been insignificant in comparison to their natural sympathizers – the disadvantaged. The nationalist chronicles probably obfuscated other reasons for unrest, gathering them all under one banner to provide a coherent narrative of resistance against imperialism. When O'Casey wrote in the *Irish Worker* that 'they can prate about the rights and liberties common to all Irishmen all they wish, but we want food and work',[6] it would be imagined that this kind of rousing statement would dismiss the idealism of revolution and gather masses to the more prosaic cause of the immediate betterment of the workers' lot. The Irish Citizen Army, formed originally from the victims of the Dublin Lockout, still found common cause with the Volunteers in ascribing most ills to the government in Britain. The puzzle is why the Volunteer force, generally acknowledged to be bourgeois in its ideology, should far outnumber the proletariat of the ICA. Partly, of course, this would arise from the peril of applying what is essentially a British or Western European social paradigm to Irish society. But there is another question, and that is why the socially and economically disadvantaged of the *petit bourgeoisie* – the shop assistants, the farm labourers and so on – should aspire to this ideology of Inis Fáil rather than a betterment of their kitchen table. Fintan Lane gives some clue in *The Origins of Irish Socialism* when he describes the agrarian nature of Irish society. 'Landlordism' exercised a baleful influence and so the aspirations were for 'a peasant proprietorship' and not the alleviation of the lot of the disadvantaged.[7] Certainly the various land acts created an ethos of pacific proprietorship but that still left a very substantial body of lumpenproletariat who seemed to have little or no representation. White himself, in 1918, presciently cautioned about the danger that 'the comparative prosperity of the farmers [might] tend to make them unite to enforce the status quo on the labourers', thereby signalling, at least in one area of society, the advent of more conservative forces.[8] But there had to be other factors.

Captain Jack White, DSO, was a considerable if unsystematic thinker who, although not professing himself to be an anarchist until the late 1930s, had an approach from the start of his life which when examined through a prism of anarchism acquires a certain coherence. Although a superficial glance at his political views would suggest he was a very radical left-winger, who despite his idiosyncratic pacifism was not averse to extreme agitation against the state, hindsight allows us to suggest that he had a perspective on the political struggle in Ireland which might have some relevance.

Son of Field Marshal Sir George White, VC, 'Hero of Ladysmith', he was a public-school boy and graduate of Sandhurst with a received pronunciation accent that must have struck the occasionally incongruous note. He associated either socially or in the line of duty with a lot of people who were regarded as important figures at the time. Chronologically, he had personal access to Lord Kitchener, had been a dinner companion of King Edward and the Kaiser, corresponded with H.G. Wells and Tolstoy, shared a platform with Shaw and Roger Casement, founded the Irish Citizen Army along with Connolly, marched (and argued) with Larkin, worked with Sean O'Casey, liaised with Countess Markievicz and socialized with most of the Irish activists and literati of the early twentieth century. Later in life, he counted Emma Goldman and other luminaries of the Left as personal friends, including the writer John Cowper Powys. It has emerged recently that T.E. Lawrence proofread his autobiography.

His personal life was, in conventional terms, disastrous; although coming into a considerable inheritance, he ended up selling vegetables in the local village to support himself and his family.[9] His estate at his death came to £82.[10] He has been described as incorrigible, and worse – Casement said he 'had a slate off'.[11] From the time at Winchester public school when he attempted to blow up his teacher, there are records of actions ranging from serious insubordination to outright rebellion. In the Boer War he pointed his gun at his superior telling him he would shoot him if the officer persisted in ordering a prisoner to be shot.[12] He features in two novels: in D.H. Lawrence's

Aaron's Rod he is represented by Jim Bricknell, an unpredictable, fractious and rather unpleasant character, and in Mary Manning's *Mount Venus* it is probably enough to note that his character is called Captain Cock-eye. His in-laws have described him as aggressive, argumentative and excessively anti-Catholic.[13] (Oddly, he married twice, both Catholics – the only two mortal sins he ever committed, he quipped.) Several people have commented on his Lothario-like qualities; there are at least two women who have recorded his offer of setting up free-love communes around the country in the 1920s.[14] His family paid to have his head literally examined and apart from his own admissions of some kind of instability there are numerous occasions where he seems to have been plain mad; one instance, reported in *The Irish Times* in 1925, describes how he decided to cross Dublin Bay in a small rowing boat, completely ignoring appalling weather conditions, because, as he explained later to the search party, he was bored with the land journey.[15]

But all of these are merely the warts (albeit interesting ones) that develop the rounded character of Jack White. He was generally indifferent to how he was perceived; the entrance criteria laid down by the pantheon of heroes were never seen by him as attributes to be aspired to.[16] His repugnance of central authoritarianism was manifested in his opposition to all sorts of constructs and one of these certainly would have been the notion that there were 'great' men and the subsequent heroic fables associated with them. Lyotard's incredulity probably best illustrates White's attitude, in the sense that he accepted nothing unquestioningly and it seemed as if it was incumbent upon him to challenge immediately any kind of received wisdom. For all that, there was a pragmatism behind what initially appeared to be ideas outside the envelope. Evidence of this occurs right from the very beginning of his life when as a young man of 16 or 17 he negotiated an amicable settlement with his headmaster at Winchester public school and was expelled, but with honour satisfied all round, so to speak.

He opposed both the Catholic Church and the nationalists. He marched with the lockout strikers, yet parleyed with William Martin Murphy. He excoriated the Carsonites and Unionists, yet clung to the principles of Presbyterianism all his life. He was violent in disposition (he even punched D.H. Lawrence) and yet spent the early years of the First World War as a pacifist driving an ambulance behind the trenches.

This, however, did not find him siding with the Unionist camp –

although a supporter of Home Rule, he envisaged it more as a prac-
tical means of Ireland being looked after by the people that lived
there rather than part of any of the loftier ideologies of Pearse. In
this he saw Connolly, who reputedly educated him in Marxism, as
the most likely of the prominent activists to put into place the ideas
he had himself which at that time would have been quite inchoate.
It was not until his epiphany in Spain, where he saw anarcho-
syndicalism in operation in Barcelona, and his meeting with Emma
Goldman that he came out of the closet, so to speak, and proclaimed
himself an anarchist. He greeted the Catalans in 1936 with the 'voice
of revolutionary Ireland, *smothered awhile*'. As he saw it, the 1916 'rising is now thought of as purely a national one, of which the aims
went no further than the national independence of Ireland'.[17] The
true nature of this revolution was 'conveniently forgotten' and he
tries to restore it when he maintains that Connolly, the international
socialist, had only 'made common cause with the Republican
separatists [because they were united] against the common Imperial
enemy'.[18]

It is here that his analysis suggests a serious critique of the
dominant ideology of this country. White's main target of contumely
was the grand narrative of what he saw as Catholic nationalism.
From the time he had his first contact with Irish nationalists at the
Civic League meetings in Trinity College, he believed they showed
an indifference to the striking workers and the conditions of the
slums in Dublin at the time of the Lockout. His experience with the
priests actively campaigning to keep the slum-dwelling children at
home caused, he said, 'the sands of his gentility to run out'.[19] He
became ardently anti-Catholic in what he perceived to be a central
authoritarian force interfering in the social affairs of Ireland. This,
combined with his difficulty with nationalism itself, his opposition to
unionism and in fact with the bigotry that arose from the essentialism that lay behind a lot of the rallying cries of the various collectives
in Ireland, distilled down to a perception of what could be called
Catholic nationalism. As a grand narrative it is a particularly potent
combination, combining basically three threads of ideology:
Catholicism, nationalism and some form of what might be termed
Celticism.

Fintan Lane points out that the clergy were drawn from the
indigenous Irish themselves, so that – unlike in Spain, for example –
they could not be suspected of allegiance to the oppressive classes.
However, White believed that Catholicism 'objectified its supreme

law in a Church and priesthood external to, and having authority over, itself'.[20] This lead to a central authoritarianism that, for all its consideration of the meek and humble, allowed little regard for those on the periphery. For example, Catholic Emancipation in 1829, although elevating the status of Catholicism in general, also resulted in the disenfranchisement of the forty-shilling smallholders; 'thus liberation for Catholics was accompanied by a drastic reduction in the county voters, from 216,000 to 37,000'.[21] While there were obviously radical clergymen down through the nineteenth century, this indifference to the voice (if not the fate) of the proletariat formed a conservative elite, led by Cardinal Paul Cullen, ill-disposed to any form of political agitation. The educational methods in Maynooth, the largest Catholic seminary in Europe, encouraged a kind of learning by rote and utilized a 'localism' where student priests were quartered with their own fellow county-men and discouraged from mixing outside – this had the effect of emphasizing a parochial outlook and produced graduates with little sympathy for abstract thought ('memorising rather than rational argument was encouraged'), but with a fierce sense of their own place and its entitlements.[22]

The most cogent nationalism of the mid-nineteenth century expressed itself in Fenianism 'nurtured on both sides of the Atlantic by the immediate and bitter memory of the Famine and by the rather longer memories of Irish historical grievances in general'.[23] Gearóid Ó Tuathaigh says the 'particular intensity of this Fenian spirit among Irish exiles in the cities of America and Britain has been seen by historians as largely the response of the overwhelmingly poor immigrant Irish to the difficulties and prejudices they encountered within their new host countries'.[24] This may suggest a partial answer to the question about where the intensity of antipathy of the lumpenproletariat at home was expressed, in the sense that they took the example of their (more adventurous?) comrades from abroad. In any case, 'the clandestine, oath-bound basis of Fenianism was anathema to [Catholicism] ... [and] from the movement's beginnings in the 1850s [they] were threatened with excommunication and subjected to the relentless public condemnation of churchmen'.[25] White, although unsympathetic to nationalism, from both upbringing and personal conviction, did concede its necessity. Writing much later, in 1919, he refers to Sinn Féin's limited objectives – he believed the nationalists wanted Britain out of Ireland but gave little thought to the new state that would emerge. He did see, however, the validity (and necessity) of their enthusiasm. 'Criticism sometimes seen in the

English press that Sinn Féin is an emotion not a policy' was mistaken, he wrote, for 'without emotion, will would be dormant and the intellect [would] lapse into a mere calculating machine'.[26] Nonetheless, he believed that Sinn Féin's idealism needed the pragmatic intellect of Labour for it to develop successfully.

The third strand of opposition to the existing hegemony drew on support from those who would – either from religion or social position – have had little empathy with the first two. There are parallels to the *Volkism* of fin de siècle Europe which manifested itself in all sorts of back-to-tradition organizations, fashions and indeed cults. These arose from the bourgeoisie's relative prosperity, finding themselves with a little time on their hands, some spare cash and a void arising from Nietzsche's 'God is Dead'. Understandable and relatively innocuous in the beginning, it examined myths and legends, traditions and folk tales in the hope of providing some kind of meaning to life, but it was later to burgeon into something more sinister and it could be argued that it was one of the roots of Fascism and Nazism.[27] Spiritualism, pantheism and beliefs propagated by people like Mrs Besant and the Order of the Golden Dawn attracted followers from Ireland. Where it could be said to have manifested itself most relevantly in Ireland was in the guise of Celticism and in cultural nationalism movements such as the Gaelic League, aided and abetted by Lady Gregory, Yeats et al. Like its counterparts on the continent it was vaguely irreligious if not actually anti-religious. White, although unimpressed, was aware of its power. He wrote: 'This spirit, though a potent intoxicant, is not the product of the local distilleries at Bushmills and Coleraine. To define it fully would take a history of Ireland and more than that. It would take one of those flashes of Kathleen Ni Houlihan's eyes, which have been known to bind even full-blooded Englishmen under a spell for life.'[28]

White believed that the more radical Catholic clergy contributed to the combining of these three strands by a tacit support of the Irish Republican Brotherhood and the later IRA. (Did this simultaneously establish an ascendancy over the lumpenproletariat?) He would not have been surprised to see that the clergy also co-opted the myths and legends of Celticism, pace earlier Christian proselytizing tactics, where feasts and pattern days and other pagan customs were commandeered in the cause of religion. This kind of faux ideology formed from a combination of mysticism and tradition provided a numinous and heady tinge to nationalism. Ironically, Yeats's poem 'Easter, 1916' articulated the inspiration for this grand narrative;[29]

ironical because the poet lived in trepidation of the *petite bourgeoisie*, those who 'fumble in a greasy till';[30] those very people who, allied with the Church, were now the dominant force of this combination.

From an anarchist's or even a socialist point of view, it is not difficult to argue that the new conservative state that emerged would prove seriously defective. Sadly, White believed, the Irish struggle had substituted one central authoritarian entity for another. Was his perspective correct on Catholic nationalism? Certainly the eventual corruption, in the sense of the disintegration of the body politic, did result in a cultural and economic wasteland in the 1950s where censorship, for example, was hardly more sophisticated than an exercise in book burning. The clientilism that pervaded all strata of political life was fostered by, and flourished in, an ethos of localism that despite all the recent upheavals has stoutly maintained its presence. Then there are the residues of what were at one time, at best, expedient political fashions. De Valera created the title of Taoiseach in the late 1930s, for example. That a man should elect to call himself 'chieftain' indicates somebody with a questionable attitude towards the democratic institution he was supposed to serve and that this title still persists when others like *El Caudillo* have long since disappeared should surely raise eyebrows.

Whether there are larger and more inhibiting inheritances of this conservative ideology is a question that will not be answered here. Even if the argument is conceded that modern Ireland has, to a substantial extent, put these beliefs and practices behind it, there still remains the residue of a legacy that has resulted in a perplexing passivity in the face of revelations of the more egregious behaviour by the dominant elite in the last few years. Did this arise from the rigid regulation of Irish Catholicism which encouraged an abdication of personal responsibility? Was it compounded by a nationalism veering into a kind of sacral republicanism which, with blind fanaticism, laid all tribulations at Britain's door? Whatever hope the country had of growing up after 1922 was seriously inhibited by a petty parochialism that evaded direct questions and hid from reality under a puritanical veil of righteousness.

On the other hand, for all its deficiencies it proved to be an ideology of extraordinary cogency in that it succeeded in putting an end to the governance of the British Empire, the greatest socioeconomic structure in history. Allowing the last word to White – in 1930 he said, in defence of James Connolly's purported nationalism:

He [Connolly] realized that the National Movement was the

reservoir of the nation's subconscious power, that amalgamating with it he could tap ore in Ireland, *even if mixed with a mass of sentimental dross.* He was a realist. He saw the British troops in Ireland. They are out of the twenty-six counties now.[31] [Italics added]

REFERENCES

Backus, M., 'More Useful Washed and Dead: James Connolly, W.B. Yeats and the Sexual Politics of Easter 1916', *Interventions: International Journal of Studies*, special issue on 'Under Which Flag: Revisiting James Connolly', 10, 1 (2008), pp.67–85.
Bartlett, T., Curtin, C., O'Dwyer, R. and Ó Tuathaigh, G. (eds), *Irish Studies: A General Introduction* (Dublin: Gill & Macmillan, 1988), p.137.
Call, L., *Postmodern Anarchism* (Oxford: Lexington Books, 2002).
Cohn, J., 'What is Anarchist Literary Theory?', *Anarchist Studies*, 15, 2 (2007), pp.115–131.
Eatwell, R., *Fascism: A History* (London: Pimlico, 2003).
Foster, R.F., *Modern Ireland, 1600–1972* (London: Penguin, 1989).
Fox, R.M., *History of The Irish Citizen Army* (Dublin: Jas Duffy, 1943).
Garvin, T., *Nationalist Revolutionaries in Ireland 1858–1928* (Dublin: Gill & Macmillan, 2005).
Kropotkin, P., *Mutual Aid* (London: Penguin, 1939).
Lane, F., *The Origins of Modern Irish Socialism 1881–96* (Cork: Cork University Press, 1997).
May, T., *The Political Philosophy of Poststructuralist Anarchism* (University Park, PA: Pennsylvania State University, 1994).
McMinn, J.R.B., *Against the Tide* (Belfast: PRONI, 1985).
Mitchell, A., *Oxford Dictionary of National Biography* (Oxford: Oxford University Press, 2004).
Ó Tuathaigh, G., 'From United Kingdom to Divided Island: Aspects of the Irish Experience', in T. Bartlett, C. Curtin, R. O'Dwyer and G. Ó Tuathaigh (eds), *Irish Studies: A General Introduction* (Dublin: Gill & Macmillan, 1988).
Newman, S., *From Bakunin to Lacan* (Oxford: Lexington Books, 2001).
White, J.R., *The Significance of Sinn Féin: Psychological, Political and Economic* (Dublin: Martin Lester, 1919).
White, J.R., *Misfit. An Autobiography* (London: Jonathan Cape, 1930).
White, J.R., *Misfit: A Revolutionary Life* (Dublin: Livewire Publications, 2005).
Yeats, W.B., *Collected Poems* (London: Papermac, 1985).

NOTES

Citations are given from two versions of White's autobiography, *Misfit*. The first is from Jonathan Cape, London, 1930 .The second, which omits the first two chapters of the original, is published by Livewire, Dublin, 2005 – however, it does have a number of invaluable reprints of articles by White.

1. There are a number of academic associations dealing specifically with theories of anarchism. Two in particular are the Anarchist Studies Network and Anarchist Academics, a discussion and mutual aid group for anarchists in academia. There is also an Anarchism Research Group at Loughborough University which provides a centre for postgraduate research on the topic and holds regular seminars.
2. J. Cohn, 'What is Anarchist Literary Theory?', *Anarchist Studies*, 15, 2 (2007), p.115.
3. T. May, *The Political Philosophy of Poststructuralist Anarchism* (University Park, PA: Pennsylvania State University, 1994); S. Newman, *From Bakunin to Lacan* (Oxford: Lexington Books, 2001); L. Call, *Postmodern Anarchism* (Oxford: Lexington Books, 2002).
4. P. Kropotkin, *Mutual Aid* (London: Penguin, 1939).

5. Call, *Postmodern Anarchism*.
6. R.M. Fox, *History of The Irish Citizen Army* (Dublin: Jas Duffy, 1943), p.10.
7. F. Lane, *The Origins of Modern Irish Socialism 1881–96* (Cork: Cork Universtiy Press, 1997), particularly chapters 1 and 3.
8. J.R. White, *The Significance of Sinn Féin: Psychological, Political and Economic* (Dublin: Martin Lester, 1919), p.5.
9. Alan White, Jack White's son, personal interview with the author, November 2007.
10. A. Mitchell, *Oxford Dictionary of National Biography* (Oxford: Oxford University Press, 2004).
11. J.R.B. McMinn, *Against the Tide* (Belfast: PRONI, 1985), p.131. Letter from J.B. Armour to his wife, September 1913.
12. Captain J.R. White, *Misfit: An Autobiography* (London: Jonathan Cape, 1930), p.45.
13. Mrs P. Wheeler, niece of Mrs Noreen White, née Shanahan (White's second wife), correspondence and personal interviews with the author, 2007.
14. Mr Rory Campbell, correspondence and personal interviews with the author, 2007.
15. *The Irish Times*, 30 October 1925.
16. White, *Misfit: An Autobiography*. See, for example, his accounts in Chapter 3 of the Boer War and in particular his being awarded the DSO for bravery, which is told in a picaresque way and not in the conventional self-deprecatory style.
17. J.R. White, 'A Rebel in Barcelona', in Captain J.R. White, *Misfit: A Revolutionary Life* (Dublin: Livewire Publications, 2005), pp.239–41.
18. White, *Misfit: A Revolutionary Life*, p.240.
19. White, *Misfit: An Autobiography*, p.219.
20. Ibid., p.166.
21. R.F. Foster, *Modern Ireland, 1600–1972* (London: Penguin, 1989), pp.301–2
22. T. Garvin, *Nationalist Revolutionaries in Ireland 1858–1928* (Dublin: Gill & Macmillan, 2005), pp.57–77.
23. G. Ó Tuathaigh, 'From United Kingdom to Divided Island: Aspects of the Irish Experience', in T. Bartlett, C. Curtin, R. O'Dwyer and Gearóid Ó Tuathaigh (eds), *Irish Studies: A General Introduction* (Dublin: Gill & Macmillan, 1988), p.137.
24. Ibid.
25. Ibid., p.138.
26. White, *Significance of Sinn Féin*, p.3.
27. R. Eatwell, *Fascism: A History* (London: Pimlico, 2003) – see pp.7ff. for *Volkisch* ideas and their link to a more emotive form of nationalism.
28. White, *Misfit: An Autobiography*, p.181.
29. M. Backus, 'More Useful Washed and Dead: James Connolly, W.B. Yeats and the Sexual Politics of Easter 1916', *Interventions: International Journal of Studies*, special issue on 'Under Which Flag: Revisiting James Connolly', 10, 1 (2008), pp.67–85.
30. W.B. Yeats, 'September 1913', in *Collected Poems* (London: Papermac, 1985), p.120.
31. White, *Misfit: An Autobiography*, p.249.

Index